JUSTICE, POLITICS, AND THE FAMILY

JUSTICE, POLITICS, AND THE FAMILY

edited by
Daniel Engster and Tamara Metz

Paradigm Publishers
Boulder • London

Published in the United States by Paradigm Publishers, 5589 Arapahoe Avenue, Boulder, CO 80303 USA.

Paradigm Publishers is the trade name of Birkenkamp & Company, LLC, Dean Birkenkamp, President and Publisher.

Library of Congress Cataloging-in-Publication Data

Justice, politics, and the family / edited by Daniel Engster and Tamara Metz.
    pages cm
  Includes bibliographical references.
  ISBN 978-1-61205-150-5 (pbk. : alk. paper)
  1. Families. 2. Family policy. 3. Marriage. 4. Parenting. 5. Parent and child.
6. Caregivers—Social conditions—21st century. 7. Globalization—Social aspects.
I. Engster, Daniel.
  HQ734.J878 2013
  306.85—dc23

2013012870

18 17 16 15 14   1 2 3 4 5

Contents

Acknowledgments

The editors wish to thank the Dean's Office of Reed College, the Charles McKinley Research Fund of the Department of Political Science of Reed College, and the Dean's Office of the University of Texas, San Antonio, for their generous support. Without it, the project would not have been possible. We are also grateful for the unflagging and competent assistance of Lucy Sexton.

Introduction

Justice and the Family in Western Political Thought

Daniel Engster and Tamara Metz

The family is one of the most important social and political institutions. In nearly all Western societies, "the family," however defined, has been one of the primary contexts in which care and socialization of the young occur, giving it tremendous influence over the development of children's attitudes and capabilities. The family has more generally served as a key source of social identity, political status, and material resources of all members of society. Today, the family is often seen—and, in fact, serves—as the chief site of intimate emotional, physical, and material support between adults, adults and young children, and adult children and their elder parents. Although often conceived of as a private institution, the family has always been a central concern of politics and home to intense social regulation, a key site of disciplinary practices of sex, sexuality, gender, class, race, and more. In short, in traditions of the English- and European-language-speaking worlds, along with the state and market, the family is one of the most important institutions of social and political life.

Although contemporary political theorists have had much to say about state and market institutions, they have given less attention to the family in their discussions of social and political justice (Kymlicka 2001, 398; Eichner 2010; Fineman 2004; McClain 2006; Okin 1989). John Rawls, for example, whose *A Theory of Justice* (1971) is widely credited with reviving discussions about justice in contemporary English- and European-language political theory, sets aside detailed discussion of the family in this work. Although he claims that a just society cannot remain stable for long without just families, he does not elaborate on the nature of such families or what the state might do to promote them (Okin 1989, 93–94). In the decades following the publication of *A Theory of Justice*, most mainstream theorists of justice similarly focused on state and market institutions and neglected the family.

Second-wave feminist theorists, children's rights advocates, and a new generation of conservative thinkers brought the family into contemporary scholarship on justice. Even though they disagreed on many points, they shared a common insight: the family *is* a matter of justice. Family relationships have broad repercussions for political justice. The justice of society as a whole is impaired and even undermined, according to these thinkers, if justice within and among families is not maintained. These thinkers split, of course, on substantive questions of what a just family looks like and how the state should be involved in maintaining it. Social conservatives tend to associate family justice with traditional ideals about marriage and two-parent families, for example, whereas feminist theorists highlight the gender injustice of such arrangements and call for more egalitarian models of family life. Children's rights advocates, in turn, focus on ensuring children's healthy development and well-being regardless of their impact on traditional family values or gender equality. Despite these differences (or perhaps in part because of them), all of these groups brought new attention to family as a crucial topic in discussions of justice.

The last thirty years have seen an explosion of new scholarship on justice, politics, and the family. This volume draws together some of the most influential of this work. Many of the selections here have been previously published. They come from a wide variety of difficult-to-access sources, hence the value in selectively reprinting from these classic pieces. In addition, new work is included from the volume editors and contributors, including Traci M. Levy, whose chapter discusses a subject not often addressed in the literature. By bringing these chapters and articles together into a single volume, this book provides an ideal introduction to this important body of literature. Underlining the significance of the family for theories of justice and highlighting key questions that arise when considering the role of family in a just society, the volume also serves as a foundation for future research into justice, politics, and the family.

To contextualize the themes and questions of the pieces included here, we offer in the remainder of the Introduction a brief summary of the views of key classical Western political philosophers on justice, politics, and the family.[1] Although many contemporary political theorists have ignored the family, the same is not true of many of the most notable of classical writers (Elshtain 1982, 4). For philosophers such as Plato, Aristotle, Locke, Mill, and others, the family is central to considerations of a just political order. Of course,

---

1. A fuller discussion can be found in Daniel Engster, "Family," in Michael Gibbon (ed.), *The Encyclopedia of Political Thought*. New York: Wiley-Blackwell, 2013. The historical discussion below is based in part on this article.

their ideas about family are often quite different from those of contemporary theorists. Most classical thinkers, for example, treat the family as natural, static, gendered, hierarchical, and heterosexual. They are hardly, if ever, concerned with protecting deep cultural diversity or thinking in global terms. Moreover, none were witness to the changes that have shaken family structures in Western societies over the past fifty years, including intensified globalization, the influx of women into paid employment, the sharp increase in single parenthood, and the emergence of groups (feminist, gay, and others) advocating for expanded definitions of marriage and family. And yet, for all these differences, we miss much if we fail to see the connections between today's scholars and those of the past. Classical authors framed enduring questions about the relationship between the family and political life that contemporary political theorists continue to build on, extend, and revise. Studying the classical authors thus allows us to engage in an ongoing conversation, to understand the roots of our own views, and, through contrasts, to become aware of our unarticulated assumptions about justice, politics, and the family.

JUSTICE AND THE FAMILY IN CLASSICAL WESTERN POLITICAL THOUGHT

Plato's (427–348 BCE) *Republic* is one of the foundational inquiries in Western political thought into the nature of justice. It is also a foundational text for thinking about the relationship between families, politics, and justice. The family, in Plato's telling, is a threat to political life. Familial ties threaten the unity and order of the city and upset justice.

In the perfectly just society of the *Republic*, each citizen performs the work that he or she is best suited for and does not meddle in the affairs of others. To achieve this perfectly just society, Plato proposes that the private household and family would have to be abolished. In the guardian and ruling classes, there could be no private property, living arrangements, or family. Philosopher-monarchs would determine who could reproduce with whom based on eugenic considerations; children would be removed from their mothers at birth and placed under the tutelage of professional caregivers. Women would be released from their traditional roles as family caregivers and, like men, assigned to the tasks best suited to their individual natures. The private family would thus disappear, and the city as a whole would come to resemble a single family, with citizens addressing each other as brother and sister and treating one another as kin.

Plato abolishes the private family and household in order to eradicate the private loyalties and affections that, in his view, threaten citizens' public loyalties and the rational governance of the polis. Writing at a time when questions about how the private family might be integrated into the polis were pressing, Plato was especially sensitive to the ways in which family attachments could undermine political unity and justice. The ancient Greek tragedy *Antigone* gives vivid expression to this tension between family and polis. Plato, however, goes beyond suggesting that the family merely needs to be better integrated into the polis. For him, the family is by its very nature a source of disorder and injustice. It encourages partiality and bias and exposes children to misguided parenting practices. Thus, the abolition of the private family is for Plato a necessary condition for the full realization of political justice.

Although Plato's position may seem extreme, it is a view that radical theorists have periodically revived and embraced over the last 2,500 years.[2] Moreover, no matter what one thinks about Plato's conclusions, he raises questions about justice, politics, and the family that remain important to this day: Can the (private) family *ever* be just? Would we all be better off without lifelong private families? Must the family exist in tension with the state? Can this tension ever be overcome?

These questions are taken up by a number of the selections included here. In Part II, Susan Moller Okin builds on Plato's insight about the deep connections between familial and political life to develop her own views on the relationship among justice, gender, and the family. In Part III, although she is responding most immediately to John Rawls, Véronique Munoz-Dardé addresses challenges at the heart of the *Republic*: "Is the Family to Be Abolished Then?" And as the title indicates, all of the readings in Part IV "Families and the State" touch on Plato's themes.

Aristotle (384–322 BCE) offers a very different view of the place of the family in a just society. In *The Politics*, he argues that the family and polity are distinct but complementary associations. The family is a natural unit, consisting of husband, wife, children, and slaves. It begins in the procreative union of male and female and exists for the reproduction of the species and satisfaction of daily recurrent needs. The natural order of the family, according to Aristotle, is for men to rule over women, children, and slaves. Political rule, by contrast, consists of relations among equals (all men), where each takes a turn in ruling and being ruled. Its aim is not merely sustaining life but promoting the good life among human beings.

For Aristotle, the family naturally gives rise to the village and ultimately to the polis, which is the final and perfect association among human beings. The polis does not, however, entirely subsume the family. Arguing against Plato's proposal to abolish private families, Aristotle maintains that the family serves an important function in the polis by providing daily, basic, and particularized material, physical, and emotional care to individuals. Moreover, he argues, because individuals care best for what is their own, Plato's proposal to abolish the private family would lead to numerous injustices, including a general indifference toward children.

---

2. In *The Dialectic of Sex* (1970), for example, Shulamith Firestone argues that the only way to achieve justice and equality for women is to abolish the nuclear biological family.

Despite these criticisms, Aristotle does not treat the family as a wholly private institution. In his discussion of the ideal polis, he argues that family must be subject to extensive public regulations, particularly with regard to the bearing and rearing of children. Legislators should take steps to encourage men and women to marry at their ideal childbearing years (thirty-seven for men, eighteen for women, by Aristotle's account). Pregnant women should be required by law to exercise regularly and follow a healthy diet for the sake of their developing fetuses. The polis should mandate that parents abandon any children born with impairments, and public superintendents of education should determine the sorts of stories that parents can tell their children. Thus, although Aristotle defends the significance and singularity of the family, he is no advocate of family privacy: His family is a gendered, hierarchical affair, subordinate to and closely regulated by political authority. Its ultimate end is its contribution to the polis, not itself or its inhabitants.

This account of the nature and place of family in political life continues as a model for many today, but also raises important questions. The readings in Parts III, IV, and V explore many of these questions, such as, How extensively should the state regulate family life and parenting practices? How much privacy should families rightfully enjoy?

In ancient Greek discussions of family, sexual desire and non-procreative sex figure rarely, if at all. Christianity changed this. For Augustine, Bishop of Hippo (354–430) and his fellow Christians, sex is the site of Original Sin. Thus, ideally, it would be avoided altogether. Yet, because few are capable of lifelong celibacy and because sex is necessary for the continuation of life, Christian marriage is an essential institution of the earthly City of God. Within its confines, sex serves the purpose of procreation. Containing sex within a divinely ordained institution elevates and orders our sin-infected drives. Shared purpose, monogamy, and fidelity of the marital family generate a society of mutual respect and affection born of restraint. These bonds, Augustine argues, provide the grounds for peaceful society among families, cities, and nations. Thomas Aquinas (1225–1274) would later outline similar views but root them in his natural law theory.

Christian ideals about the family and marriage continue to exercise a strong influence over personal and public practices in countries such as the United States. Some scholars argue that the companionate marriage of the modern period grows directly out of early Christian views. Several of the selections in Part I, "What Is the 'Family'?," and Part IV, "Families and the State," directly engage with and challenge these ideals, arguing for a more diverse understanding of the family and marriage.

In the early modern period, John Locke (1632–1704) offered a more egalitarian and voluntaristic vision of family and justice that has also remained influential to the present day. Like Aristotle, he distinguishes between family and politics. Parental power, he argues, exists for the sake of raising and educating children; political power, for the sake of preserving the lives, liberty, and property of citizens. Unlike Aristotle or Christian thinkers, however, Locke contends that both family and state power rest on artificial grounds: consent. The only legitimate and, therefore, for Locke, just basis of political authority is the consent of the people. Similarly, "conjugal society" consists of a "voluntary compact between man and woman" for "so long as is necessary to the nourishment and support of the young" (Locke 1980, 7.78–79). Because the marriage contract is consensual, Locke maintains that its terms might be varied as long as they are consistent with the goals of procreation and child rearing. There is, for example, no reason why a marriage contract might not be set to expire at a predetermined date, or be terminated by its signatories, once procreation, education, and inheritance have been secured (Locke 1980, 7.81–83).

Although Locke expressly conceives of marriage and the family in conventional, contractual terms, he nonetheless ultimately treats them as rooted in natural ends of procreation and child rearing. Thus, there are inherent limits, in his account, to the malleability of the marriage contract. Likewise, equal consent notwithstanding, Locke asserts that within the family, the husband, "as the abler and stronger," should have the final determination in important matters, thus maintaining a gendered, hierarchical element in his understanding of family relations (Locke 1980, 7.82). Finally, because, in his view, the family is an association that exists prior to and independent of political society, he suggests the state ought to have limited authority over it (Shanley 1982, 80–95). With these three claims, Carole Pateman argues, Locke helped to establish the modern patriarchal tradition within liberal political thought whereby the family is conceived of as a private, patriarchal, and heterosexual institution within a relatively free and equal political society. Feminist and other egalitarian theorists (Parts II and IV of this work), in particular, have challenged these views and worked to envision a more thoroughly egalitarian liberal theory of society and the family.

The most influential treatments of the family in eighteenth- and nineteenth-century English political thought challenged the prevailing patriarchal assumptions. Feminist theorists Mary Wollstonecraft (1759–1797) and John Stuart Mill (1806–1873) both argued that the power that men wielded over women in the Victorian family was as artificial and unjust as the power that despots wielded over their subjects and had similar corrupting effects on society. The subjection of women in the family violates individual liberty—of wives—and, perhaps even worse, teaches injustice to all that inhabit it. It contributes to poorly educated children, unhappy marriages, a waste of women's talents, and, in general, vanity, frivolity, and sloth among both men and women. For both theorists, justice and progress require the full extension of equal rights to women in all areas of life, including both politics and the family. Indeed, Mill argues, individuals will never be fully prepared to participate in a free democratic society "until they practice in the family the same moral rule which is adapted to the normal constitution of human society" (Mill 1991,

518–519). Anticipating contemporary feminist arguments, both held that political justice starts at home. Equalizing personal relationships within the family was crucial for achieving a more fully equal and free democratic society.

Yet, despite their feminist innovations, both Wollstonecraft and Mill retain elements of the older conceptions of family. Wollstonecraft claims, for example, that women are naturally suited for raising children and tending the household and should remain as homebound helpmates to their husbands. Mill assumed that within marriage most women would continue to devote themselves primarily to domestic life and child rearing. Like most political theorists up until the mid-twentieth century, both regarded the division of labor between men and women within the family as natural and did not foresee the far-reaching consequences that extending full political and social equality to women might have for structure of family life, and vice versa. Contemporary theorists (including most contained in this volume) tend to view Wollstonecraft's and Mill's theories as incomplete and favor a more equal division of labor within the family. Wollstonecraft's and Mill's arguments nonetheless represent an implicit challenge to current thinking about the family: Is the traditional gendered division of labor within families entirely conventional? Is it realistic to expect men and women to equally share in all family tasks? Are there any negative consequences (for children? for society?) of equalizing family life?[3]

Friedrich Engels (1820–1895) outlined a radically different understanding of the family that also deserves brief mention. The patriarchal, monogamous pair at the heart of the modern family, he argues—presaging arguments such as Judith Stacey's in Part I here—is the result not of sexual necessity or romantic love, but rather, of economics. Monogamy represents "the victory of private property over original, naturally developed common ownership" (Engels 1978, 739). Before the invention of private property, "communistic" households were the norm. In that context, women ruled the family: as the known origin of all the children, women naturally occupied the dominant position of esteem and influence in the family. As wealth increased, so too, the power of men and the imperative of identifying paternity. Engels argues that monogamy developed as a response to the need for individual men to know, confidently, which children were theirs, so that they could pass their private wealth on to just their children. He calls the invention of monogamy "the overthrow of mother right … [and] the world-historic defeat of the female sex" (Engels 1978, 736). This new family form represents, for Engels, not only the first division of labor (for breeding) but also the first class antagonism and first class oppression. Thus, real justice, that is, the justice of true communism, starts and ends, for Engels, in the family.

Although many of the particulars of Engels's account have been rejected or ignored, some remain influential even today. Many contemporary theorists

---

3. One writer who explicitly defends gender inequality within the family is David Blankenhorn, *Fatherless America*. New York: Basic Books, 1995.

accept some version of his argument that family form derives not from nature but from economics. That the patriarchal family serves to oppress women as a sex class was a view taken up by radical feminists in the 1960s and beyond. Okin (1989, 14), for example, calls the patriarchal family the "linchpin" (170) of the unjust gender system. Stacey, Traci Levy, and Tamara Metz all likewise endorse Engels's view that the construct of the monogamous, nuclear family undergirds social class divisions. Whereas few today see communism as the solution to family and social injustice, many political theorists of the family—including, here, Nancy Fraser, Levy, and others—advocate for much more robust social welfare policies than exist in most postindustrial polities, and, hence, the partial socialization of the family. And finally, the claim that the way we talk about family obscures and perpetuates structural injustice is also widely accepted by scholars of all stripes.

Definitions of justice, accounts of family, and the relationship between the two have changed over the course of the last two and a half millennia. Key questions, however, remain the same: What is a "family"? How is political justice related to life within and among families? What role should the state play in families? What role does the family play in political justice? A threat? A foundation? The answers of classical authors inform—often unwittingly— much of contemporary discourse about the family, politics, and justice.

JUSTICE AND THE FAMILY IN CONTEMPORARY WESTERN POLITICAL THOUGHT

When political theorists reflect on the family today, they encounter a very different world from that of the past: complex global economies, the massive administrative state, the dominance of liberal democratic rhetoric (if not policies), longer life expectancy, powerful reproductive technologies, and postindustrial economies that assume two-income households. In 2010, for example, 62 percent of working-age women in the United States were in paid employment (compared with around 19 percent in 1900), roughly 40 percent of all children were born outside of marriage, and more than one-quarter of all children lived in single-parent homes (the vast majority with single mothers).[4] These new social circumstances challenge us to reconsider the relationships among justice, politics, and the family in both some familiar and some quite novel ways. Familiar questions include those relating to the definition of the family, the tension between family privacy and political justice, and the role of the state in regulating family life. New questions arise regarding the role of the administrative state in supporting families and tensions between families and global capitalism. Above all, in the twentieth- and twenty-first-century context, questions of gender and diversity take on central significance. So, for instance,

---

4. US Census Bureau, http://factfinder2.census.gov/faces/nav/jsf/pages/index.xhtml.

the old question of what is "the family" is overlaid with concern about the implications of different family forms for gender equality.

The readings in Part I begin appropriately enough with the definitional question: What is the family? The family is obviously not just any assortment of cohabiting individuals. Some cohabiting individuals (e.g., roommates) are not usually considered a family, and some families do not all live in one location (perhaps because one or more family members work in another city, state, or country). A family is also not necessarily a group of biologically related individuals, because married couples are not biologically related, and adopted children have no biological link with their parents. What, then, marks off a family from other groups of individuals? Many take an expansive approach to this question, defining "family" in the broadest terms possible. But this raises a second important question that frames the readings in this part: What are the implications for society of broadening the definition of families? Does society have an interest in promoting all family forms or only some?

Part II explores the connection between gender relations within the family and political justice. The readings in this part argue that unequal gender relations within the family—particularly the traditional division between male breadwinners and female homemakers/caregivers—underlie broad economic, social, and political inequalities between men and women. Both selections maintain that social and political justice cannot be achieved without significant reforms both to family life and to public policy and, thus, make the case for the centrality of the family to any theory of justice. They offer a variety of proposals for achieving greater gender equality in the family, including some that challenge the justice of allowing individuals to structure their family lives as they alone see fit.

Part III shifts the focus from gender to children. The treatment of children within the family is an important political concern; as we have seen, it was a *central* concern for Plato and Aristotle. Parents may abuse and neglect their children. Less dramatically, they may also raise them in ways that stunt their abilities to work, form relationships, and function in liberal democratic societies. The readings in this part examine the nature of children's rights and the implications of these rights for legitimate parenting practices as well as various reforms that states might undertake to improve the just treatment of children.

Part IV addresses two central elements of state-family relationships. First, should families enjoy a right to privacy from state interference? If so, why? Locke and other modern political theorists generally defended the family's right to privacy based in part on the father's prerogative to rule over his wife and children. If this sexist assumption is removed, is there any reason for the state to continue to accord special privacy rights to family relations? The first reading in this part challenges the notion that families can be entirely free of state influence and argues, thus, that state action should be expressly guided by the best interests of individuals and society. The second and third readings take up the heated question of state recognition of marriage. Should the legal definition of marriage be expanded from its current emphasis on heterosexual couples to include same-sex couples? What about polygamous unions or groups of people? Alternatively, should the state give up its role in recognizing and regulating marriage altogether?

Part V reexamines all the themes from the preceding three sections (gender, children, family privacy, and marriage) in light of multicultural family practices. Owing in part to globalization, Western societies have become increasingly diverse ethnically and culturally. Citizens of liberal democracies now often have different—sometimes radically different—ideas about gender equality, child rearing practices, and marriage arrangements. What, then, should liberal democratic states do about non-liberal or nondemocratic family arrangements and practices? How far should liberal democratic states go in tolerating cultural diversity in family life? The two readings in this part outline interesting challenges for thinking about these large and complicated questions.

Part VI explores most directly some of the new challenges that arise for thinking about justice, politics, and the family as a result of the developments associated with globalization. The intertwining of national economies and greater ease with which individuals travel across borders have dramatic implications for family life. With greater frequency, women from poorer countries are traveling to wealthier countries to work as nannies, child care providers, and family caregivers, often leaving their own children behind. At least in the United States, because of high rates of unregulated immigration, the government is increasingly faced with the prospect of deporting parents whose children are legal citizens. The readings in this final part discuss the implications of these new developments for politics and family justice.

The readings in this book represent only the tips of very large bodies of research. At the end of each section, we offer a "Suggested Further Readings" list to facilitate more detailed investigation of these topics. Although the readings included here provide a fairly comprehensive introduction to family justice issues, it should also be said that they are not exhaustive. Broadly conceived, the topic of family justice might be understood to include questions about abortion, artificial insemination, surrogacy, and other issues relating to sex, sexuality, pregnancy, and birth. Although these topics are certainly important for thinking about family justice, we were able to include only a limited number of selections in this volume. Our goal has been to select readings that have laid the foundations for existing research into justice, politics, and the family and raise interesting questions that pave the way for future investigations into this topic. Due to space constraints, many of the pieces in this volume have been edited. Ellipses indicate where material has been cut, and all notes and references have been omitted—please consult the originals for complete citation information. The core ideas, we believe, remain clear and true to the original.

WORKS CITED

Aristotle. *The Politics.* Trans. by Ernest Barker. Oxford: Oxford University Press, 1995.

Blankenhorn, David. *Fatherless America.* New York: Basic Books, 1995.

Eichner, Maxine. *The Supportive State: Families, the State, and American Political Ideals.* Oxford: Oxford University Press, 2010.

Elshtain, Jean Bethke, ed. *The Family in Political Thought.* Amherst: The University of Massachusetts Press, 1982.

Engels, Friedrich. *The Origin of the Family, Private Property, and the State* (1884). In *Marx-Engels Reader.* Edited by Robert C. Tucker. New York: W. W. Norton & Co., 1978.

Engster, Daniel. "Family." In *The Encyclopedia of Political Thought.* Edited by Michael Gibbon. New York: Wiley-Blackwell, 2013.

Fineman, Martha. *The Autonomy Myth: A Theory of Dependency.* New York: The New Press, 2004.

Firestone, Shulamith. *The Dialectic of Sex: The Case for Feminist Revolution.* New York: Morrow, 1970.

Kymlicka, Will. *Contemporary Political Theory: An Introduction.* 2nd ed. Oxford: Oxford University Press, 2001.

Locke, John. *Second Treatise of Government.* Edited by C. B. McPherson. Indianapolis, IN: Hackett Publishing, 1980.

McClain, Linda. *The Place of Families: Fostering Capacity, Equality, and Responsibility.* Cambridge, MA: Harvard University Press, 2006.

Mill, John Stuart. "The Subjection of Women." In *On Liberty and Other Essays.* Edited by John Gray. Oxford: Oxford University Press, 1991.

Okin, Susan Moller. *Justice, Gender, and the Family.* New York: Basic Books, 1989.

Pateman, Carole. *The Sexual Contract.* Cambridge, UK: Polity Press, 1988.

Plato. *Republic.* Trans. by G. M. A. Grube. Indianapolis, IN: Hackett Publishing Company, 1992.

Rawls, John. *A Theory of Justice.* Cambridge, MA: The Belknap Press, 1971.

Shanley, Mary Lyndon. "Marriage Contract and Social Contract in Seventeenth-Century English Political Thought." In *The Family in Political Thought.* Edited by Jean Elshtain. Amherst: The University of Massachusetts Press, 1982.

Suggested Further Readings

CLASSICAL POLITICAL THOUGHT

Aristotle, *The Politics* (especially Books I and VII).

Augustine, *The Good of Marriage*; *The City of God*; *The Confessions*.

Friedrich Engels, *The Origin of the Family, Private Property, and the State* (1884).

G. W. F. Hegel, *Elements of the Philosophy of Right* (1821) (especially Sections 158–181).

Thomas Hobbes, *Leviathan* (1651) (especially Chapter 20).

John Locke, *The Second Treatise of Government* (1690) (especially Chapters 6–7).

John Stuart Mill, "Subjection of Women" (1869).

Plato, *Republic* (especially Book V).

Jean-Jacques Rousseau, *Discourse on the Origin of Inequality* (1755); *Emile* (1762).

Alexis de Tocqueville, *Democracy in America* (1835/1840) (especially Vol. I, Part 1, Chapter 3; Vol. II, Part 3, Chapters 8–12).

Mary Wollstonecraft, *A Vindication of the Rights of Woman* (1792).

CONTEMPORARY POLITICAL THOUGHT

David Archard, *The Family: A Liberal Defense* (New York: Palgrave Macmillan, 2010).

Jean Bethke Elshtain, *Public Man, Private Woman* (Princeton, NJ: Princeton University Press, 1981).

Jean Bethke Elshtain, ed., *The Family in Political Thought* (Amherst: The University of Massachusetts Press, 1982).

Valerie Lehr, *Queer Family Values: Rethinking the Myth of the Nuclear Family* (Philadelphia, PA: Temple University Press, 1999).

Linda McClain, *The Place of Families: Fostering Capacity, Equality, and Responsibility* (Cambridge, MA: Harvard University Press, 2006).

Susan Okin, *Women in Western Political Thought* (Princeton, NJ: Princeton University Press, 1979).

Diana Tietjens Meyers, Kenneth Kipnis, and Cornelius Murphy Jr., *Kindred Matters: Rethinking the Philosophy of the Family* (Ithaca, NY: Cornell University Press, 1993).

I

What Is the "Family"?

Introduction to Part I

The readings in this first part deal with questions that are basic to the theme of the volume: What *is* a family? What intimate relational groupings should the state recognize as such? And why? Is the family best defined in terms of function or form, and what are the implications for the well-being of society as a whole?

In "Postmodern Families," Judith Stacey argues that the modern nuclear family ideal was an ephemeral and not entirely desirable phenomenon to begin with. She then adds that this ideal was destined to collapse under pressure from the forces of individualism, democracy, and romantic love in modern societies. By her account, we should not resist or regret the diversification of family forms, or what she calls the emergence of "postmodern families," but celebrate it, because postmodern family forms provide individuals with new opportunities for democratic self-expression and personal fulfillment.

In "The Family and Civic Life," Jean Bethke Elshtain takes a rather more dim view of these developments. By her account, democratic societies rightly privilege traditional family arrangements—nuclear, heterosexual, and monogamous—over other alternative groupings, because society depends on these traditional family arrangements to provide children with the moral education required for democratic citizenship. This does not mean, Elshtain is careful to note, that individuals ought not to be free to pursue different relational arrangements in their private lives. Yet, she argues that these alternative groupings should not be publicly or legally accorded the same benefits and rights as

13

"families" and suggests that they should perhaps even be discouraged when children are involved. The two-parent, heterosexual family is, by her estimation, the best environment for raising children in a democratic society.[1] Thus, justice weighs in favor of the state privileging that family form.

In a piece original to this volume, Traci Levy's "Families as Relationships of Intimacy and Care" offers a radically different perspective. Because US public policy has failed to adapt its definition of families to changing social circumstances, Levy argues, it has contributed to a crisis in family care, leaving many individuals without the personal support they need. Rather than relying on outmoded family ideals, justice and prudence recommend that "the family" be redefined in functional terms as intimate relational units based on natural or self-chosen caregiving responsibilities. Public policies should be reformed and expanded, according to Levy, so that they apply to all such caregiving units.

---

1. A large body of social science research exists on the effects of alternative family arrangements (single-parent families, same-sex couples, stepparents) on children's health, development, and well-being. Interpretations of this research are invariably controversial. Elshtain interprets this research as indicating the superiority of intact, heterosexual, two-parent families in supporting the development of children well-suited to life in democratic societies. Others read the research differently.

1

Postmodern Families

Judith Stacey

THE MAKING AND UNMAKING OF MODERN FAMILIES

> *On a spring afternoon half a century from today, the Joneses are gathering to sing "Happy Birthday" to Junior.*
>
> *There's Dad and his third wife, Mom and her second husband, Junior's two half brothers from his father's first marriage, his six stepsisters from his mother's spouse's previous unions, 100-year-old Great-Grandpa, all eight of Junior's current "grand-parents," assorted aunts, uncles-in-law and stepcousins.*
>
> *While one robot scoops up the gift wrappings and another blows out the candles, Junior makes a wish—that he didn't have so many relatives.*
>
> *The family tree by the year 2033 will be rooted as deeply as ever in America's social landscape, but it will be sprouting some odd branches.*
>
> —*U.S. News & World Report*

In the summer of 1986 I attended a wedding ceremony in a small Christian pentecostal church in the Silicon Valley. The service celebrated the same "traditional" family patterns and values that two years earlier had inspired a "profamily" movement to assist Ronald Reagan's landslide reelection to the presidency of the United States. At the same time, however, the pastor's rhetoric displayed substantial sympathy with feminist criticisms of patriarchal marriage. "A ring is not a shackle, and marriage is not a relationship of domination," he instructed the groom. Moreover, complex patterns of divorce, remarriage, and stepkinship linked the members of the wedding party and their guests. The group bore far greater resemblance to the postmodern family of the

15

imaginary twenty-first-century Joneses than it did to the image of "traditional" family life that arouses the nostalgic fantasies so widespread among critics of contemporary family practices.

In the final decades before the twenty-first century, passionate contests over changing family life in the United States have polarized vast numbers of citizens. Outside the Supreme Court of the United States, righteous, placard-carrying Right-to-Lifers square off against feminists and civil libertarians demonstrating their anguish over the steady dismantling of women's reproductive freedom. On the same day in July 1989 when New York's highest court expanded the legal definition of a family to extend rent-control protection to gay couples, a coalition of conservative clergymen in San Francisco blocked implementation of their city's new "domestic partners" ordinance. "It is the totality of the relationship," proclaimed the New York judge, "As evidenced by the dedication, caring and self-sacrifice of the parties which should, in the final analysis, control" the definition of family. But just this concept of family is anathema to "profamily" activists. Declaring that the attempt by the San Francisco Board of Supervisors to grant legal status to unmarried heterosexual and homosexual couples "arbitrarily redefined the time-honored and hallowed nature of the family," the clergymen's petition was signed by sufficient citizens to force the ordinance into a referendum battle. The reckoning came in November 1989, when the electorate of the city many consider to be the national capital of family change narrowly defeated the domestic partners law.

Most popular, as well as many scholarly, assessments of family change anxiously and misguidedly debate whether "the family" will survive the twentieth century at all. Anxieties like these are far from new. "For at least 150 years," historian Linda Gordon writes, "there have been periods of fear that 'the family'—meaning a popular image of what families were supposed to be like, by no means a correct recollection of any actual 'traditional' family—was in decline; and these fears have tended to escalate in periods of social stress." The actual subject of this recurring, fretful discourse is a historically specific form and concept of family life, one that most historians identify as the "modern" family. Students in a course I teach called "The Making and Unmaking of Modern Families" helped me realize that many of us who write and teach about American family life have not abetted public understanding of family change with our counterintuitive use of the concept, the "modern" family. The "modern" family of sociological theory and historical convention designates a form no longer prevalent in the United States—an intact nuclear household unit composed of a male breadwinner, his full-time homemaker wife, and their dependent children. This is precisely the form of family life that many mistake for an ancient, essential, and now-endangered institution.

"How many of you grew up in a modern family?" I used to ask my students at the beginning of each term. I expected the proportion of raised hands to decline, like the modern family, with the years. It baffled me at first to receive precisely the inverse response. Just when demographers were reporting that twice as many American households were headed by divorced, separated, and never-married individuals as were occupied by "modern" families, increasing numbers of my students claimed to have grown up in "modern" ones. This seemingly anomalous finding was the product, of course, of my poorly conceived survey question. Just as I had anticipated, over the years fewer and fewer of my students were coming of age in Ozzie and Harriet families. Quite sensibly, however, unlike me, they did not regard such families as "modern"; to them they were archaic "traditional" ones. Those contemporary family relationships that my students took to be modern comprise the "postmodern" family terrain. [...]

THE EPHEMERAL MODERN FAMILY

Now that the "modern" family system has almost exited from its historical stage, we can perceive how peculiar, ephemeral, and internally contradictory was this once-revolutionary gender and kinship order. Historians place the emergence of the modern American family among white middle-class people in the late eighteenth century; they depict its flowering in the nineteenth century and chart its decline in the second half of the twentieth. Thus, for white Americans, the history of modern families traverses the same historical trajectory as that of modern industrial society.[1] What was modern about upper-middle-class family life in the half century after the American Revolution was the appearance of social arrangements governing gender and kinship relationships that contrasted sharply with those of "traditional," or premodern, patriarchal corporate units.

The premodern family among white Colonial Americans, an institution some scholars characterize as "the Godly family," was the constitutive element of Colonial society. This integrated economic, social, and political unit explicitly subordinated individual to corporate family interests, and women and children to the authority of the household's patriarchal head. Decisions regarding the timing and crafting of premodern marriages served not the emotional needs of individuals but the economic, religious, and social purposes of larger kin

---

1. The family histories of subjugated, "nonwhite" populations in the United States—Native Americans, African Americans, Mexican Americans, and Asian Americans—are also intertwined with that of industrial capitalist development. Yet cultural differences and systemic racial-ethnic subordination produce major differences in the substance and timing of each group's process of family change. I portray the history of the ideal-typical family order of the dominant white population because, until recently, it represented this nation's culturally mandated gender and kinship system. This family regime has been denied to most members of racial and ethnic minorities, and their diverse family arrangements frequently have been judged and found wanting when compared with it. For more comprehensive and comparative texts that treat a broad range of American families, see Mintz and Kellogg, *Domestic Revolutions*; Evans, *Born for Liberty*; Baca-Zinn and Eitzen, *Diversity in American Families*; and Coontz, *Social Origins of Private Life*.

groups, as these were interpreted by patriarchs who controlled access to land, property, and craft skills. Nostalgic images of "traditional" families rarely recall their instability or diversity. Death visited Colonial homes so frequently that second marriages and blended households composed of stepkin were commonplace. With female submission thought to be divinely prescribed, conjugal love was a fortuitous bonus, not a prerequisite of such marriages. Similarly the doctrine of innate depravity demanded authoritarian parenting to break the will and save the souls of obstinate children, a project that required extensive paternal involvement in child rearing. Few boundaries between family and work impeded such patriarchal supervision, or segregated the sexes who labored at their arduous and interdependent tasks in close proximity. Boundaries between public and private life were equally permeable. Communities regulated proper family conduct, intervening actively to enforce disciplinary codes, and parents exchanged their children as apprentices and servants.

Four radical innovations differentiate modern from premodern family life among white Americans: (1) Family work and productive work became separated, rendering women's work invisible as they and their children became economically dependent on the earnings of men. (2) Love and companionship became the ideal purposes of marriages that were to be freely contracted by individuals. (3) A doctrine of privacy emerged that attempted to withdraw middle-class family relationships from public scrutiny. (4) Women devoted increased attention to nurturing fewer and fewer children as mothering came to be exalted as both a natural and demanding vocation.

The rise of the modern American family accompanied the rise of industrial capitalist society, with its revolutionary social, spatial, and temporal reorganization of work and domestic life. The core premises and practices of the new family regime were far more contradictory than those of the premodern family order. Coding work as masculine and home as feminine, modern economic arrangements deepened the segregation of the sexes by extracting men from, and consigning white married women to, an increasingly privatized domestic domain. The institutionalized subordination of these wives to their husbands persisted; indeed, as factory production supplanted domestic industry, wives became increasingly dependent on their spouses' earnings. The doctrine of separate gender spheres governing the modern family order in the nineteenth century was so potent that few married women among even the poorest of native white families dared to venture outside their homes in search of income.

The proper sphere of working-class married white women also was confined to the home. Yet few working-class families approximated the modern family ideal before well into the twentieth century. Enduring conditions of poverty, squalor, disease, and duress rivaling those in industrializing England, most immigrant and native white working-class families in nineteenth-century America depended on supplementary income. Income from women's out work, child labor, lodgers, and the earnings of employed unmarried sons and daughters supplemented the meager and unreliable wages paid to working men.

Not until the post–World War II era did substantial numbers of working-class households achieve the "modern family" pattern.

If the doctrine of separate, and unequal, gender spheres limited women's domain and rendered their work invisible, it also enhanced their capacity to formulate potent moral and political challenges to patriarchy. Men ceded the domains of child rearing and virtue to "moral" mothers who made these responsibilities the basis for expanding their social influence and political rights. This and the radical ideologies of individualism, democracy, and conjugal love, which infused modern family culture, would lead ultimately to its undoing. It is no accident, historians suggest, that the first wave of American feminism accompanied the rise of the modern family.

With rearview vision one glimpses the structural fragility of the modern family system, particularly its premise of enduring voluntary commitment. For modern marriages, unlike their predecessors, were properly affairs not of the purse but of the heart. A romantic "until death do us part" commitment volunteered by two young adults acting largely independent of the needs, interests, or wishes of their kin was the vulnerable linchpin of the modern family order. It seems rather remarkable, looking back, that during the first century of the modern family's cultural ascendancy, death did part the vast majority of married couples. But an ideology of conjugal love and companionship implies access to divorce as a safety valve for failures of youthful judgment or the vagaries of adult affective development. Thus, a statistical omen of the internal instability of this form of marriage lies in the unprecedented rise of divorce rates that accompanied the spread of the modern family. Despite severe legal and social restrictions, divorce rates began to climb at least as early as the 1840s. They have continued their ascent ever since, until by the middle of the 1970s divorce outstripped death as a source of marital dissolution. A crucial component of the modern family system, divorce would ultimately prove to be its Achilles' heel.

For a century, as the cultural significance of the modern family grew, the productive and even the reproductive work performed within its domain contracted. By the end of the "modern" industrial era in the 1950s, virtually all productive work had left the home. While advances in longevity stretched enduring marriages to unprecedented lengths, the full-time homemaker's province had been pared to the chores of housework, consumption, and the cultivation of a declining number of progeny during a shortened span of years.

Those Americans, like myself, who came of age at that historic moment were encouraged to absorb a particularly distorted impression of the normalcy and timelessness of the modern family system. The decade between the late 1940s and the late 1950s represents an aberrant period in the history of this aberrant form of family life. Fueled in part, as historian Elaine May has suggested, by the apocalyptic Cold War sensibilities of the post–World War II nuclear age, the nation indulged in what would prove to be a last-gasp orgy of modern nuclear family domesticity. Three-fifths of American households conformed to the celebrated breadwinner–full-time homemaker modern form in 1950, as substantial sectors of working-class men began at long last to secure access to a family wage. A few years later Walt Disney opened the nation's first family theme park in southern California, designed to please and profit from the socially conservative fantasies of such increasingly prosperous families.

The aberrant fifties temporarily reversed the century's steady decline in birth rates. The average age of first-time visitors to the conjugal altar also dropped to record lows. Higher percentages of Americans were marrying than ever before or since, and even the majority of white working-class families achieved coveted homeownership status. It was during this time that Talcott Parsons provided family sociology with its most influential theoretical elaboration of the modern American family, of how its nuclear household structure and complementary division of roles into female "expressive" and male "instrumental" domains were sociologically adaptive to the functional demands of an industrial society. Rare are the generations, or even the sociologists, who perceive the historical idiosyncrasies of the normal cultural arrangements of their time.

The postwar baby boom was to make the behaviors and beliefs of that decade's offspring disproportionately significant for the rest of their lives. The media, the market, and all social and political institutions would follow their development with heightened interest. Thus, a peculiar period in US family history came to set the terms for the waves of rebellion against, and nostalgia for, the passing modern family and gender order that have become such prominent and disruptive features of the American political landscape. The world's first generation of childhood television viewers grew up, as I did, inundated by such weekly paeans to the male breadwinner nuclear household and modern family ideology as *Father Knows Best, Leave It to Beaver,* and *Ozzie and Harriet.* […]

[B]eneath the sentimental gloss that the fifties enameled onto its domestic customs, forces undermining the modern family of the 1950s accelerated while those sustaining it eroded. In the midst of profamily pageantry, nonfamily households proliferated. As the decade drew to a close, the nation entered what C. Wright Mills, with characteristic prescience, termed its "postmodern period." The emergent postindustrial economy shifted employment from heavy industries to nonunionized clerical, service, and new industrial sectors. Employers found themselves irresistibly attracted to the nonunionized, cheaper labor of women and, thus, increasingly to that of married women and mothers.

One glimpses the ironies of class and gender history here. For decades industrial unions struggled heroically for a socially recognized male breadwinner wage that would allow the working class to participate in the modern gender order. These struggles, however, contributed to the cheapening of female labor that helped gradually to undermine the modern family regime. Escalating consumption standards, the expansion of mass collegiate coeducation, and the persistence of high divorce rates then gave more and more women ample cause to invest a portion of their identities in the "instrumental" sphere of paid labor. Thus, middle-class women began to abandon their confinement in the modern family just as working-class women were approaching its access ramps. The former did so, however, only after the wives of working-class men had pioneered the twentieth-century revolution in women's paid work. Entering employment during the catastrophic 1930s, participating in defense industries in the 1940s, and raising their family incomes to middle-class standards by returning to the labor force rapidly after child rearing in the 1950s, working-class women quietly modeled and normalized the postmodern family standard of employment for married mothers. Whereas in 1950 the less a man earned, the more likely his wife was to be employed, by 1968 wives of middle-income men were the most likely to be in the labor force.

Thus, the apotheosis of the modern family only temporarily concealed its imminent decline. Breadwinners as well as homemakers were renegotiating the terms and tempos of their conjugal commitments. Cultural constraints that tethered women and men to lifelong vows continued to loosen. Writing about the origins of "the virgin and the state," anthropologist Sherry Ortner once theorized that the domestication of men represented a major social evolutionary watershed, which was achieved at considerable cost to the sexuality and autonomy of women. If this is correct, the historic bargain came apart during the sexual revolution of the 1960s. Even in the familistic fifties, as social critic Barbara Ehrenreich has suggested, beats and playboys rebelled against the monogamous breadwinner mold for culturally mandated masculinity. Advances in contraception paved the path for revolutionary changes in women's sexual behavior during the 1960s, changes that feminists alternately depict as the feminization or the masculinization of sex.

The aberrant and contradictory features of fifties' familial culture prepared the ground for the family revolution of the 1960s and 1970s from whose shock effects American society has not yet recovered. The gap between dominant cultural ideology and discordant behaviors generated radical challenges to the modern family. A social movement for gay liberation coincided with the legalization of abortion. Both posed the ultimate challenges to the cultural bond between sexuality and procreation. Particularly important for the fate of the modern family, a massive and militant movement for the liberation of women also revived in those years. And this "second wave" of American feminism made family politics central to its project.

FEMINISM AS MIDWIFE TO POSTINDUSTRIAL SOCIETY

Feminists intentionally accelerated the modern family's demise. *The Feminine Mystique,* Betty Friedan's best-selling critique of "the problem that has no name," inspired the awakening women's movement to launch a full-scale attack on the exploitative and stultifying effects of women's confinement and dependency as homemaker. Soon feminist scholars were warning women that "in truth, being a housewife makes women sick." This backward-looking critique of a declining institution and culture, one that I personally embraced wholeheartedly and helped to disseminate, colluded unwittingly in postindustrial processes, and at considerable political cost to the feminist movement. Although we intended the institutions of domesticity and their male beneficiaries to be the targets of our critique, we placed housewives on the defensive just when sizable numbers of working-class women were attaining this long-denied status. Feminists provided ideological support for divorce and for the soaring rates of female-headed households. Feminist enthusiasm for female autonomy encouraged women's massive entry into the postindustrial labor market. This, in turn, abetted the corporate deunionization strategies that have accompanied the reorganization of the US economy.

Millions of women like myself derived enormous, tangible benefits from the changes in postindustrial home and work life and from the ways in which feminist ideology encouraged us to initiate and cope with such changes. The lioness's share of these benefits, however, fell to privileged women. As postindustrial society became entrenched, many women, perhaps the majority, found their economic and personal conditions worsening. While unionized occupations and real wages began to decline, women were becoming the postindustrial "proletariat," performing most of the nation's low-skilled, poorly paid jobs. As the overall percentage of jobs that were secure and well paying declined, particularly within blue-collar occupations, increasing numbers of even white men swelled the ranks of the under- and unemployed. Nonetheless, most white male workers still labored at jobs that were skilled and comparatively well paid. The devastating economic effects on women and children of endemic marital instability became widely known. Increasing percentages of women were rearing children by themselves, generally with minimal economic contributions from former husbands and fathers. Yet rising numbers of single mothers who worked full time, year-round, were not earning wages sufficient to lift their families above the official poverty line.

Even as marriage bonds lost their adhesive, they came to serve as a major axis of economic and social stratification. Increasingly, families required two incomes to sustain a middle-class way of life. The married female "secondary" wage earner can lift a former working-class or middle-class family into relative affluence, while the loss or lack of access to a male income drove millions of women and children into poverty. In short, the drastic increase in women's paid employment in the postindustrial period yielded lots more work for mother, but with very unevenly distributed economic benefits and only modest improvements in relative earnings between women and men.

In the context of these developments, many women (and men) became susceptible to the profamily appeals of an antifeminist backlash. Because of our powerful and highly visible critique of the modern family, and because of the sensationalized way by which the media disseminated this critique, feminists received much of the blame for family and social crises that attended the transition from an industrial to a postindustrial order in the United States.

"Feminist ideology told women how foolish and exploited they were to be wives and mothers," turning them into "a vicious cartoon," wrote Connaught Marshner, "chairman" of the National Pro-Family Coalition, in her manifesto for the profamily movement, *The New Traditional Woman.*

Had white feminists identified earlier with the plight of the Black "matriarch," we might have been forewarned of our fate. In 1965 Daniel Patrick Moynihan's explosive report, *The Negro Family: The Case for National Action,* blamed Black "matriarchs" for much of the "tangle of pathology" he found in the nation's African American households. The Moynihan report ignited an acrimonious and deeply sexist debate over the crisis in African American families, which eventually derailed a planned White House conference on Black families and rights. Debates over feminism and the crisis in white families later caused President Jimmy Carter to scuttle plans for a White House Conference on the Family in the late 1970s. Raging political contests over emergent gender and family arrangements splintered the intended unified conference on "the family" into deeply polarized regional forums on "famil*ies*." In this pluralist definition, liberals and feminists may have won one of the last of our rhetorical victories in the family wars, while the profamily movement of the New Right began to rehearse the antifeminist script that helped to fuel the Reagan revolution of the 1980s.

Ronald Reagan was an undeserving beneficiary of the profamily reaction, as humorist Delia Ephron observes in a book review of Maureen Reagan's dutiful memoir: "It is funny and a bit pathetic that Ronald and Nancy Reagan keep finding out their family secrets by reading their children's books. It is also ironic that this couple who symbolized a return to hearth, home and l950's innocence should, in reality, be candidates for a very 1980s study on the troubled family." The former president's less dutiful daughter, Patti Davis, agrees: "Anyone who hasn't been living in a coma for the past eight years knows that we're not a close-knit family." It seems an astonishing testimony to Reagan's acclaimed media magic, therefore, that despite his own divorce and his own far-from-happily blended family, he and his *second* lady managed to serve so effectively as the symbolic figureheads of a profamily agenda, which his economic and social policies helped to further undermine.

The demographic record demonstrates that postmodern gender and kinship changes proceeded unabated throughout the Reagan era. The proportion of American households headed by single mothers grew by 21 percent, while rates of employment by mothers of young children continued their decades of ascent. When "profamily" forces helped elect Reagan to his first term in 1980, 20 percent of American children lived with a single parent, and 41 percent of mothers with children under the age of three had joined the paid labor force. When Reagan completed his second term eight years later, these figures had climbed to 24 and 54 percent, respectively. The year of Reagan's landslide reelection, 1984, was the first year that more working mothers placed their children in public group child care than in family day care. Reaganites too hastily applauded a modest decline in divorce rates during the 1980s—to a level at which more than half of first marriages still were expected to dissolve before death. But demographers who studied marital separations as well as divorce found the years from 1980 to 1985 to show "the highest level of marital disruption yet recorded for the U.S." Likewise, birth rates remained low, marriage rates fell, and homeownership rates, which had been rising for decades, declined throughout the Reagan years.

Moreover, changes in African American family patterns that Moynihan's report had treated as pathology, particularly unmarried childbearing and single motherhood, escalated in the Reagan era among whites as well as Blacks. By the time that profamily administration left office, single-parent households were far more numerous than modern families. Little wonder that the profamily movement misrepresented those modern families as "traditional" ones. The Reagan period was indeed the time when the once-modern familial and social order had become the past.

As the modern family order exited, the debate over the meaning of its passing shifted decidedly to the right. Nostalgia for the modern family, and even for premodern patriarchal kinship patterns, generated a backlash literature within feminism as well as elsewhere. Although the antifeminist, profamily movement failed to halt the disintegration of the modern family, it placed feminists and liberals on the defensive and achieved major political gains. So visible and politically effective has been this counterwomen's movement that it has obscured the fact that feminist sympathies and support for changing family life continued among all major age and social groups of Americans throughout the Reagan era. Many feminists ourselves were surprised when a poll conducted by the *New York Times* six months after Reagan left office found that more than two-thirds of the women and even a majority of the men agreed that the United States still needs a strong women's movement.

RECOMBINANT FAMILY LIFE

[...] Women and men have been creatively remaking American family life during the past three decades of postindustrial upheaval. Out of the ashes and residue of the modern family, they have drawn on a diverse, often incongruous array of cultural, political, economic, and ideological resources, fashioning these resources into new gender and kinship strategies to cope with postindustrial challenges, burdens, and opportunities. [...]

I call the fruits of these diverse efforts to remake contemporary family life "the postmodern family." I do this, despite my reservations about employing such a fashionable and elusive cultural concept, to signal the contested, ambivalent, and undecided character of contemporary gender and kinship arrangements. "What is the post-modern?" art historian Clive Dilnot asks rhetorically in the title of a detailed discussion of literature on postmodern culture, and his answers apply readily to the domain of present family conditions in the United States. The postmodern, he maintains, "is first, an uncertainty, an insecurity, a doubt." Most of the "post-" words provoke uneasiness, because they imply simultaneously "both the end, or at least the radical transformation of, a familiar pattern of activity or group of ideas" and the emergence of "new fields of cultural activity whose contours are still unclear and whose meanings and implications … cannot yet be fathomed." The postmodern, moreover, is "characterized by the process of the linking up of areas and the crossing of the boundaries of what are conventionally considered to be disparate realms of practice."

Like postmodern culture, contemporary family arrangements are diverse, fluid, and unresolved. Postindustrial social transformations have opened up such a diverse range of gender and kinship relationships as to undermine the claim in the memorable opening line from Tolstoy's *Anna Karenina*: "All happy families are alike, but every unhappy family is unhappy after its own fashion." Today even happy families no longer are all alike! No longer is there a single culturally dominant family pattern to which the majority of Americans conform and most of the rest aspire. Instead, Americans today have crafted a multiplicity of family and household arrangements that we inhabit uneasily and reconstitute frequently in response to changing personal and occupational circumstances. […]

We are living, I believe, through a transitional and contested period of family history, a period *after* the modern family order, but before what we cannot foretell. Precisely because it is not possible to characterize with a single term the competing sets of family cultures that coexist at present, I identify this family regime as postmodern. *The* postmodern family is not a new model of family life, not the next stage in an orderly progression of family history, but the stage when the belief in a logical progression of stages breaks down. Rupturing evolutionary models of family history and incorporating both experimental and nostalgic elements, "the" postmodern family lurches forward and backward into an uncertain future.

Analogous features of contemporary economic arrangements generated the concept of postindustrial society. "This is a strange period in the history of the United States," economic sociologist Fred Block explains, "because people lack a shared understanding of the kind of society in which they live. For generations, the U.S. was understood as an industrial society, but that definition of reality is no longer compelling. Yet in its absence, no compelling alternative has emerged." Postindustrial society, therefore, designates "that historical period that begins when the concept of industrial society ceases to provide an adequate account of actual social developments." Under postindustrial conditions more people work in clerical, sales, and services than produce goods, and computer-based automation drastically revises the organization, experience, and distribution of work. While in 1959, 60 percent of total employment in the United States was in goods production and 40 percent in services, by 1985 a dramatic reversal had occurred, with 74 percent of employment in services and only 26 percent in the production of goods. Economists continue to debate the long-term implications, but evidence is mounting that this shift is shrinking middle-income employment and polarizing the occupational structure into a "two-tier workforce" of "good" and "bad" jobs.

While all of the "post-" words are controversial, it is my use of the third of these, postfeminism, that has generated the most spirited objections. The term offends many of my feminist friends who believe the media coined it to sound a premature death knell for the women's liberation movement and "to give sexism a subtler name." Whatever the motives of the media, I regard postfeminism as distinct from sexism or antifeminism. Postfeminism, I believe, is a useful way to characterize this contested period in the history of gender relationships. It can be used as a historical concept, as historian Barbara Bardes notes, to suggest that "the feminist movement is accepted, and to ask, 'Where do you go in the post-feminist age?'" To use it this way, however, understates the continuing need for feminist political efforts as well as the ongoing grass-roots struggles for gender justice that can be found throughout our society and the globe. The term postfeminism serves better, I believe, to describe the gender consciousness and strategies of vast numbers of contemporary women and men—those legions of subscribers to the doctrine, "I'm not a women's libber, but ..." While they hold their distance from feminist identity or politics, they have been profoundly influenced by feminist ideology. Feminism, antifeminism, and postfeminism coexist uneasily in the current period, and the last of these has altered and complicated the political challenges that advocates of the first must confront. [...]

WHOSE FAMILY CRISIS?

Ironically, while women are becoming the new proletariat and some men are increasing their participation in housework and childwork, the postmodern family, even more than the modern family it is replacing, is proving to be a woman-tended domain. There is some empirical basis for the enlightened father imagery celebrated by films like "Kramer versus Kramer." Indeed my fieldwork corroborates evidence that the determined efforts by many working women and feminists to reintegrate men into family life have had some success. There are data, for example, indicating that increasing numbers of men would sacrifice occupational gains in order to have more time with their families, just as there are data documenting actual increases in male involvement in child care. The excessive media attention which the faintest signs of new paternity enjoy, however, may be symptomatic of a deeper, far less comforting reality it so effectively obscures. We are experiencing, as demographer Andrew Cherlin aptly puts it, "the feminization of kinship." Demographers report a drastic decline in the average numbers of years that men live in households with young children. Few of the women who assume responsibility for their children in 90 percent of divorce cases in the United States today had to wage a custody battle for this privilege. We hear few proposals for a "daddy track." And few of the adults providing care to sick and elderly relatives are male. Yet ironically, most of the alarmist, nostalgic literature about contemporary family decline impugns women's abandonment of domesticity, the flipside of our tardy entry into modernity. Rarely do the anxious outcries over the destructive effects on families of working mothers, high divorce rates, institutionalized child care, or sexual liberalization scrutinize the family behaviors of men. Anguished voices, emanating from all bands on the political spectrum, lament state and market interventions that are weakening "the family." But whose family bonds are fraying? Women have amply demonstrated our continuing commitment to sustaining kin ties. If there is a family crisis, it is a male family crisis.

The crisis cannot be resolved by reviving the modern family system. While nostalgia for an idealized world of *Ozzie and Harriet* and *Archie Bunker* families abounds, little evidence suggests that most Americans genuinely wish to return to the gender order these symbolize. [...]

Responding to new economic and social insecurities as well as to feminism, higher percentages of families in almost all income groups have adopted a multiple-earner strategy. Thus, the household form that has come closer than any other to replacing the modern family with a new cultural and statistical norm consists of a two-earner, heterosexual married couple with children. It is not likely, however, that any single household type will soon achieve the measure of normalcy that the modern family long enjoyed. Indeed, the postmodern success of the voluntary principle of the modern family system precludes this. The routinization of divorce and remarriage generates a diversity of family patterns even greater than was characteristic of the premodern period when death prevented family stability or household homogeneity. Even cautious demographers judge the new family diversity to be "an intrinsic feature ... rather than a temporary aberration" of contemporary family life.

"The family" is *not* "here to stay." Nor should we wish it were. On the contrary, I believe that all democratic people, whatever their kinship preferences, should work to hasten its demise. An ideological concept that imposes mythical homogeneity on the diverse means by which people organize their intimate relationships, "the family" distorts and devalues this rich variety of kinship stories. And, along with the class, racial, and heterosexual prejudices it promulgates, this sentimental fictional plot authorizes gender hierarchy. Because the postmodern family crisis ruptures this seamless modern family script, it provides a democratic opportunity. Efforts to expand and redefine the definition of family by feminists and gay liberation activists and by many minority rights organizations are responses to this opportunity, seeking to extend social legitimacy and institutional support to the diverse patterns of intimacy that Americans have already forged.

If feminist identity threatens many and seems out of fashion, struggles to reconstitute gender and kinship on a just and democratic basis are more popular than ever. If only a minority of citizens are willing to grant family legitimacy to gay domestic partners, an overwhelming majority subscribe to the postmodern definition of a family by which the New York Supreme Court validated a gay man's right to retain his deceased lover's apartment. "By a ratio of 3-to-1" people surveyed in a Yale University study defined the family as "a group of people who love and care for each other." And while a majority of those surveyed gave negative ratings to the quality of American family life in general, 71 percent declared themselves "at least very satisfied" with their own family lives.

There is bad faith in the popular lament over family decline. Family nostalgia deflects social criticism from the social sources of most "personal troubles." Supply-side economics, governmental deregulation, and the right-wing assault on social welfare programs have intensified the destabilizing effects of recent occupational upheavals on flagging modern families and emergent postmodern ones alike. [...] If the postmodern family crisis represents a democratic opportunity, contemporary economic and political conditions enable only a minority to realize its tantalizing potential.

The bad faith revealed in the discrepant data reported in the Yale study indicates how reluctant most Americans are to fully own the genuine ambivalence we feel about family and social change. Yet ambivalence, as sociologist Alan Wolfe suggests, is an underappreciated but responsible moral stance, and one well suited for democratic citizenship: "Given the paradoxes of modernity, there is little wrong, and perhaps a great deal right, with being ambivalent— especially when there is so much to be ambivalent about."

Certainly [...] there are good grounds for ambivalence about postmodern family conditions. Even were a feminist family revolution to succeed, it could never eliminate all family distress. At best, it would foster a social order that could invert Tolstoy's aphorism by granting happy families the freedom to differ, and even to suffer. Truly postfeminist families, however, would suffer only the "common unhappiness" endemic to intimate human relationships; they would be liberated from the "hysterical misery" generated by social injustice. No nostalgic movement to restore the modern family can offer as much. For better and/or worse, the postmodern family revolution is here to stay.

2

The Family and Civic Life

Jean Bethke Elshtain

Democracy and the family always exist in tension with one another, as do capitalism and the family. Moreover, socialism and the family are not a happy mix. Perhaps this tells us something about the family. In *Spheres of Justice*, Michael Walzer criticizes all attempts to restructure the family, whether from defenders or opponents of the market or the state, in order to make the family "fit" neatly with some scheme of total justice or some overarching macroeconomic theory. Such attempts, he argues, are always problematic, even disastrous. Perhaps a few examples are in order.

PLATO AND HIS CHILDREN

Consider the Plato of *The Republic*. As with all subsequent attempts to control social reality and to reshape it according to an overarching schema, Plato must eliminate the family if the ideal city is to come into being. The ruler-philosophers must take "the dispositions of human beings as though they were a tablet ... which, in the first place, they would wipe clean." Women must be held "in common." If a powerful, all-encompassing bond between individuals and the state can be achieved, social conflict disappears. Discord melts away. The state resembles a "single person," a fused, organic entity. Private loyalties and purposes are eliminated.

Plato constructs a rationalist meritocracy that strips away all considerations of sex, race, age, class, family ties, tradition, and history. People are fit

29

into their appropriate social slots, performing only that function to which each is suited. Children outside the ruler class can be shunted upward or downward at the will of the "Guardian," for they are raw material to be turned into instruments of social "good." A system of eugenics is devised for the Guardians. Children are removed from their mothers at birth and placed in a child ghetto, tended to by those best suited for the job. No parental loyalties emerge. No child knows who his or her parents are.

What is all this for? What is it a defense against? Plato seeks to eradicate motives for discord. Private homes and sexual attachments, devotion to friends, dedication to individual or group aims and purposes—all of these militate against devotion to the city. Particular Lies are a great evil. Only those that bind the individual to the state are good.

Who, today, would try to implement such an ideal, with all its frightening consequences? Totalitarians of all stripes, social engineers of various hues, revolutionaries of several flavors, and a small army of contemporary philosophers. Here are several examples, drawn from feminist politics and philosophy.

Shulamith Firestone's radical feminist "classic," *The Dialectic of Sex,* depicts a world of stark lovelessness in which coercion, manipulation, and crude power roam undifferentially over the landscape. Within the family, the "female sex-class" is dominated by the "male sex-class," and thus the family must be destroyed. In Firestone's scenario, test-tube babies replace biological reproduction. Every aspect of life rests in the beneficent hands of the "new elite of engineers, cybernetricians." The child, no longer "hung up" by authoritarian parents (parents having pretty much melted away), is "free" to bargain for the best deal in contracted households.

Firestone's vision has been attacked as a nightmare by many feminist critics in the past few years because

> it rests on conceptual foundations that have much in common with the presuppositions of researchers and policymakers who would ... support technological intervention for the sake of the monopoly of power it would make possible.... Both see human biology as a limitation to be overcome—for Firestone, because she takes the relations of procreation to be ... the source of women's oppression; for those who would support "a brave new world," because the diffusion of power among women and families threatens their own power hegemony.

But despite such critiques, the philosophic drumbeat continues: the radical feminist future requires a family-less world. Indeed, Alison M. Jagger, in her widely hailed *Feminist Politics and Human Nature,* even foresees the elimination of gender. She calls for the "ultimate transformation of human nature"—an actual biological reformation of the human species.

> This transformation might even include the capacities for insemination, for lactation and for gestation so that, for instance, one woman could inseminate

another, so that men and nonparturitive women could lactate and so that fertilized ova could be transplanted into women's or even into men's bodies. These developments may seem farfetched, but in fact they are already on the technological horizon.

That which is technologically possible is politically and ethically desirable so long as these new means of control are controlled by women, because women are oppressed by "having to be women."

In these examples, we see the animus of philosophers and revolutionaries directed toward the personal lives and ties, especially family ties, of ordinary human beings. Martha Nussbaum, in her remarkable work *The Fragility of Goodness*, offers a wise discussion of why Plato (and, by extension, all later universalizing philosophers) had to destroy the family. Plato's urge to deconstruct is linked to his animus against the poets and tragedians who must be banished from the ideal city. Thus it seems that families, as do tragedians and poets, stir up strong emotions; they rouse pity and fear, excite longing and love. But Plato aspired to "rational self-sufficiency." He would make the lives of human beings immune to the messy fragilities of ordinary existence. The ideal of self-sufficiency was mastery: the male citizen was to be imbued with a "mythology of autochthony that persistently, and paradoxically, suppressed the biological role of the female and therefore the family in the continuity of the city." (Consider the irony of late twentieth-century feminist philosophers embracing this relentlessly anti-body, anti-female model.) For Plato, moral conflicts suggest irrationalism, which must be "discarded as false." If one cannot be loyal both to families and to the city, loyalty to the family must be bent to serve the city. For Plato and subsequent Platonists of every variety, including Marxists, "Our ordinary humanity is a source of confusion rather than of insight [and] the philosopher alone judges with the right criterion or from the appropriate standpoint." Hence the ascetic plan of *The Republic* aims to purify and to control by depriving human beings of "the nourishment of close ongoing attachments, of the family, of dramatic poetry."

Subsequent universalists take a similar tack. But what drives these attempts to diminish the family for the good of the state? Clearly, it is the suspicion and condemnation of all relationships that are not totally voluntary, rationalistic, and contractual. It is the conviction that the traditional family is the example *par excellence* of imbedded particularity. It is the view that the world will attain the ideal of justice and order only when various proposals to "wipe the slate clean" have been implemented and human beings are no longer constrained and limited by special obligations and inherited (nonvoluntary) duties.

It seems that we must choose. On the one hand, we have visions of total order and rationalistic harmony; on the other, an open, complex, conflicted receptivity to the rich plurality of values that exist in the world of nature and of history. The family contributes to this plurality of values in a way no other social institution can.

PHILOSOPHERS FOR THE FAMILY

In this chapter, I propose a philosophic argument in support of the family in civic life. Furthermore, I sketch a normative vision of the family—mothers, fathers, and children—that is not only *not* at odds with democratic civil society but is in fact, now more than ever, a prerequisite for that society to function. Yet I do not seek to eliminate all tensions, to create some overarching ideal of "The Family" and "The Democratic Order." Rather, I aim to preserve a necessary and fruitful tension between particular and universal commitments, as embodied in the family, without which democratic society cannot flourish.

Consider my basic questions: In what ways is the family issue also a civic issue with public consequences? What is the relationship between democratic theory and the intergenerational family? What ideals of the human person are imbedded in contrasting visions of intimate life? Do we have a stake in sustaining some visions as compared with others? What do families do that no other social institution can? How does current public discourse in the United States undermine family obligations and downgrade the moral vocation of parenting?

In answering these questions, I seek a method of interpretive complexity that is grounded in moral commitments. The philosopher must be interested in the problems created by any way of life and in how human beings deal with those problems. If the political thinker is to avoid being arrogant and lofty, contemptuous of the values and judgments people make, she must philosophize in a way that resembles the complexity and content of our actual beliefs and actions. The only alternative is performing philosophical surgery—cutting and restitching reality—in the hope that actual life may one day be brought into line.

THE DILEMMA OF DEMOCRATIC POLITICS AND THE FAMILY

Democrats are suspicious of traditional authority, from kings and chiefs to popes and lords. And properly so, for democracy requires self-governing citizens rather than obedient subjects. In a democracy, holding authority is a temporary gift, granted only through the consent of the governed.

Democratic authority emerged unevenly over several centuries, as late medieval and early modern cosmologies faltered. Its distinguishing features included the principle that citizens possess inalienable rights. Possession of such rights empowered citizens to offer assent to the governors and the laws, including those procedural guarantees that protected them from the abuses of authority. Equality between and among citizens was assumed. Indeed, the citizen was, by definition, equal to any other citizen. (Not everyone, of course, could be a citizen, but that's another story.) Democratic citizenship required the creation of persons with qualities of mind and spirit necessary for civic participation. Early liberal theorists viewed this creation of citizens as neither simple nor automatic. Many, in fact, insisted upon a structure of education tied to a particular understanding of "the sentiments." This education should usher in a moral autonomy that stresses self-chosen obligations, thereby casting further suspicion upon relations and loyalties deemed unchosen, involuntary, or natural.

Not surprisingly, within such systems of civic authority, the family emerges as a problem. For one does not enter a family through free consent but rather is born into a world unwilled and unchosen by oneself, beginning life as a helpless and dependent infant. Eventually one reaches "the age of consent." But in the meantime one is a child, not a citizen. This situation vexed liberal and democratic theorists, some of whom believed, at least abstractly, that the completion of the democratic ideal required bringing all of social life under the sway of a single principle of democratic authority.

During the sixteenth and seventeenth centuries, political thought slowly shifted from a patriarchal to a liberal-contractarian discourse. Patriarchalist discourse in its paradigmatic form—for example, Robert Filmer's *Patriarcha*—concerned itself preeminently with authority, defined as singular, absolute, patriarchal, natural, and political. In Filmer's world there is no differentiation between public and private, family and politics. Indeed, there is no private sphere at all, in the sense of a realm demarcated from political life. Nor is there a separate political sphere, in the sense of a realm diverging from exigencies of the private world. Power, authority, and obedience are fused within God's original grant of dominion to Adam at the Creation. Accordingly, the father has dominion over his wife, his children, and his servants in his own little kingdom. But he, in turn, is subject to the First Father, the lordly King.

In the realm of civil society, countering this patriarchal philosophy proved relatively easy for liberals and democrats. But the issue became trickier when new conceptions of authority seemed to challenge the family. Is a family dominated by patriarchy, however softened in practice, legitimate within the new civic world framed by ideas of consent? If liberals sought to end conditions of perpetual political childhood, were they required to eliminate childhood itself?

Adhering to a strong version of the liberal ideal, "free consent" from birth, was deeply problematic given the nature of human infants. Liberal contractarians were often cautious in carrying their political principles into domestic life. Some contented themselves with contractarianism in politics and economics and with traditionalism in families, not, however, without considerable discursive maneuvering. Filmer's caustic query to his liberal interlocutors concerning whether people sprang up like "so many mushrooms" and his incredulous insistency—"How can a child express consent?"—continued to haunt liberals, in part because they shared with Filmer the presumption that authority must be singular in form if a society is to be coherent and orderly.

John Locke, who was more subtle than many early liberal thinkers, softened his demands for consistency in social practices, arguing instead for the coexistence of diverse authoritative forms. Conjugal society originates through the consent of two adults. But "parental" or "paternal" power within the family (Locke recognizes both but privileges the latter) could not serve as a model for the liberal polity any more than could the norms constituting civil society provide an apposite model for families. Locke strips the father-husband of patriarchal absolutism by denying him sovereignty, which includes the power of life and death. That prerogative is reserved only for democratically legitimized public authority. A father's power is "conjugal ... not Political" and these two are "perfectly distinct and separate ... built upon so different Foundations and given to so different Ends."

The child's status is that of "not-yet-adult," hence the child is not part of the consensual civil order. But the education of the child into moral sentiments is vital to that wider order. Locke avoids the seductions of patriarchal authority as an all-encompassing norm. He refuses to launch a mimetic project that mirrors patriarchalism, nor does he demand an overreaching liberal authority principle that turns the family into a political society governed by the same principles that guide liberal public life.

This incongruence between democracy and the family continued to vex post-Lockean thinkers. The position of women, for example, presented philosophical contradictions. For women, having reached the age of consent, could enter freely into a marriage only to find future consent foreclosed. Moreover, because the family itself was perceived as a blemish by those who foresaw the ultimate triumph of rationalism in all spheres of human existence, liberals continued to focus on the relations between the family and politics.

In the nineteenth century, however, John Stuart Mill, in contrast with Locke, insisted that familial and civic orders be drawn into a tight mesh with one another. For Mill, the family remained a despotic sphere governed by a "law of force" whose "odious source" was rooted in pre-enlightened and barbaric epochs. By revealing the origins of family relations, thus bringing out their "true" character, Mill hoped to demonstrate that the continued subjection of women blunts social progress. He proposed a leap into relations of "perfect equality" between the sexes as the only way to complete the teleology of liberal individualism and equality, to assure the promise of progress.

In his tract *The Subjection of Women*, Mill argued that his contemporaries, male and female alike, were tainted by the atavisms of family life with its illegitimate (because unchosen and prerational) male authority as well as its illegitimate (because manipulative and irrational) female quests for private power. The family would become a school in the virtues of freedom only when parents lived together without power on one side or obedience on the other. Power, for Mill, was repugnant: true liberty must reign in all spheres.

But what about children? Mill's children emerge as rather abstract concerns: blank slates on which parents must encode the lessons of obedience in the aim of authoritatively inculcating the lessons of freedom. Stripped of undemocratic authority and privilege, the parental union serves as a model of democratic probity.

Mill's paean to liberal individualism can be interestingly contrasted to Alexis de Tocqueville's concrete observations of family life in nineteenth-century America. He found a society that already exhibited the effects of the extension of democratic norms and the breakdown of patriarchal and Puritan ethics. The fathers of Tocqueville's America were fathers in a different mode: stern but forgiving, strong but flexible. They listened to their children and humored them. They educated them as well as demanded their obedience.

Like the new democratic father, the American political leader did not lord it over his people. Citizens were not required to bend the knee or stand transfixed in awe. Yet the leader was owed respect. If he urged a course of action, his fellow citizen, following democratic consultation and procedure, had a patriotic duty to follow.

Tocqueville's discerning eye perceived changing public and private relationships in liberal, democratic America. Although great care was taken "to trace two clearly distinct lines of action for the two sexes," Tocqueville claimed that women, in their domestic sphere, "nowhere occupied a loftier position of honor and importance." The mother is the chief inculcator of democratic values in her offspring. "No free communities ever existed without morals and, as I observed ... morals are the work of women."

Although the father was the family's "natural head," his authority was neither absolute nor arbitrary. In contrast with the patriarchal authoritarian family, in which the parent not only has a "natural right" but acquired a "political right" to command his children, a democratic family is one in which the authority of parents is a *natural right* alone. For Tocqueville, in contrast with Mill, this natural authority presents no problem for democratic practices. Indeed, the "right to command" is natural, not political. It is a right of a special and temporary nature: once the child becomes self-governing, the right dissolves. In this way, paternal authority and maternal education reinforce a political order that values flexibility, freedom, and the absence of absolute rule, but requires order and stability.

"Child experts" in Tocqueville's America emphasized kindness and love as the preferred technique of nurturance. Obedience was necessary—to parents, elders, God, "just government and one's conscience"—but the child was no longer constructed as a depraved, sin-ridden, stiff-necked little creature who needed harsh instruction and reproof. Notions of infant depravity faded along with Puritan patriarchalism. The problem of discipline grew more, rather than less, complex. Parents were enjoined to win obedience without corporal punishment or rigid methods, casing affection, issuing their commands in gentle voices while insisting quietly on their authority lest contempt and chaos rule in the domestic sphere.

In Tocqueville's image of the "democratic family," children are both ends in themselves and means to the end of a well-ordered society. A widespread moral consensus reigned in the America of that era—a kind of Protestant civic religion. When this consensus began to corrode under the force of rapid social change (and analogues to the American story appear in all modern democracies), certainties surrounding familial life and authority were shaken as well.

Today, no force of authority can be taken for granted. In light of modern challenges to the norms that govern both the familial and civil spheres, a case for the family as a good in itself and as a precondition for democratic society becomes difficult to mount. One can opt for restorationism. Or one can celebrate rationalist hopes that the time is finally ripe to bring society under the sway of wholly voluntarist norms.

If restorationists seek a return to traditional norms, voluntarists seek to nullify the moral significance of all "unchosen" obligations. One might, however, find each of these alternatives to be unrealistic, undesirable, or both. If this is so, the task is to mount a defense of the family within, and for, a world whose members no longer share a single overriding conception of the good life or even repose deep faith in the future of most human institutions. This task is not easy.

There are two possible directions. The first option might be termed the strong case: an unambiguous defense of familial authority in the modern world. By evaluating objections to the strong case, we arrive at the second option, a more ambiguous set of family affirmations. Such qualifications permit us to evaluate whether the strong case remains compelling or, alternatively, whether a softened defense of the family better serves the social goods at stake.

DEMOCRATIC AUTHORITY AND THE FAMILY: THE STRONG CASE

Familial authority, though seemingly at odds with the presumptions of democracy, is nonetheless a prerequisite for the survival of democracy. Family relations could not exist without familial authority. Such relations remain the best way we know to create citizens, that is, adults who offer ethical allegiance to the principles of democratic society. Family authority is the best way to structure the relationships between adults and dependent children who slowly acquire capacities for independence. Modern parental authority, moreover, is shared by the mother and father. Some may take strong exception to this claim, arguing that the family is patriarchal, even today, or that the authority of the mother is *less* decisive than that of the father, or that Mill was right.

Children, however, exhibit little doubt that their mothers are powerful and authoritative, though perhaps not in ways identical to fathers. This ideal of parental equality does not presuppose sameness between the mother and father. Each can be more or less a private or a public person, yet be equal in relation to children.

What makes family authority distinctive is the quality of stewardship: the recognition that parents undertake solemn obligations, under authority that is special, limited, and particular. Parental authority, like all authority, can be abused. But unless it exists, the activity of parenting is itself impossible. Parental authority is essential to democratic political morality, because parents are the primary providers of the moral education required for democratic citizenship.

The *Herzenbildung*—education of the heart—that takes place in families should not, however, be viewed as merely one item in a larger political agenda. To construe it as such is to treat the family merely instrumentally, affirming it only insofar as it can be shown to serve external purposes. Yes, the family helps sustain the democratic order. But it also offers alternatives, even resistance, to many policies that a public order may throw up at any given time.

The loyalties and moral imperatives nurtured in families may often clash with the demands of public authority. For example, a young man may refuse to serve in a war because to do so violates the religious beliefs taught by his mother and father. This, too, is vital for democracy. Democracy emerged as a form of revolt. Keeping alive a potential for revolt, keeping alive the space for particularity, for difference, for pluralism, sustains democracy in the long run. It is no coincidence that all twentieth-century totalitarian orders labored to destroy the family as a locus of identity and meaning apart from the state. Totalitarianism strives to govern all of life; to allow for only one public identity; to destroy private life; and most of all, to require that individuals never allow their commitments to specific others—family, friends, comrades—to weaken their commitment to the state. To this idea, which can only be described as evil, the family stands in defiance.

Familial authority simply does not exist in a direct homologous relation to the principles of civil society. To establish an identity between public and private lives would weaken, not strengthen, democratic life. The reason for this is children. They need particular, intense relations with specific beloved others. If a child is confronted prematurely with the "right to choose" or situated too soon inside anonymous institutions that minimize that special contact and trust with parents, that child is much less likely to be "free to choose" later on. To become capable of posing alternatives, a person requires a sure and certain place from which to start. In Mary Midgley's words, "Children … have to live now in a particular culture; they must take some attitude to the nearest things right away." The family is the social form best suited to provide children with a trusting, determinate sense of "self." Indeed, it is only through identification with concrete others that children can later identify with nonfamilial human beings and come to see themselves as members of a wider community.

Familial authority is inseparable from parental care, protection, and concern. In the absence of such ties, familial feelings would not be displaced throughout a wider social network; they would, instead, be vitiated, perhaps lost altogether. And without the human ties and bonds that the activity of parenting makes possible, a more general sense of "brotherhood" and "sister-hood" simply cannot emerge.

The nature and scope of parental authority changes over time. Children learn that being a child is not a permanent condition. Indeed, the family teaches us that no authority on this earth is omnipotent, unchanging, or absolute. Working through familial authority, as children struggle for identity, requires that they question authority more generally. Examples of authoritarian parents do not disconfirm this ideal case; they do, however, show that familial authority, like any constitutive principle, is subject to abuse. Yet granting particular instances of abuse, familial authority, in both ideal and actual forms, remains uniquely capable of keeping alive that combination of obligation and duty, freedom and dissent, that is the heart of democratic life.

Any further erosion of the ethical life embodied in the family bodes ill for democracy. For example, we can experience the plight of homelessness as a human tragedy only because we cherish an ideal of what it means to have a home. We find it easier to love others if we ourselves have been loved. We learn self-sacrifice and commitment as we learn so many things—in small, manageable steps, starting close to home. Thus, the family, at its best, helps foster a commitment to "do something" about a whole range of social problems. The ideal of family, then, is a launching pad into more universal commitments, a civic *Moralität*. The child who emerges from such a family is more capable of acting in the world as a complex moral being.

To destroy the family would create a general debacle from which we would not soon recover. The replacement for parents and families would not comprise a happy, consensual world of children coequal with adults. It would be a world in which children would become clients of bureaucrats and engineers of all sorts, many of whom would, inevitably, regard children largely as grist for the mill of extrafamilial schemes and ambitions.

DEMOCRATIC AUTHORITY AND
THE FAMILY: AMBIGUITIES

The strong case presumes a family that is secure in its authoritative role—a family that serves as the bearer of a clear *telos*. This is spine-stiffening stuff, but it assumes a wide social surrounding that no longer exists. American society ceased long ago to endorse unambiguously the shouldering of family obligations or to locate honor in long-term moral responsibilities. Authoritative norms have fallen under relentless pressures that promote individualistic, mobile, and tentative relations between self and others. Modern life enjoins us to remain as untrammeled as possible in order to attain individual goals and to enjoy our "freedom."

Constraints today are more onerous than they were when it was anticipated that everyone would share them: that is, all women, almost without exception, would become mothers; all men, almost without exception, would become supportive fathers. Young people, finding themselves surrounded by a social ethos that no longer affords clear-cut moral and social support for familial relations, choose in growing numbers to postpone or evade these responsibilities.

In acknowledging these transformations, the case for familial authority is softened but not abandoned. Taking account of shifts in the social ethos does not mean that one succumbs to them as if they comprised a new authoritative norm simply by virtue of their existence. But some alterations are warranted, including articulation of less dauntingly rigorous normative requirements for being a "parent" than are implied by the strong argument. The changes I suggest here are not, I hope, facile reassurances that modern human beings can be both unfettered individualists and encumbered parents in some happy, perfect harmony. Parental authority both constrains and makes possible; it locates mothers and fathers in the world in a way that must be different from that of nonparenting adults. This fact need not lock parents into some dour notion of duty that encourages them to overstate both their power to shape their children and their responsibility for doing so. The modern family is a porous institution, one open to a variety of external influences. Parents are no longer the sole moral guardians. A defense of modern familial authority must take this, too, into account.

Critics might insist that even a softened defense of family authority—indeed, any defense at all—is "arbitrary" in several ways because it privileges procreative heterosexual unions, thereby excluding a variety of other intimate arrangements, whether "nonexclusive," "open" marriages and families, or homosexual unions; because it posits the child as a dependent who requires discipline and restriction, thus shoring up paternalism ostensibly in behalf of children but in reality to deny them their rights; because it limits parental choices by stressing dependability, trust, and loyalty to the exclusion of adventure, unpredictability, and openness; and because it constructs a case for ethical development that is self-confirming in assuming that a set of authoritative norms is essential to personal life.

Perhaps, this critic might go on, behavior modification is a less strenuous and more effective shaper of a child's action. Perhaps children transferred at an early age out of the home and into a group context emerge less burdened by individual conscience and moral autonomy and hence are freer to act creatively without incessant, guilt-ridden ruminations about responsibility and consequence. Perhaps children who learn at an early age to be cynical and not trust adults will become skeptics and better prepared to accept the rapid changes of modernity than are the trusting, emotionally bonded, slowly maturing children of the authoritative family.

Admittedly, a defense of familial authority should recognize that every set of norms contains contingent features, "in the sense that, while they are indispensible to this way of life, there are other forms of living … in which this special set would not be necessary." But contingent does not mean arbitrary. In the absence of authoritative rules, the social world would be more rather than less dominated by arbitrary violence, coercion, or crass manipulation.

Take, for example, the incest taboo. It can be construed as wholly arbitrary. A number of radical social critics have described this taboo as both "illegitimate" and "indefensible," contrary to freedom of expression and action. Exposing its arbitrariness, they would liberate children from paternalistic despotism and parents from ancient superstition. Chafing at restrictions of sexual exploration, these antiauthoritarians celebrate total freedom of sexuality.

Their mistake, one might wish to argue, is not their insistence that we recognize the conventional or "arbitrary" features of our social arrangements. It is rather their insistence that such recognition requires elimination of the rules in question. In assuming that some better form of existence might flourish in the absence of authoritative restrictions, the "antis" emerge as naive and dangerous. They would open up social life to more, rather than less, brutalization, including targeting children as acceptable resources for adult sexual manipulation. Yes, acceptance of the incest taboo implicates one in a conventional normative standard. But that standard sustains a social good—protecting children from abuse by the more powerful. We punish abusive parents precisely because we accept the idea that adult power must be limited. Adult power, shorn of the internal moral limits of, for example, the incest taboo, would become more generalized, less accountable, and dangerously unlimited.

A second criticism holds that in defending the family, one privileges a restrictive ideal of intimate relations. More people in America are coming to believe that a society should stay equally open to all alternative arrangements, treating "life-styles" as so many morally identical peas in a pod. To be sure, families coexist with other life-style forms, whether heterosexual and homosexual unions that are by choice or by definition childless, communalists who diminish individual parental authority in favor of the preeminence of the group, and so on. *But the acceptance of plural possibilities does not mean each alternative is equal to every other regarding specific social goods.* No social order has ever existed that did not privilege certain activities and practices as preferable to others. Every social order forges terms of inclusion and exclusion. Ethically responsible challenges may loosen those terms, but they do not negate a normative endorsement of family life. In defining family authority, then, we acknowledge that we are privileging relations of a particular kind in which certain social goods are at stake.

Those excluded by, or who exclude themselves from, these norms should not be denied social space and tolerance. And if that which is at stake were, say, seeking out and exploring those creations of self that enhance an aesthetic construction of life and sensibility, the romantic bohemian or rebel might well get higher marks than the Smith family of Fremont, Nebraska. But regarding what families do, those explorations are not at stake.

Accordingly, we should be cautious about going too far in the direction of a wholly untrammeled pluralism of intimate relations. It is possible to become so vapid that we no longer distinguish between the moral weightiness of, say, polishing one's Porsche and sitting up all night with a sick child. The intergenerational family creates irreplaceable and invaluable social goods by nurturing recognition of human frailty, mortality, and finitude and by inculcating moral limits and constraints. A revamped defense of family authority, then, takes account of challenges to its normalizing features. It also opens it to ambiguities and paradox. But the essential defense remains.

NEATNESS ISN'T EVERYTHING

What about the worries of liberal thinkers historically about the family's anomalous position within a civic world governed by contractarian and voluntarist norms? It seems to me, finally, that those worries are misplaced. Ironically, what such analysts fear is what I here endorse: a form of familial authority that does not mesh perfectly with democratic principles. That form, I contend, remains vital to the sustaining of a diverse and morally decent culture. This paradox is one of many that social life throws up and that civic philosophers would be well advised to recognize and to nourish. For the discordance embodied in this uneasy coexistence of familial and democratic authority sustains the struggles over identity, purpose, and meaning that form the very stuff of democratic life. To resolve this untidiness, we could simply declare a set of unitary authoritative norms. Or we could simply eliminate all norms as arbitrary and oppressive. But to do either is to jeopardize the social goods that democratic and familial authority—paradoxical in relation to one another—promise to citizens and their children.

3

Families as Relationships of Intimacy and Care

Traci M. Levy

INTRODUCTION—SOCIAL SUPPORTS AND FAMILIES IN THE UNITED STATES

American public policies that impact families have two major shortcomings: the support they provide is meager, and it is only directed at a very narrow and exclusionary understanding of family.[1] Indeed, the United States is a clear outlier among similarly affluent (and even some less affluent) nations in the paucity of support it provides families. This lack of support can be explained, at least in part, by dominant interpretations of American liberalism that construe care as a family affair. Families, in this way of thinking, are supposed to be self-sufficient. Although families have been in flux—affected by changes in composition and longevity, new population demographics, and the increased visibility of "nontraditional" relationships—American law and public policies have not adequately adjusted how they define family. By failing to keep pace with changes, the policies intended to provide public support to families have been allowed to "drift," thereby further burdening care practices. To meaningfully address this care crisis, redefining the family is one important step. This chapter builds on the work of feminist theorists by applying a public ethic of care to reconceptualize families as relationships of intimacy and care.

---

1. Owing to space limitations, footnotes have been cut to a minimum. Hence, standard qualifications and elaborations are missing.

AMERICAN FAMILIES: REALITY
VERSUS STATE RECOGNITION

Classifying a social group as a family can take two main approaches. A formal approach defines family by identifying whether a group's members are related biologically or in a legally recognized marriage, civil union, or adoption. A functional approach defines family by examining the character of the group and activities its members undertake. Many groups not recognized as "traditional" families behave as such in terms of sharing resources, caring for dependents, and so on. American federal public institutions and policies (and those of a majority of the states) tend to focus on formal understandings of family in a way that recognizes and accords rights only to heterosexual married couples and a narrow set of biological and adoptive relationships. The US Census Bureau's (2012) "Current Population Survey: Definitions and Explanations," for example, equates family with a "group of two people or more (one of whom is the householder) related by birth, marriage, or adoption and residing together."[2] The Family and Medical Leave Act of 1993 (FMLA) allows qualifying employees unpaid leave to care for only a spouse, child, or parent, in certain circumstances (US Department of Labor, Wage and Hour Division 2012), unless a current or recent military service member needs care, in which case, the types of family members that can qualify for the leave are extended to next of kin (US Department of Labor, WHD 2010). On the federal level, rights and privileges are often focused on heterosexual, married couples. For example, in 2004 the General Accounting Office of the United States determined there were at least "1,138 federal rights, responsibilities, and privileges automatically accorded to couples based on marital status. In addition, state and local governments as well as private organizations provide hundreds of additional rights based on marital status" (American Bar Association 2004, 8). In practice, then, there is a considerable gap between the families accorded legal recognition, rights, and benefits, and the families in which large segments of the population live with and care for each other.

US public policy has not adequately adjusted to changes in family composition, purposes, and duration, or changing population demographics. State and municipal legislatures have taken widely different approaches to the issue. For example, some accord legal recognition and extensive rights and responsibilities to same-sex partners, whereas others have passed legislation restricting marriage to heterosexual couples and have firmly rejected domestic partnership registries and the like (National Conference of State Legislatures 2012). Jacob Hacker (2004) refers to the failure of public policies to adjust to changing social circumstances as policy "drift" (246). He shows that although the American welfare state may be "retrenched" in many areas, some advocacy groups have managed to limit or even decrease the size and impact of social

---

2. By mentioning living together, the Census definition also includes an element of function.

welfare programs by deliberately pursuing a policy of drift. In other words, although established social welfare programs may be difficult to eradicate, by failing (or refusing) to adjust them to changing circumstances, risks that were once shared collectively have been shifted back to the private realm, with the burden falling primarily or exclusively on individuals and families (Hacker 2004, 252). This phenomenon is exactly what has occurred in the United States with informal (unpaid) relationships of intimacy and care: care work has been largely assigned to families, while public policies and institutions have failed to adequately adjust to contemporary manifestations of families.[3]

Legal scholars are engaged in vigorous debates over if and how laws should change to address "nontraditional" families. One of the main fault lines in these debates is between those who support the practice of restricting formal legal recognition to the heterosexual nuclear family (for example—Hafen 1991; Wagner 2001; and Gallagher 2004) and those who advocate extending recognition to a greater variety of personal relationships (Minow [1991] 1998; Woodhouse 1996; Fineman 2001, 2004; Polikoff 2003).

Courts have variously applied formal and functional approaches to families. A "Note" in the *Harvard Law Review* (1991) and Minow (1998) highlight two cases that epitomize the different approaches. A formal approach was used in *Alison D. v. Virginia M.* Alison and Virginia had been cohabitating same-sex partners for several years. During that time, Virginia became pregnant through artificial insemination. Alison acted as a parent to the child, starting at birth and persisting for several years, until she and Virginia separated, and Virginia eventually denied Alison permission to visit the child. The court ruled that Virginia, the child's biological mother, had the exclusive right to control or even deny visitation to her former partner, because Alison was "a biological stranger" to the child. Thus, no consideration was given to the relationship of intimacy and care that existed between Alison and the child. Since the ruling in *Alison D.*, many courts, motivated by concerns of keeping a child from losing a parent, began looking more at the nature, or function, of the relationship between the adult and child rather than simply their formal status (National Center for Lesbian Rights 2012, 5–6); however, some scholars are concerned that recent court rulings (e.g., *Debra H. v. Janice R.*) and what they consider as a disproportionate focus on advocating same-sex marriage, is moving the United States back toward a definition of family based solely on form. The formal definition of family, following this trend, may be slightly expanded and may (unevenly) add married same-sex families (and some in officially registered civil unions). But, this limited expansion of the legal/formal definition still ignores or denies the parental bonds in same-sex families in which couples

---

3. In implementing federal policies, some state and local agencies have adjusted to administer benefits in ways that explicitly or implicitly recognize a more diverse conception of family, but this patchwork response is limited, uneven, and uncoordinated. Thus, it leaves many families vulnerable. I do not mean to suggest that a standardized federal response is necessarily the (only) answer.

do not or cannot marry or form officially registered civil unions (Josephson 2010; Polikoff 2012).

A functional approach to defining family, by contrast, was employed in *Braschi v. Stahl Associates*. In that case, the court's ruling allowed the same-sex partner of a deceased tenant to keep the apartment the two men had lived in together, even though the surviving member of the couple was not the tenant of record. In this case, the court determined that the relationship must be recognized as familial for the purposes of the New York City rent control law, because the two men had behaved (i.e., functioned) like a married couple. This piece will advocate an approach that is largely sympathetic to the so-called functionalist approach in law applied in the *Braschi* case and will focus on how a public ethic of care can provide a coherent and ethical philosophical rationale for moving in the direction of this approach. (Section VI fleshes out some of the differences between legal functionalism and the position taken here.)

Instead of defining families through the narrow lens of the heterosexual able-bodied, married couple (or even adding the same-sex married couple) and their biological and adoptive children, I agree with those feminist theorists and legal functionalists who support a more diverse and fluid conception of family. Situating my approach within the framework of a feminist public ethic of care, I argue in favor of reconceptualizing the family with a focus on intimate relationships of care. This change will help shift the emphasis away from certain formal familial structures to what the programs should be supporting—relationships of intimacy and care. To develop this understanding of family, I first flesh out what I mean by *care*.

CARE THEORY AND VALUES

Public Ethic of Care

Contemporary feminist care theory provides useful insights and analyses of families and the politics of care. This chapter relies most heavily on the work of contemporary feminist care theorists who are more explicitly *political* than early proponents of care. To paraphrase Berenice Fisher and Joan Tronto, care entails activities and practices through which we attempt to sustain and repair ourselves, our world, and those around us, so that we may survive and thrive (Fisher and Tronto 1991; Tronto [1993] 1994). Daniel Engster (2009) provides more specificity, arguing "*caring means most basically helping individuals to meet their basic needs, develop or sustain their basic capabilities, and avoid and alleviate unwanted suffering in attentive, responsive, and respectful ways*" (64). Interpretations of care can vary by time, place, and heritage, so a definitive list of activities is difficult to compile; however, some examples of care in relationship with others could include feeding an infant, directing a paid personal assistant while she or he helps one dress, bathing a spouse recovering from a serious illness, or cleaning house for a frail elderly couple.[4] In order for a practice to be characterized as care, it must include an element of vulnerability, but not necessarily complete dependence. In other words, without assistance, the person in need must be unable to fulfill, or have considerable difficulty fulfilling, his or her own needs.

To discuss care in the context of families, as Eva Feder Kittay (1999) has pointed out, is not to concede that all families can or should be self-sufficient or without public supports for their care work. In fact, what is so useful about a feminist ethic of care is the way it moves the activities of care from the margin to the center of our field of vision and disrupts the status-quo boundaries between public and private care roles (Tronto [1993] 1994). To flesh out a working "public ethic of care" (Kittay 1999), it is necessary to identify some core care values that productively guide thinking about families and apply these values to rethinking the relationships recognized as familial. Specifically, social connectedness, difference, equality, and voice are four care values especially important to promoting human survival and flourishing.

Social Connectedness as a Care Family Value

Care theory addresses social connectedness both descriptively and normatively. Descriptively, it acknowledges our social natures and needs. Part of what it means to be human is to have and make connections to others. Some facets of human existence make humans necessarily interdependent—for example, the vulnerability of infancy and childhood, the desire for human companion-ship, the tendency to strive for things and accomplishments beyond what we could make or achieve alone, the aging process, and periodic sickness. It is a rare individual who can and does remove herself from society to lead the solitary and completely self-sufficient life of a hermit. We are born into this world already connected to certain people and some places differently from others. These connections come into play as we form and maintain our family and care relationships. Over time, these relationships can change, and we can become agents who create, enhance, and/or redefine our relationships and orientation to the world (Young 2000, 99).

Prescriptively, an important objective of care theory is to facilitate social connectedness through just and meaningful care relationships that can func-tion well and fairly for all the parties involved. We cannot just *try* to perform care—it must be done effectively and responsively in order for needs to be met, justice fulfilled, and human dignity respected. These values are in step with the general ethical commitments of liberal democracy and major reli-gions around the world, but a feminist care approach highlights a public way to systematically address and implement such commitments.

---

4. Some basic needs are culturally and historically constant, but how we fulfill these needs varies. For a more comprehensive treatment of how to acknowledge the self-care and agency of many people with disabilities, see Little and Levy (2012).

Difference as a Care Family Value

A care perspective is well situated to recognize the distinctive contributions and burdens of women, people of color, people with disabilities, the poor, and other groups that have been socially marginalized—without allowing those who do not fall into these categories to cast it as the issue of "others." Care requires attention to the context and particularities of diverse people and situations (Tronto [1993] 1994, 136–137). As part of care theory's insistence on "attentiveness" and "responsiveness"—that is, recognizing a need for care and paying attention to how the care-receiver responds to various care initiatives[5]—care theory stresses the necessity of recognizing and responding to differences. Tronto (1998) suggests, for example, that we should ask: "What construction of 'otherness' ... contributes to perceptions of caring?" Acknowledging how different groups of people define and form families contributes to respecting diversity and helping to tackle the inequality that often comes from being "other" than the more privileged groups in society.

Equality as a Care Family Value

Care theory makes equality an explicit political goal. It recognizes that all people are fundamentally connected and interdependent beings who have needs and are morally engaged. As Eva Feder Kittay argues, we start by recognizing that "both receiving and giving care are ... essential goods, as fundamental and irreducible as political liberty and economic well-being" (Kittay 1999, 182). Acceptance of this realization requires that we both give care and support caregivers in ways that do not make them "unable to be equals in a society of equals" (Kittay 1999, 182). Framing issues with this care value in mind pushes us to examine the inequalities that permeate caregiving and to work to change the extent to which care is poorly supported, unpaid or ill paid, and disproportionately the duty of women, people of color, and the poor (see, e.g., Tronto [1993] 1994, 112–117; Mignon Duffy 2007). Equality becomes a political goal rather than an assumed state of affairs. Equality in this sense is not to be equated with sameness. Rather, it is to ensure, where possible, an adequate minimum level of functioning for all citizens. It creates a certain "floor" beneath which it is morally objectionable and physically ruinous to allow people to fall.

Voice as a Care Family Value

"Voice" involves the ability to meaningfully participate in determining one's own role in relationships of care and to have a say in the processes by which

---

5. Attentiveness and responsiveness are especially required in relationships where due to age (e.g., infancy) or type of disability (i.e., extreme cognitive impairment), the person receiving care cannot express their own needs or how they would like them met.

choices are created and public programs designed (see, e.g., Levy 2006). It is vitally important in a democratic society and integrally related to the afore-mentioned care values. As Julie White (2000) argues in *Democracy, Justice, and the Welfare State*, many public programs tend to treat care-receivers as permanently and necessarily dependent, as people who are unable or unworthy of articulat-ing their own needs. For example, where inequality is pronounced, "difference" is often treated as "less worthy" or "less able" and works to "muffle" voice. Gender, race, and disability stereotypes (among other things) often encourage this type of misperception and oppression. For example, many people assume that physically disabled or seriously ill people are only on the receiving end of care. But, many people with disabilities are also taking care of others (Little and Levy 2012). Disabled mothers, for instance, often remain responsible for thinking about and arranging care for their households, even from hospital beds following spinal cord injury (Morris 1989).

FAMILIES AS RELATIONSHIPS OF INTIMACY AND CARE

A Care Approach to Defining Families

Contemporary care theory offers useful insights for sorting out which relation-ships a caring political community should recognize as family. Much of care work is performed within families. The connections among family members are forged largely by what families do (and how they do it). The task is to craft a definition of family that includes so-called traditional families and cap-tures what it is that makes many of the "chosen families," "fictive kin," and other arrangements, warrant the classification of "family." This would help distribute rights and public support more equitably. As I define them, *families are composed of: (a) those who have an intimate relationship in which they care for, or are committed to caring for, each other to the best of their abilities without being motivated by material gain or profit; and/or (b) biological parents and children whose parental rights and responsibilities have not been waived or removed.*[6] *In other words, families are formed by emotional intimacy and the willingness to participate in the activities of care and/or genetic ties. Families are relationships of intimacy and care.* The first component of the definition ensures the recognition of groups, conventional or otherwise, that have relationships of intimacy that cause them to be willing to embrace caregiving responsibilities—and indeed, often experience the need to perform care in the context of specific relationships as an ethical and practical *imperative*. The second component of the definition ensures holding adults accountable in certain relationships—that is, requiring that they take some responsibility for either providing care or ensuring that others provide it.

---

6. This definition resonates with Mary Shanley (1997).

"Intimacy," in the sense of closeness, is integral to families. The lives of family members are significantly intertwined. This intimacy can come from living together, from a significant sharing of resources, and/or from a long, robust, and extensively cultivated relationship. Were any of these practices undertaken with a conscious intention of temporality—that is, knowing and desiring that one would only be intimately involved for a short, fixed time before moving on—it would violate the character of the relationship. Family members are more than just casual friends or people whose general dispositions or specific skills motivate them to pursue a career in the caring professions. They exhibit a special bond to a particular person or persons. Thus, a paid nanny or nursing assistant is not family, even though he or she performs a vital care role. This aspect of intimacy enlarges the circle of relationships we acknowledge as familial by including, for example, "chosen families," multi-generational families, and "fictive kin" relations. Broadening intimacy in this way removes some of the explicit heterosexism and implicit ethnocentrism from our definition of family. Notably, this aspect of intimacy does not rely on a sexual or biological component.

Sexual relationships and/or biological ties *may* play roles in family for-mation. A couple engaging in a sexual relationship may develop the type of closeness and strong ties that characterize the intimacy just discussed. If they do, then they would theoretically qualify as family; however, if a sexual rela-tionship does not lead a couple to develop the extremely strong ties, affection, and understanding of the substantive sort that characterizes *being close*, then the sexual partners do not have the feelings or experiences that are usually necessary to make people obligate themselves to each other the way family members do. Because they do not exhibit a level of emotional closeness, legally declared commitment, or significant sharing of resources—that is, because they have neither taken on nor committed themselves to the responsibilities of care—they are legitimately excluded as family. Rights and recognition should come with the willingness to undertake the responsibilities inherent in intimate relationships of care.

As for the biological component of families, children clearly cannot choose whether, to whom, or under what circumstances they are born or adopted. This fact, combined with the issue of children's overwhelming physical and emotional dependence on adults, makes it clear that society has a strong and legitimate interest in ensuring that someone cares for children. Also, the unequal responsibility and risks placed on women during pregnancy, childbirth, and the termination of pregnancy make it necessary that some aspect of sexual intimacy must be acknowledged in our understanding of a responsibility to care. Thus, I propose recognizing that the genetic relation-ship to a child born of a consensual sexual union brings with it the automatic presumption of family between the child and each biological parent (with the attendant rights and responsibilities). This presumption would remain unless the rights of each parent are waived (as in adoption) or removed (as in cases of serious abuse). In other words, including a biological component as a sufficient (but not necessary) component of family makes it clear that creating a child imposes parental responsibilities and rights that *may* be relinquished or diminished through a series of legal and ethical actions, but cannot simply be abandoned or removed carelessly.[7]

Form, Function, and Same-Sex Families

A major development in the legal and public understanding of family in the last decade has been the growing awareness and acceptance of same-sex families. That is not to say that this issue is no longer controversial—it is. But, despite the fact that almost half of Americans support same-sex marriage (Pew Research Center 2012), only a handful of states have legalized it. These developments bring into focus an important question for the care approach to defining families: How do same-sex parenting and partnerships relate to a more functional care approach to family?

In terms of moving toward a definition of family that takes seriously the way people relate to each other, that is, taking function seriously, there has been mixed progress dealing with same-sex parenting and partnerships. In the *Alison D. v. Virginia M.* ruling, which I cited earlier as an example of a strict "formal" understanding of family, the court disregarded the nature of Alison's relationship to the child, denying her standing as a parent, simply because she neither had a biological tie nor was legally bound to the child's biological parent. Interestingly, although public policies have not done much to adjust this inflexible definition of family, Nancy Polikoff (2012) notes that after *Alison D.*, "most appellate courts had created a mechanism for ensuring that a child would not lose a parent when the couple's relationship ended" (725). This movement represented a step forward, in favor of greater recognition of relationships of intimacy and care with nonbiological and nonlegal ties. In other words, a more functional understanding of family had been gaining ground.

A recent high-profile court case, *Debra H. v. Janice R.*, by contrast, arguably moved the courts away from a functional approach and back toward a more formal (albeit expanded) definition of family. Polikoff (2012) describes the court's decision as an example of "winning backward" (for the cause of recognizing a more flexible understanding of families, particularly for LGBT families). The ruling emphasized the fact that Debra H. and Janice R. had legally registered a civil union (the only status available for same-sex couples in the United States at that time) before the child was born. Although Debra's legal counsel and numerous friend of the court briefs argued that the relationship of intimacy and care that Debra had formed with the child (with the biological

---

7. For more details about the handling of biological ties in complex situations, see Levy (2005, 83–85).

parent's permission) should give her standing as a parent, in its ruling, the court stuck to what Polikoff (2012) calls the "easy, but wrong, approach" of focusing on "marriage—or an equivalent formal status" (725–726, 729). In other words, the court reverted back toward a formal understanding of family that was stretched to include same-sex couples in registered unions.

ADVANTAGES TO APPROACHING FAMILIES AS RELATIONSHIPS OF INTIMACY AND CARE

Enlarging the types of relationships that receive public recognition and support for undertaking the demanding and critical work of care would help bring policy and reality closer together, thereby better facilitating care practices in intimate relationships and creating a society that better enables social connectedness, values difference, promotes equality, and cultivates voice.

Families and Social Connectedness

Policies that facilitate and sustain relationships of care are critical. Current US public policies tend to focus on the narrowly defined legal and biological configurations of relationships when determining who qualifies as a family, and who will, thus, be entitled to the benefits that facilitate care. In the case of the FMLA, for example, the right to take leave from work turns on whether one is a spouse, parent, or child of someone with a pronounced need for assistance (unless one qualifies for the more expansive military caregiver leave). If so, a full-time worker in a qualifying business can theoretically take unpaid leave through FMLA. Although passing the FMLA represented a major advance by helping more people perform their caregiving responsibilities better, for most Americans it still focuses on enabling care in restricted biological and legal circumstances.[8] A care approach to family, by contrast, focuses on function and actual care relationships to expand those to whom public policies would extend rights and benefits in response to their commitments. To follow through on the care definition of family, one would ask: Does s/he need the time off to care for a person to whom she has a relationship of intimacy and care? If so, the employee is eligible for the leave on the same terms as "traditional" spouses and parents.[9] There are legitimate concerns that some people might be dishonest and try to take leave without actually undertaking the obligations of

---

8. There are other problems with the FMLA. The fact that it is unpaid means most economically vulnerable families will not be able to take advantage of the leave. Also, because the FMLA does not cover part-time workers or those employed in small businesses, many people are ineligible for the leave (Kittay 1999, 133–140).

9. Not all care benefits should be directed through employers. Given employment trends in the United States, as Frances Fox Pivens (2002) notes, attaching important supports to workers through their jobs could be self-defeating.

care. Presumably, however, measures can be taken to discourage and uncover such cases. The most challenging issue will be determining who is eligible. This issue could be achieved in a variety of ways—for instance, legalizing same-sex marriage, creating domestic partnership registries (including for those without a presumption of sexual intimacy), or judicial functionalism. Not all people who are in relationships of intimacy and care can, or want to, be married. So, it is important to note that adding same-sex marriage will not resolve the question of "drift," even if it gets us a little closer.

Families and Difference

By acknowledging and supporting more diverse relationships of intimacy and care as valuable manifestations of social connectedness, difference is valued—not cast as something that should be ignored or eradicated. In this way, the care approach that focuses on functioning (how people behave and relate to each other) resonates with the work of thinkers such as Young (1990 and 2000), who treat difference as a resource and something to be respected. Given the infinitely complex reasons and circumstances that influence people to form one type of family rather than another, valuing difference and taking it into account are important. There are real advantages to be gained from greater acceptance and respect for the diversity of relationships that people actually develop. It could, for example, help change social climates that cast many as members of "alternative families," where *alternative* implies a deficiency (Nicholson 1997). By expanding the groups of people that we recognize as family, the benefits, rights, and responsibilities could be extended to a larger circle of people. As Karen Struening (1999) argues, expanding our definition of family strengthens society by facilitating networks of care.

Families and Equality

Care theory is particularly helpful because it rejects the false dichotomy between those who seek to raise the status of women by raising the status of care and those who want to raise the status of women by distributing care work more fairly between the sexes. By stressing care as part of the good life for all human beings and making a case for public support, care theory both values the work that women have traditionally done (and continue to do) more often than men[10] *and* advocates distributing this work more equitably.

Care theory, furthermore, can fruitfully address more than gender inequality. Sexual orientation, race, and ethnic identity (among other factors) can influence the formation of families. In valuing social connectedness and opening up the definition of family to incorporate a variety of intimate, caring

---

10. See Duffy (2007) for caveats about types of paid care now performed disproportionately by minority men.

relationships—including "chosen families," "fictive kin," and extended families—we move in the direction of greater equality for traditionally marginalized groups. Still, expanding those relationships that are recognized as familial does not necessitate recognition for every type of relationship imaginable. Following the care value of equality, one could argue, for example, that polygyny violates gender equality.

Families and Voice

The issue of voice is important, but not straightforward. Simply having the public decide on legal rules that govern public policies and practices that impact families will not necessarily result in an outcome that favors an understanding of family that corresponds with the approach and values outlined here. For example, there has been a large increase in the number of Americans that support legalizing same-sex marriage, and recent polls show that more people support it than oppose it (Pew Research Council 2012). If it were possible, however, to have a national referendum (which, of course, it is not), it is not clear that those who support legalization would win. This realization points to two important considerations. First, voting is not the only way that "voice" plays a role in the political process. Ideally, a conversation in which diverse viewpoints are expressed and explained can form part of a communicative process by which people may adjust their ideas. Secondly, the understanding of family that flows from the care approach serves both as a description of the human situation *and* as a prescription for just and effective care practices. Care advocates need to exercise their voices to make the case for change.

IMPLEMENTING A FUNCTIONAL CARE APPROACH

The understanding of family advocated here—as defined by relationships of intimacy and care, and carefully weighing biological connections—could hypothetically be implemented through various measures. One way would be to create domestic partnership registries that expand the type of relationships that can get formal legal recognition of familial status. In general, this approach is often only discussed in terms of recognizing same-sex couples. Although this addition would be a step in the right direction, a care-analysis suggests that this approach would fall short, because it would unfairly exclude people in relationships of intimacy and care by assuming that intimacy can only be defined sexually (or biologically). As implemented in certain jurisdictions, some domestic registry schemes even exclude cohabiting heterosexual partners. This restriction also ignores (or rejects) the possibility that heterosexual partners might refrain from marriage for different reasons, but are still enmeshed in a relationship of intimacy and care. Thus, adding domestic registries would not do enough to expand familial recognition.

A second approach is to cultivate legal thought and rulings that (consistently) employ a functional legal approach. Under this regime, individuals or groups could petition for recognition of their intimate caregiving relationships. But, critics and proponents alike have pointed out some shortcomings of judicial functionalism. They include:

- unpredictability—people in "nontraditional" relationships cannot be sure what functionalist criteria the courts will use and/or whether their relationships will be judged to meet the criteria;
- intrusiveness and privacy concerns—relationships without "preapproved" legal status will have to allow public authorities to critically examine their intimate relationships to obtain familial status;
- suspect history—in the past, public authorities have employed functionalist approaches selectively to enhance control over immigrants, the poor, and people of color;
- freeloading—some people may try to "play" the system to win familial benefits without taking on familial responsibilities.[11]

A public ethic of care provides a working definition of the family as a relationship of intimacy and care. By paying more attention to care work and applying care values, the definition outlined here could be further refined to provide more specific criteria useful for functionalist legal approaches. Still, how particular courts would apply the criteria to specific relationships would remain an open question for a large segment of the population in relationships of care that would not be automatically accorded formal legal recognition. Care theory, by valuing diversity and voice, and by working to facilitate just and equitable social connectedness, could help purge the residues of discrimination from functionalist approaches. Finally, the problem of minimizing or eliminating instances of people trying to manipulate the system to their advantage is a legitimate concern; however, this challenge is neither unique to family law and policy nor an insurmountable barrier. Care theory and legal functionalism, in other words, have a considerable area of overlap; however, the need to rectify functionalism's shortcomings calls for considering other options.

A third approach to implementing a public ethic of care could be to combine the creation of public registries for a much broader array of relationships—taking into consideration the caveats about biology raised earlier—with a functionalist approach in law to address those relationships that will unavoidably fall outside of the registration scheme. (See, e.g., *Beyond Conjugality*, by the Law Commission of Canada 2001.) Although part of this approach is about extending formal/legal definitions of family, this extension would involve a comprehensive rethinking of family that focuses on

---

11. Minow ([1991] 1998, 11–12) identifies criticisms a–d; The *Harvard Law Review's* "Note" (1991) acknowledges criticisms a and b.

expanding legal understandings based on how relationships of intimacy and care function. So, it would entail formalizing a more functional approach. This move would expand any proposed registration scheme to allow individuals to register relationships of intimacy and care that do not (necessarily) include sexual intimacy—for example, a relationship between a woman and her ex-husband's great-aunt, where the two have undertaken extensive obligations of care.[12] This proposal could be called an "RIC registry," where RIC stands for "relationship of intimacy and care." Combining an extensively expanded registry for care relationships with a functionalist approach in law would have the advantage of increasing predictability for those involved in intimate relationships of care without behaving as if the only relationships worthy of recognition and state support are those that can fit easily into whatever models eventually end up in the resulting registration scheme. Cultivating both the inclusive RIC registry *and* judicial functionalism would not lead to what Polikoff (2012) calls "winning backwards." Relationships that did not fit in the registry, or that failed to register, would still be examined from the point of view of function, should a need arise.

The focus in this piece has been on expanding recognition and rights because so many people are already undertaking care work in relationships that lack both of these; however, the obligations of these new relationships also need to be fleshed out in ethics, law, and policy. When rights *and responsibilities* are specified for these new registered partnerships, it would help those who are undertaking the work of care in intimate relationships while making ineligible or deterring those who might be tempted to register for the benefits but do not want the corresponding obligations.

As for other approaches, there are reasons to argue against suggestions like Martha Albertson Fineman's (2004) to allow, on one hand, consenting adults to be radically free to make their own contracts, akin to expanding the use and scope of prenuptial agreements, and, on the other, for a more regulated "caregiver-dependent" status for other relationships. There are several concerns. First, even with the legal remedies she mentions to protect weaker members of the relationship, there is the potential for forming contracts that would be exploitative in ways that individuals might not be able to predict early in their relationships and could only (possibly) be remedied through legal action. Additionally, a contractual approach seems too inherently individualistic. Like Martha Minow ([1991] 1998), "I do not favor leaving the content of family obligations to the private choices of those individuals. I think people should be free to enter family relationships but not be free to rewrite the terms of those relationships" (14). A more productive way to implement this approach is to couple an expansive RIC registry with a functional legal approach to catch unregistered relationships that meet the care family values for recognition and support.

---

12. In *Beyond Conjugality*, the Law Commission of Canada (2001) advocates an expansive registration scheme that is sympathetic to the approach advocated here.

Also, dividing relationships into either "consenting adults" or "caregiver-dependents" categories, as Fineman does, creates a greater sense of disparity between the two than actually exists and distorts how relationships of intimacy and care often function. Contrasting the "consenting adults" category to the "caregiver-dependent" unit seems to imply a sense of static autonomy and independence for the former and separate and nonreversible roles for the latter. *Everyone* has needs. Even those whose needs may be comparatively minimal or easily filled at one moment will eventually see a slow or sudden change. So, to distinguish "consenting adults" from more active or demanding care relationships may be accurate at a particular point in time, but not characteristic of most relationships over any reasonable space of time. Similarly, to focus on a "caregiver-dependent" unit misleadingly suggests that a person is either one or another, whereas these roles can change over time and can even be fluid or shared in the moment. For example, what about the mother recovering from spinal cord surgery, mentioned earlier, who is arranging care for her family from her hospital bed (Morris 1989)? Is she a caregiver or a dependent? What about a family in which a ten-year-old child fixes a meal for her frail grandfather, while the latter calls the child's mother to let her know the child made it home safely from school? How do we categorize the participants in these actions as either, or only, caregivers or dependents? Of course, there are relationships where a great disparity in the ability to give or to need care exists, but a more flexible and comprehensive designation—"relationship of intimacy and care" or "RIC"—can cover these kinds, too.

WORKS CITED

American Bar Association, Working Group on Same-Sex Marriages and Non-Marital Unions. "White Paper: An Analysis of the Law Regarding Same-Sex Marriage, Civil Unions, and Domestic Partnerships." 2004. Accessed on July 12, 2012, from www.americanbar.org/content/dam/aba/migrated/family/reports/WhitePaper.authcheckdam.pdf.

Duffy, Mignon. "Doing the Dirty Work: Gender, Race, and Reproductive Labor in Historical Perspective." *Gender & Society* 21, no. 3 (2007): 313–336.

Engster, Daniel. *The Heart of Justice: Care Ethics and Political Theory.* Oxford: Oxford University Press, 2009.

Fineman, Martha Albertson. "Contract and Care." *Chicago-Kent Law Review* 76, no. 3 (2001): 1403–1440.

———. *The Autonomy Myth: A Theory of Dependency.* New York: New Press, 2004.

Fisher, Berenice, and Joan C. Tronto. "Toward a Feminist Theory of Care." In *Circles of Care: Work and Identity in Women's Lives.* Edited by Emily Abel and Margaret Nelson. Albany: State University of New York Press, 1991.

Gallagher, Maggie. "Does Sex Make Babies? Marriage, Same-Sex Marriage and Legal Justifications for the Regulation of Intimacy in a Post-*Lawrence* World." *Quinnipiac Law Review* 23 (2004): 447–472.

Hacker, Jacob S. "Privatizing Risk without Privatizing the Welfare State: The Hidden Politics of Social Policy Retrenchment in the United States." *American Political Science Review* 98, no. 2 (2004): 243–260.

Hafen, Bruce C. "Individualism and Autonomy in Family Law: The Waning of Belonging." *Brigham Young University Law Review* 1 (1991): 32–42.

Harvard Law Review. "Note: Looking for a Family Resemblance: The Limits of the Functional Approach to the Legal Definition of Family." *Harvard Law Review* 104 (1991): 1640–1660.

Josephson, Jyl. "Romantic Weddings, Diverse Families." *Politics & Gender* 6, no. 1 (2010): 128–134.

Kittay, Eva Feder. *Love's Labor: Essays on Women, Equality, and Dependency.* New York: Routledge, 1999.

Law Commission of Canada. *Beyond Conjugality: Recognizing and Supporting Close Personal Adult Relationships,* 2001.

Levy, Traci. "At the Intersection of Intimacy and Care: Redefining 'Family' through the Lens of a Public Ethic of Care." *Politics & Gender* 1, no. 1 (2005): 65–95.

———. "The Relational Self and the Right to Give Care." *New Political Science* 28, no. 4 (2006): 547–570.

Little, Deborah, and Traci Levy. "Who Cares: Integrating Disability Experiences into Care Theory." Paper presented at the Annual Meeting of the Western Political Science Association in March 2012 in Portland, Oregon. Accessed July 11, 2012, from: http://wpsa.research.pdx.edu/meet/2012/littleandlevy.pdf.

Minow, Martha. "Redefining Families: Who's In and Who's Out?" Chapter One in *Families in the US Kinship and Domestic Politics.* Edited by Karen V. Hansen and Anita Ilta Garey, 7–19. Philadelphia, PA: Temple University Press, [1991] 1998.

Morris, J. "Being a Mother." In *Able Lives: Women's Experience of Paralysis.* Edited by J. Morris. London: The Women's Press, 1989.

National Center for Lesbian Rights. "Legal Recognition of LGBT Families," 2012. Accessed on June 27, 2012, from www.nclrights.org/site/DocServer/Legal_Recognition_of_LGBT_Families.pdf?docID=2861.

National Conference of State Legislatures. "Defining Marriage: Defense of Marriage Acts and Same-Sex Marriage Laws." Last updated November 2012. Accessed on November 15, 2012, from: www.ncsl.org/issues-research/human-services/same-sex-marriage-overview.aspx.

Nicholson, Linda. "The Myth of the Traditional Family." In *Feminism and Families.* Edited with an introduction by Hilde Lindemann Nelson. New York: Routledge, 1997.

Pew Research Center. "More Support for Gun Rights, Gay Marriage Than in 2008 or 2004," 2012. Accessed on June 26, 2012, from www.people-press.org/2012/04/25/more-support-for-gun-rights-gay-marriage-than-in-2008-or-2004/?src=prc-headline.

Pivens, Frances Fox. "Policy Matters." *Boston Review,* February/March 2002. Accessed on July 15, 2012, from http://bostonreview.net/BR27.1/piven.html.

Polikoff, Nancy D. "Conference on Marriage, Families, and Democracy: Ending Marriage as We Know It." *Hofstra Law Review* 32 (2003): 201–232.

———. "The New 'Illegitimacy': Winning Backward in the Protection of the Children of Lesbian Couples." *Journal of Gender, Social Policy & the Law* 20, no. 3 (2012): 721–740.

Shanley, Mary Lyndon. "Fathers' Rights, Mothers' Wrongs: Reflections on Unwed Fathers' Rights and Sex Equality." In *Feminist Ethics and Social Policy.* Edited by Patrice DiQuinzio and Iris Young. Bloomington: Indiana University Press, 1997.

Struening, Karen. "Familial Purposes: An Argument against the Promotion of Family." *Policy Studies Journal* 27, no. 3 (1999): 477–493.

———. *New Family Values.* Lanham, MD: Rowman & Littlefield Publishers, 2002.

Tronto, Joan. *Moral Boundaries: A Political Argument for an Ethic of Care.* New York: Routledge, [1993] 1994.

———. "An Ethic of Care." *Generations* 22, no. 3 (Fall 1998): 15–20.

US Census Bureau. "Current Population Survey: Definitions and Explanations." Last revised June 8, 2012. Accessed on June 21, 2012, from www.census.gov/cps/about/cpsdef.html.

US Department of Labor, Wage and Hour Division (WHD). "Family and Medical Leave Act National Defense Authorization Act for FY 2010 Amendments." Last updated February 2010. Accessed June 21, 2012, from www.dol.gov/whd/fmla/2010ndaa.htm

———. "Family and Medical Leave Act (FMLA)," 2012. Accessed on June 21, 2012, from www.dol.gov/whd/fmla/index.htm.

Wagner, David M. "Balancing 'Parents Are' and 'Parents Do' in the Supreme Court's Constitutionalized Family Law: Some Implications of ALI's Proposals on De Facto Parenthood." *Brigham Young University Law Review,* no. 3 (2001) 1175–1187.

White, Julie Anne. *Democracy, Justice, and the Welfare State.* University Park: Pennsylvania State University Press, 2000.

Woodhouse, Barbara Bennett. "'It All Depends on What You Mean by Home': Toward a Communitarian Theory of the 'Nontraditional' Family." *Utah Law Review* 569 (1996): 569–612.

Young, Iris Marion. *Justice and the Politics of Difference.* Princeton, NJ: Princeton University Press, 1990.

———. *Inclusion and Democracy.* New York: Oxford University Press, 2000.

Suggested Further Readings for Part I

David Blankenhorn, *Fatherless America* (New York: Basic Books, 1995).

Pierre Bourdieu, "On the Family as a Realized Category," *Theory, Culture & Society* 13 (August 1996): 19–26.

Patricia Hill Collins, "It's All in the Family: Intersections of Gender, Race, and Nation," *Hypatia* 13, no. 3 (1998): 62–82.

Nancy Dowd, *In Defense of Single Families* (New York: New York University Press, 1999).

Uma Narayan and Julia Bartowiak, eds., *Having and Raising Children: Unconventional Families, Hard Choices and the Social Good* (University Park: Pennsylvania State University Press, 1999).

Nancy D. Polikoff, "This Child Does Have Two Mothers: Redefining Parenthood to Meet the Needs of Children in Lesbian-Mother and Other Nontraditional Families," *Georgetown Law Journal* 78 (1990): 459, 527–543.

David Popenoe, *Life Without Father* (New York: Free Press, 1996).

Mary Shanley, *Making Babies, Making Families: What Matters Most in an Age of Reproductive Technologies, Surrogacy, Adoption, and Same-Sex and Unwed Parents* (Boston, MA: Beacon Press, 2001).

Kath Weston, "Families We Choose," in *Families We Choose: Lesbians, Gays, Kinship* (New York: Columbia University Press, 1991).

II

Justice, Gender, and the Family

Introduction to Part II

Part II explores the family from the perspective of gender justice. The distribution of economic and political resources and connections between public and private life are central concerns of this scholarship. Echoes of Plato, Aristotle, Wollstonecraft, Mill, and Engels are hard to miss here.

Although a number of feminist theorists helped to bring the family to the attention of political theorists and highlight its importance for justice theories, probably no work has been more influential than Susan Moller Okin's *Justice, Gender, and the Family*. Okin argues that the gendered character of traditional marriage and family life disadvantages women (and their charges) and makes them vulnerable to an assortment of harms: poverty, abuse, manipulation, and worse. These injustices are frequently ignored, she argues, because of the "private" place of the family in most political theories, and yet they affect not only women but also children and society as a whole. Justice, therefore, demands that theorists and policy makers attend to power dynamics within, as well as outside of, the family. From her perspective, the creation of a more just society literally begins at home with the reform of gender relations within the family.

Because Okin's book was published more than twenty years ago, the editors of this volume have included notes updating some of the statistics that are key to her analysis. Reading the piece in light of these new figures generates a number of questions: How has our society changed since Okin wrote her book? How do these changes affect the relevance of her argument? If one were to rewrite Okin's argument today, what would it look like?

The second reading in this part, Nancy Fraser's widely cited, "After the Family Wage," addresses the theme of justice, gender, and the family from a broader social and philosophical perspective. Fraser argues that the traditional gender order based on the male-breadwinner-female-caregiver family form has become obsolete in the face of late-twentieth-century economic and social changes. In search of a new family ideal suited for promoting gender equality under these postindustrial circumstances, she compares three different models—the "Universal Breadwinner Model," the "Caregiver-Parity Model," and the "Universal Caregiver Model." Although all three improve on the traditional family model, Fraser argues, only the Universal Caregiver Model would deliver full gender equality. And yet, for this model to be a real possibility for most people, she argues, the state would have to take on a much more active role in dismantling the gendered opposition between caregiving and breadwinning and, in effect, make "women's current life-patterns the norm for everyone." Fraser concludes by noting that "much more work needs to be done to develop this third—Universal Caregiver—vision of a postindustrial welfare state."

4

Justice, Gender, and the Family

Susan Moller Okin

[…] Neither mainstream theorists of social justice nor their critics (with rare exceptions) have paid much attention to the internal inequalities of the family. They have considered the family relevant for one or more of only three reasons. Some have seen the family as an impediment to equal opportunity. But the focus of such discussion has been on class differentials among families, not on sex differentials within them. While the concern that the family limits equality of opportunity is legitimate and serious, theorists who raise it have neglected the issue of gender and therefore ignored important aspects of the problem. Those who discuss the family without paying attention to the inequalities between the sexes are blind to the fact that the gendered family radically limits the equality of opportunity of women and girls of all classes—as well as that of poor and working-class children of both sexes. Nor do they see that the vulnerability of women that results from the patriarchal structure and practices of the family *exacerbates* the problem that the inequality of families poses for children's equality of opportunity. As I shall argue in this chapter, with the increasing prevalence of families headed by a single female, children suffer more and more from the economic vulnerability of women.

Second and third, theorists of justice and their critics have tended either to idealize the family as a social institution for which justice is not an appropriate virtue, or, more rarely, to see it as an important locus for the development of a sense of justice. I have disagreed strongly with those who, focusing on an idealized vision of the family, perceive it as governed by virtues nobler than justice and therefore not needing to be subjected to the tests of justice to which

63

we subject other fundamental social institutions. While I strongly support the *hope* that families will live up to nobler virtues, such as generosity, I contend that in the real world, justice is a virtue of fundamental importance for families, as for other basic social institutions. An important sphere of distribution of many social goods, from the material to the intangible, the family has a history of distributing these goods in far from just ways. It is also, as some who have overlooked its internal justice have acknowledged, a sphere of life that is absolutely crucial to moral development. If justice cannot at least begin to be learned from our day-to-day experience within the family, it seems futile to expect that it can be developed anywhere else. Without just families, how can we expect to have a just society? In particular, if the relationship between a child's parents does not conform to basic standards of justice, how can we expect that child to grow up with a sense of justice?

It is not easy to think about marriage and the family in terms of justice. For one thing, we do not readily associate justice with intimacy, which is one reason some theorists idealize the family. For another, some of the issues that theories of justice are most concerned with, such as differences in standards of living, do not obviously apply among members of a family. Though it is certainly not the case in some countries, in the United States the members of a family, so long as they live together, usually share the same standard of living. As we shall see, however, the question of who earns the family's income, or how the earning of this income is shared, has a great deal to do with the distribution of power and influence within the family, including decisions on how to spend this income. It also affects the distribution of other benefits, including basic security. Here, I present and analyze the facts of contemporary gender-structured marriage in the light of theories about power and vulnerability and the issues of justice they inevitably raise. I argue that marriage and the family, as currently practiced in our society, are unjust institutions. They constitute the pivot of a societal system of gender that renders women vulnerable to dependency, exploitation, and abuse. When we look seriously at the distribution between husbands and wives of such critical social goods as work (paid and unpaid), power, prestige, self-esteem, opportunities for self-development, and both physical and economic security, we find socially constructed inequalities between them, right down the list. [....]

VULNERABILITY BY ANTICIPATION OF MARRIAGE

In many respects, marriage is an institution whose tradition weighs upon those who enter into it. The cycle of women's vulnerability begins early, with their anticipation of marriage. Almost all women and men marry, but marriage has earlier and far greater impact on the lives and life choices of women than on those of men. Socialization and the culture in general place more emphasis on marriage for girls than for boys and, although people have recently become less negative about remaining single, young women are more likely than young men to regard "having a good marriage and family life" as extremely important to them. This fact, together with their expectation of being the parent primarily responsible for children, clearly affects women's decisions about the extent and field of education and training they will pursue, and their degree of purposiveness about careers. It is important to note that vulnerability by anticipation of marriage affects at least as adversely the futures of many women who do not marry as it affects those who do. This is particularly significant among disadvantaged groups, particularly poor urban black women, whose actual chances of marrying and being economically supported by a man are small (largely because of the high unemployment rate among the available men), but who are further burdened by growing up surrounded by a culture that still identifies femininity with this expectation.

Even though the proportion of young women who plan to be housewives exclusively has declined considerably, women's choices about work are significantly affected from an early age by their expectations about the effects of family life on their work and of work on their family life. As is well known, the participation of women in the labor force, especially women with small children, has continued to rise. But, although a small minority of women are rapidly increasing the previously tiny percentages of women in the elite professions, the vast majority of women who work outside the home are still in low-paying jobs with little or no prospect of advancement.[1] This fact is clearly related to girls' awareness of the complexity they are likely to face in combining work with family life. As the authors of one study conclude: "the occupational aspirations and expectations of adolescents are highly differentiated by sex ... [and this] differentiation follows the pattern of sexual segregation which exists in the occupational structure." They found not only that the high school girls in their large-scale study were much less likely than the boys to aspire to the most prestigious occupations, but that the girls who had such aspirations displayed a much lower degree of confidence than the boys about being able to attain their goals.

As the women Kathleen Gerson recently studied looked back on their girlhood considerations about the future, virtually all of them saw themselves as confronting a choice: *either* domesticity and motherhood or career. Given the pervasiveness of sex-role socialization (including the mixed or negative messages that girls are often given about their future work lives), the actual obstacles that our social structures place in the way of working mothers, and the far greater responsibility, both psychological and practical, that is placed on mothers than on fathers for their children's welfare, it is not surprising that

---

1. In 2010–2011 in the United States, roughly 30 percent of doctors and 31 percent of lawyers were women. Women were CEOs of twelve of the Fortune 500 companies. Seventy-six out of 435 members of the House of Representatives were women, and seventeen out of one hundred senators. By contrast, almost 98 percent of preschool and kindergarten teachers were women.

these women perceived a conflict between their own work interests and the interests of any children they might have. While many reacted against their own mothers' domestic lives, very few were able to imagine successfully combining motherhood with a career. And those who did generally avoided confronting the dilemmas they would have to face. But most grew up with the belief that "a woman can have either a career or children, but not both." Not surprisingly, many of them, assuming that they would want to have children, followed educational and work paths that would readily accommodate the demands of being a primary parent. The only way that those who were career-oriented came to believe that they might avoid the difficult choice, and even attempt to combine their work with mothering, was by deciding to be trailblazers, rejecting strongly ingrained beliefs about the incompatibility of the two.

Needless to say, such a choice does not confront boys in their formative years. *They* assume—reasonably enough, given our traditions and present conditions and beliefs—that what is expected of them as husbands and fathers is that, by developing a solid work life, they will provide the primary financial support of the family. Men's situation can have its own strains, since those who feel trapped at work cannot opt for domesticity and gain as much support for this choice as a woman can. For those who become unemployed, the conflict of their experience with society's view of the male as provider can be particularly stressful. But boys do not experience the dilemma about work and family that girls do as they confront the choices that are crucial to their educations, future work lives and opportunities, and economic security.

When women envisage a future strongly influenced by the demands on them as wives and particularly as mothers, they are likely to embark on traditionally female fields of study and/or occupational paths. The typical route for women is still to finish their education with high school and to marry and have children in their early twenties, though a growing minority are continuing their education, establishing themselves in careers, and marrying later. Some of those who are primarily family-oriented foresee their wage work as temporary or intermittent, while some envisage trying to combine some continued work in the marketplace with traditionally female family responsibilities. But whether such women enter clerical, sales, or service work, or train for one of the predominantly female professions such as teaching or nursing, they are heading not only for the relatively more flexible hours or greater replaceability that most of these jobs afford but also for low pay, poor working conditions, and, above all, blocked mobility. In 1987, women who worked year-round at full-time jobs earned a median wage of $15,704—71 percent of the $22,204 earned by full-time working men.[2] The fact that women's educational achievement is becoming equal to men's, through the level of master's degrees, is clearly affecting women's *participation* in the work

---

2. The median annual earnings for full-time, year-round women workers in 2012 in the United States was $36,931—77 percent of the $47,715 earned by full-time working men.

force. But, though it could also potentially affect their earnings relative to men's, it has done so very little up to now, in part because the professional and service occupations that are more than two-thirds female—such as education, humanities, home economics, library science, and health science—are far worse paid than those that are still more than two-thirds male—such as science and engineering. Occupational sex segregation cancels out women's educational advances: in 1985, the average full-time working white woman with a college degree or higher earned $2,000 less than the average white man who had only a high-school diploma; and the average black woman with some college education earned slightly less than the average white man who had only an elementary school education.[3]

Regardless of educational achievement, women are far more likely than men to work in administrative support jobs, as a secretary, typist, or bookkeeper, for example, which in most cases hold no prospects for advancement.[4] Almost 30 percent of employed women worked in this category in 1985, compared with fewer than 6 percent of men. A study of workplaces during the late 1960s and the 1970s (*after* the 1963 Equal Pay Act and Title VII of the 1964 Civil Rights Act) found the sex segregation of specific jobs and occupational ladders in both manufacturing and nonmanufacturing firms to be so pervasive that more than 90 percent of women would have had to change jobs in order for women to share equally the same job titles as men. Frequently, workplaces had only one or two job titles that included members of both sexes. On top of all this, recent research has shown that large discrepancies exist between male and female wages for the same job title. While female secretaries earned a median wage of $278 per week in 1985, the median for male secretaries was $365; moreover, in twenty-four other narrowly defined occupations in which females earned less than they would have as secretaries, males earned *more* in every case than a female secretary. Indeed, some firms designate particular jobs as male and others designate the same jobs as female, and the wage rates differ accordingly. It seems, therefore, that "the wage level for a particular job title in a particular establishment is set *after the employer decides whether those jobs will be filled by women or men.*" Barbara Bergmann's detailed study of sex segregation in the workplace leads her to conclude:

---

3. In 2008 in the United States, the median income of a full-time, year-round white male worker age twenty-five to thirty-four with only a high school diploma was $36,300. The median income for a white male with a bachelor's degree was $54,200. The median income of a full-time, year-round white female worker age twenty-five to thirty-four with a bachelor's degree was $41,500, and the median income for a full-time, year-round black or Hispanic female worker age twenty-five to thirty-four with a bachelor's degree was $41,000.

4. The top five occupations for women in the United States in 2010 were: (1) secretaries and administrative assistants, (2) elementary and middle school teachers, (3) registered nurses, (4) nursing and home health aides, and (5) cashiers.

> Women are fenced off from a disproportionate share of what we might call "labor market turf." ... [Thus] the supply and the demand in the markets for men's and women's labor are powerfully affected by discrimination.... The exclusion of women from a big share of all of the jobs in the economy is what creates two labor markets where there should be only one. The discriminatory assignment of jobs to one sex or the other is what sets the level of demand in each market ... [and] force[s] women to have to sell their labor at a low price.

Thus workplace discrimination per se is very significant. In addition, as I have suggested, some of the segregation of wage work by sex is attributable to the individual choices that women and men make in the context of their own socialization and with knowledge of the gender structure of the family in particular. M. Rivka Polatnick has recently summarized the situation:

> Not only during the period of childrearing do women become economically or professionally disadvantaged vis-à-vis men; most women's lives have already been constructed in anticipation of that period. "Helpful advice" from family, friends, and guidance counselors, and discriminatory practices in schools and in the job market steer women toward jobs and interests compatible with a future in childrearing.

It is no wonder, then, that most women are, even before marriage, in an economic position that sets them up to become more vulnerable during marriage, and most vulnerable of all if their marriage ends and—unprepared as they are—they find themselves in the position of having to provide for themselves and their children.

VULNERABILITY WITHIN MARRIAGE

Marriage continues the cycle of inequality set in motion by the anticipation of marriage and the related sex segregation of the workplace. Partly because of society's assumptions about gender, but also because women, on entering marriage, tend already to be disadvantaged members of the work force, married women are likely to start out with less leverage in the relationship than their husbands. As I shall show, answers to questions such as whose work life and work needs take priority, and how the unpaid work of the family will be allocated—if they are not simply assumed to be decided along the lines of sex difference, but are live issues in the marriage—are likely to be strongly influenced by the differences in earning power between husbands and wives. In many marriages, partly because of discrimination at work and the wage gap between the sexes, wives (despite initial personal ambitions and even when they are full-time wage workers) come to perceive themselves as benefiting from giving priority to their husbands' careers. Hence they have little incentive

4 / <i>Justice, Gender, and the Family</i>

to question the traditional division of labor in the household. This in turn limits their own commitment to wage work and their incentive and leverage to challenge the gender structure of the workplace. Experiencing frustration and lack of control at work, those who thus turn toward domesticity, while often resenting the lack of respect our society gives to full-time mothers, may see the benefits of domestic life as greater than the costs.

Thus, the inequalities between the sexes in the workplace and at home reinforce and exacerbate each other. It is not necessary to choose between two alternative, competing explanations of the inequalities between men and women in the workplace—the "human capital" approach, which argues that, because of expectations about their family lives, women *choose* to enter lower-paid and more dead-end occupations and specific jobs, and the workplace discrimination explanation, which blames factors largely outside the control of female employees. When the pivotal importance of gender structured marriage and the expectation of it are acknowledged, these explanations can be seen, rather, as complementary reasons for women's inequality. A *cycle of power relations and decisions pervades both family and workplace, and the inequalities of each reinforce those that already exist in the other.* Only with the recognition of this truth will we be able to begin to confront the changes that need to occur if women are to have a real opportunity to be equal participants in either sphere.

Human capital theorists, in perceiving women's job market attachment as a matter of voluntary choice, appear to miss or virtually to ignore the fact of unequal power within the family. Like normative theorists who idealize the family, they ignore potential conflicts of interest, and consequently issues of justice and power differentials, *within* families. This means that they view the question of whether a wife works solely in terms of the total aggregate costs and benefits for the family unit as a whole. They assume that if a wife's paid work benefits the family more (in terms, say, of aggregate income and leisure) than her working exclusively within the household, her rational choice, and that of her husband, will be that she should get a job; if the reverse is true, she should not. But this simplistic attention to the family's "aggregate good" ignores the fact that a wife, like a husband, may have an independent interest in her own career advancement or desire for human contact, for example, that may give her an incentive to work even if the family as a whole may on that account find its life more difficult. Further, the human capital approach overlooks the fact that such goods as leisure and influence over the expenditure of income are by no means always equally shared within families. It also fails to recognize that the considerable influence that husbands often exert over their wives' decisions on whether to take paid work may be motivated not by a concern for the aggregate welfare of the household but, at least in part, by their desire to retain the authority and privilege that accrues to them by virtue of being the family's breadwinner. Thus the decisions of married women about their participation in the job market, even when they are choices, may not be such simple or voluntary choices as human capital theory seems to imply.

In addition, those who seek to explain women's comparative disadvantage in the labor market by their preference for domestic commitments do not consider whether at least some of the causality may run in the opposite direction. But there is considerable evidence that women's "choices" to become domestically oriented, and even whether to have children, may result at least in part from their frequently blocked situations at work. Kathleen Gerson's study shows that, though they usually did not notice the connection, many of the women in her sample decided to leave wage work and turn to childbearing and domesticity coincidentally with becoming frustrated with the dead-end nature of their jobs. Conversely, she found that some women who had initially thought of themselves as domestically oriented, and who had in many cases chosen traditionally female occupations, reversed these orientations when unusual and unexpected opportunities for work advancement opened up to them.

Even if these problems with the human capital approach did not exist, we would still be faced with the fact that the theory can explain, at most, half of the wage differential between the sexes. In the case of the differential between white men and black women, 70 percent of it is unexplained. At *any* given level of skill, experience, and education, men earn considerably more than women. The basic problem with the human capital approach is that, like much of neoclassical economic theory, it pays too little attention to the multiple constraints placed on people's choices. It pays too little attention to differentials of power between the sexes both in the workplace and in the family. It thus ignores the fact that women's commitment and attachment to the workplace are strongly influenced by a number of factors that are largely beyond their control. As we have seen, a woman's typically less advantaged position in the work force and lower pay may lead her to choices about full-time motherhood and domesticity that she would have been less likely to make had her work life been less dead-ended. They also give her less power in relation to her husband should she want to resist the traditional division of labor in her household and to insist on a more equal sharing of child care and other domestic responsibilities. Those who stress the extent to which both husbands and wives cling to the "male provider/female nurturer" roles as unobjectionable because efficient and economically rational for the family unit need to take a step back and consider the extent to which the continued sex segregation of the work force serves to perpetuate the traditional division of labor within the household, even in the face of women's rising employment. [....]

Wives and Wage Work

While theorists of justice have largely ignored it, women's double burden and its effects have long been recognized by feminists. Largely because of the unequal distribution of housework and child care, married women's opportunities in the work force are considerably more constrained than men's. As Gerson notes, "the simple fact of [women's] working ... does not by itself entail significant social change." Though women are now less inclined than they were a generation ago to be part-time and sporadic workers, there is a wide gap between the increase in their labor force participation and their labor force attachment and position. Because of their lower level of labor force attachment, their tendency to work part-time and at jobs that in other respects bend to meet the needs of the family, and their propensity to accommodate their own employment to their husbands', women's wages become lower in relation to men's as they get older. Whereas the ratio between an average full-time working woman's earnings and a full-time working man's is 83:100 between the ages of twenty-one and twenty-nine, the wage gap by ages forty-five to sixty-four has increased to 60:100.

The constraints placed on wives as workers are strengthened by the fact that many full-time employers assume, in innumerable ways, that "someone" is at home at least part-time during the day to assume primary responsibility for children. The traditional or quasi-traditional division of labor is clearly assumed in the vast discrepancy between normal full-time working hours and children's school hours and vacations. It is assumed by the high degree of geographical mobility required by many higher-level management positions. It is also implicit in the structure of the professions, in which the greatest demands are placed on workers at the very peak of the child-rearing years. Academia and the law are two clear examples; both tenure and partnership decisions are typically made for a person between the ages of thirty and thirty-five, with obvious discriminatory implications for the professional parent (almost always a woman) who does not have a partner willing to assume the major responsibility for children.

Because the structure of most wage work is inconsistent with the parenting responsibilities chiefly borne by women, far fewer women (especially married women) than men *do* work full-time. Only 27 percent of all wives in families with children worked full-time year-round in 1984, compared with 77 percent of husbands.[5] Some mothers conclude that, given the demands of their work, the only reasonable answer to the needs of their children is to take time out of the workplace altogether. Others work part-time. But the repercussions of either of these choices, given the current structure and attitudes of the workplace, are often serious and long-lasting. The investment in career assets is by far the most valuable property owned by most couples. To the extent that wives work part-time or intermittently, their own career potential atrophies, and they become deeply dependent on their husbands' career assets. Even when a wife maintains her career, her husband's work needs—in terms of time, freedom from other preoccupations, education and training, and geographical mobility—usually take priority. This is often the case even with dual-career couples who are similarly qualified and claim to be committed to an egalitarian ideology. In relation to the outside world

---

5. By 2000, about 35 percent of women with children under six worked full time.

of employment, therefore, the notion that husbands and wives are equals is myth. Typically, women as workers are disadvantaged by marriage itself, and the more so the longer the duration of the marriage.

Power in the Family

There are very few studies of power within marriage. Of those few, the one most frequently cited until recently—Robert O. Blood Jr. and Donald M. Wolfe's 1960 *Husbands and Wives*—though informative, is now outdated and unreliable in the way it interprets its own findings. The study in itself is of considerable interest for the question of power and gender, given its influential character, not only because of what it purports to discover but also because these findings are both distorted and blurred by the authors' initial assumption that a moderate degree of male dominance is the desirable norm within families. This assumption leads them to define what their own scale indicates to be moderate male dominance as "relative equalitarianism" in family decision making. When reinterpreted in the absence of this sexist normative assumption, we find that what Blood and Wolfe's study of married life in the 1950s discovered was not, as they claimed, that "the American family has changed its authority pattern from one of patriarchal male dominance to one of equalitarian sharing," but rather that male dominance was still the norm, though its extent varied in accordance with a number of factors. The most important of these was the discrepancy in income and wage-work success between the husband and the wife.

As Blood and Wolfe report their findings about what variables affect family power, they are again misleading, due to their implicit assumptions. They conclude that the distribution of power, and its ebb and flow during the course of a marriage, vary with the "resources" that each spouse contributes to the family. But they completely fail to notice that the only resources that affect marital power are those—such as income, success, and prestige—that are valued in the world *outside* the marriage. Resources such as domestic services and childbearing and child-rearing capacities, skills, and labor are not only not positively correlated with marital power but are in fact *negatively* correlated with it. While Blood and Wolfe note that the housewife with preschool children is at the least powerful point in her marriage, and that her power decreases as the number of children rises, they do not question why she should be so powerless at a time when she is contributing so much to the family. Because of their unstated sexist assumptions about what constitutes a "resource," they explain her lack of power in terms of her extreme financial dependence on her husband, and fail to perceive her husband as dependent on her for any resources at all.

Only recently, with the publication of Blumstein and Schwartz's *American Couples,* have we had a large-scale and more neutral account of the power picture behind decision making by couples. They asked thousands of couples to respond on a scale of 1 to 9 (with 5 defined as "both equally") to the question: "In general, who has more say about important decisions affecting your relationship, you or your partner?" Clearly, what this new study reveals about married couples confirms the major findings that Blood and Wolfe's earlier study discovered but obscured. First, though the number of marriages in which spouses consider that they share decision-making power relatively equally has increased considerably, the tendency in others is still distinctly toward male rather than female dominance. Second, it is still clearly the case that the possession by each spouse of resources valued by the *outside* world, especially income and work status, rather than resources valuable primarily within the family, has a significant effect on the distribution of power in the relationship.

Blumstein and Schwartz preface their findings about couples, money, and power by noting that they are not likely to accord with "cherished American beliefs about fairness and how people acquire influence in romantic relationships." Perhaps this is why, as they point out, although "economic factors tend to be involved in every aspect of a couple's life," standard textbooks on marriage and the family are unlikely to devote more than five pages to this subject. Just as political and moral theorists have been extremely reluctant to admit that questions of justice pertain to family life, a similar tendency to idealize—and to conceal dominance—has apparently characterized sociologists of the family until recently, too. But Blumstein and Schwartz's study establishes quite decisively that "in three out of four of the types of couples ... studied [all types except lesbian couples], ... the amount of money a person earns—in comparison with a partner's income—establishes relative power." Given that even the 26 percent of all wives who work full-time earn, on average, only 63 percent as much as the average full-time working husband, and the average wife who works for pay (full- or part-time) earns only 42 percent as much, it is therefore not at all surprising that male dominance is far more common than female dominance in couples who deviate from a relatively egalitarian distribution of power. When women are employed, and especially when their earnings approach those of their husbands, they are more likely to share decision-making power equally with their husbands and to have greater financial autonomy. In marriages in which the husband earned over $8,000 more than the wife (more than half the marriages in the Blumstein and Schwartz sample), the husband was rated as more powerful (as opposed to an equal sharing of power or to the wife's being more powerful) in 33 percent of cases. In marriages in which the incomes of husband and wife were approximately equal, only 18 percent of the husbands were rated as more powerful. The workplace success of wives, then, helps considerably to equalize the balance of power within their marriages and gains them greater respect from their husbands, who often have little respect for housework. Success at work, moreover, can reduce the expectation that a wife will do the vast bulk of family work. Nevertheless, the full-time employment, and even the equal or greater earnings, of wives do not guarantee them equal power in the family, for the male-provider *ideology* is sometimes powerful enough to counteract these factors.

Given these facts about the way power is distributed in the family, and the facts brought out earlier about the typical contentiousness of the issue of housework, it is not difficult to see how the vulnerability of married women in relation to the world of work and their inequality within the family tend to form part of a vicious cycle. Wives are likely to start out at a disadvantage, because of both the force of the traditions of gender and the fact that they are likely to be already earning less than their husbands at the time of marriage. In many cases, the question of who is responsible for the bulk of the unpaid labor of the household is probably not raised at all, but *assumed*, on the basis of these two factors alone. Because of this "nondecision" factor, studies of marital power that ask only about the respective influence of the partners over *decisions* are necessarily incomplete, since they ignore distributions of burdens and benefits that may not be perceived as arising from decisions at all.

However, there *is* often conflict about how much time each partner should devote to wage work and how much to family work. This may include disagreement over the issue of whether the wife should have a job at all, whereas this is almost always taken for granted (a "nondecision") in the case of the husband. Since the partner whose wage work is given priority and who does far less unpaid family work is likely to increase the disparity between his and his spouse's earnings, seniority, and work status, his power in the family will tend to grow accordingly. Hence if, as is likely, he wishes to preserve a traditional or semitraditional division of labor in the family, he is likely to be able to do so. This need not involve constant fighting, with the man always winning; his "man" power and his earning power combined may be so pre-eminent that the issue is never even raised. Either way, his wife is likely to find it difficult to reallocate the family work so as to make him responsible for more of it so that she can take a job or expend more time and energy on the one she has. In addition, the weight of tradition and of her own sex-role socialization will contribute to her powerlessness to effect change.

VULNERABILITY BY SEPARATION OR DIVORCE

The impact of the unequal distribution of benefits and burdens between husbands and wives is hardest and most directly felt by the increasing numbers of women and children whose families are no longer intact. In 1985, 28 percent of ever-married white women and 49 percent of ever-married black women in the United States were separated, divorced, or widowed.[6] Marital disruption through the death of a spouse, divorce, or separation is consistently rated as the most psychologically stressful life event for men and women alike. But in women's lives, the personal disruption caused by these events is frequently

---

6. In 2009 in the United States, roughly 40 percent of ever-married white women were divorced from their first marriage, 48 percent of black women, and 34 percent of Hispanic women.

exacerbated by the serious social and economic dislocation that accompanies them.

Every year, divorce disrupts the lives of more than three million men, women, and children in the United States. The annual divorce rate per 1,000 married women increased from 9.2 in 1960 to 22.6 in 1981; it has leveled off and even declined slightly during the 1980s.[7] Half of all marriages contracted in the 1970s are projected to end in divorce, and between 50 and 60 percent of the children born in the early 1980s are likely to experience the breakup of their parents' marriage by the age of eighteen. Rates of separation and divorce are much higher for black than for white women: in 1983 there were 126 divorced white women for every 1,000 married women; for black women, the ratio was 297 to 1,000. In 1985, about 23 percent of children under the age of eighteen lived with only one parent—in about 90 percent of cases, the mother.[8] Contrary to popular prejudice, female-maintained families with children consist in only a fairly small percentage of cases of never-married women raising children alone. They are in the vast majority of cases the result of separation or divorce.

Not only has the rate of divorce increased rapidly but the differential in the economic impact of divorce on men and women has also grown. Divorce and its economic effects contribute significantly to the fact that nearly one-quarter of all children now live in single-parent households, more than half of them, even after transfer payments, below the poverty level. Moreover, partly because of the increased labor force participation of married women, there has been a growing divergence between female-maintained families and two-parent families. These dramatic shifts, with their vast impact on the lives of women and children, must be addressed by any theory of justice that can claim to be about all of us, rather than simply about the male "heads of households" on which theories of justice in the past have focused.

There is now little doubt that, while no-fault divorce does not appear to have caused the increasing rate of divorce, it has considerably affected the economic outcome of divorce for both parties. Many studies have shown that whereas the average economic status of men improves after divorce, that of women and children deteriorates seriously. Nationwide, the per-capita income of divorced women, which was only 62 percent that of divorced men in 1960, decreased to 56 percent by 1980. The most illuminating explanation of this is Lenore Weitzman's recent pathbreaking study, *The Divorce Revolution.* Based on a study of 2,500 randomly selected California court dockets between 1968 and 1977 and lengthy interviews with many lawyers, judges, legal experts, and 228 divorced men and women, the book both documents and explains the differential social and economic impact of current divorce law on men, women, and children. Weitzman presents the striking finding that in the first

---

7. In 2009 in the United States, the annual divorce rate per 1,000 married women was 16.4.

8. In 2010 in the United States, 23 percent of children lived with only their mothers, and 3 percent lived with only their fathers.

year after divorce, the average standard of living of divorced men, adjusted for household size, increases by 42 percent while that of divorced women falls by 73 percent.[9] "For most women and children," Weitzman concludes,

> divorce means precipitous downward mobility—both economically and socially. The reduction in income brings residential moves and inferior housing, drastically diminished or nonexistent funds for recreation and leisure, and intense pressures due to inadequate time and money. Financial hardships in turn cause social dislocation and a loss of familiar networks for emotional support and social services, and intensify the psychological stress for women and children alike. On a societal level, divorce increases female and child poverty and creates an ever-widening gap between the economic well-being of divorced men, on the one hand, and their children and former wives on the other.

Weitzman's findings have been treated with disbelief by some, who claim, for example, that California, being a community property state, is atypical, and that these figures could not be projected nationwide without distortion. However, studies done in other states (including common law states and both urban and rural areas) have corroborated Weitzman's central conclusion: that the economic situation of men and that of women and children typically diverge after divorce.

The basic reason for this is that the courts are now treating divorcing men and women more or less as equals. Divorcing men and women are not, of course, equal, both because the two sexes are not treated equally in society and, as we have seen, because typical, gender-structured marriage makes women socially and economically vulnerable. The treatment of unequals as if they were equals has long been recognized as an obvious instance of injustice. In this case, the injustice is particularly egregious because the inequality is to such a large extent the result of the marital relationship itself. Nonetheless, that divorce as it is currently practiced in the United States involves such injustice took years to be revealed. There are various discrete parts of this unjust treatment of unequals as if they were equals, and we must briefly examine each of them.

The first way in which women are unequally situated after divorce is that they almost always continue to take day-to-day responsibility for the children. The increased rate of divorce has especially affected couples between the ages of twenty-five and thirty-nine—those most likely to have dependent children.

---

9. Weitzman's figures have been challenged and recalculated. A 1996 study found that women in the United States had an average 27 percent decline in their standard of living and men an average 10 percent increase in their standard of living after divorce. The issue remains controversial. A 2009 US Census Report, *Marital Events of Americans*, nevertheless found clear evidence that women's financial situation tends to be worse than men's in the year after divorce: women who divorced in the past twelve months were more likely to receive public assistance than recently divorced men (23 percent and 15 percent, respectively), to live in poverty (22 percent to 11 percent), and to have less than $25,000 in household income (27 percent to 17 percent).

And in approximately 90 percent of cases, children live with mothers rather than fathers after divorce. This is usually the outcome preferred by both parents. Relatively few fathers seek or are awarded sole custody, and in cases of joint custody, which are increasing in frequency, children still tend to live mainly with their mothers. Thus women's postdivorce households tend to be larger than those of men, with correspondingly larger economic needs, and their work lives are much more limited by the needs of their children.

Second, as Weitzman demonstrates, no-fault divorce laws, by depriving women of power they often exerted as the "innocent" and less willing party to the divorce, have greatly reduced their capacity to achieve an equitable division of the couple's tangible assets. Whereas the wife (and children) typically used to be awarded the family home, or more than half of the total tangible assets of the marriage, they are now doing much worse in this respect. In California, the percentage of cases in which the court explicitly ordered that the family home be sold and the proceeds divided rose from about one-tenth of divorces in 1968 to about one-third in 1977. Of this one-third, 66 percent had minor children, who were likely on this account to suffer significantly more than the usual dislocations of divorce. James McLindon's study of divorcing couples in New Haven, Connecticut, confirms this effect of no-fault divorce. In the case of an older housewife, forced sale of the family home can mean the loss of not only her marriage, occupation, and social status, but also her home of many years, all in one blow. Whether what is supposed to be happening is the "equal" division of property, as in the community property states, or the "equitable" division, as in the common law states, what is in fact happening is neither equal nor equitable. This is partly because even when the division of *tangible* property is fairly equal, what is in fact most families' principal asset is largely or entirely left out of the equation. This leads us to the third component of injustice in the current practice of divorce.

As we have seen, most married couples give priority to the husband's work life, and wives, when they work for wages, earn on average only a small fraction of the family income, and perform the great bulk of the family's unpaid labor. The most valuable economic asset of a typical marriage is not any tangible piece of property, such as a house (since, if there is one, it is usually heavily mortgaged). In fact, "the average divorcing couple has less than $20,000 in net worth." By far the most important property acquired in the average marriage is its career assets, or human capital, the vast majority of which is likely to be invested in the husband. As Weitzman reports, it takes the average divorced man only about *ten months* to earn as much as the couple's entire net worth. The importance of this marital asset is hard to overestimate, yet it has only recently begun to be treated in some states as marital property for the purposes of divorce settlements. Even if "marital property" as traditionally understood is divided evenly, there can be no equity so long as this crucial piece is left in the hands of the husband alone. Except for the wealthy few who have significant material assets, "support awards that divide income, especially future income, are the most valuable entitlements awarded at divorce." Largely because of the division of labor within marriage, to the extent that divorced women have to fall back on their own earnings, they are much worse off than they were when married, and than their ex-husbands are after divorce. In many cases, full-time work at or around the minimum wage, which may be the best a woman without much job training or experience can earn, is insufficient to pull the household out of poverty. As Bianchi and Spain state, "women's labor market adjustments to accommodate children, which are often made within a two-parent family context and seem economically rational at the time, cause difficulty later when these same women find themselves divorced and in great need of supporting themselves and their children."

For reasons that seem to have been exacerbated by no-fault divorce laws, most separated or divorced women *do* have to fall back on their own earnings. These earnings—as opposed to spousal support payments or public transfer payments—make up the major portion of the income of female-maintained families. In 1980, they constituted the entire income of almost half such households. The major reason for this is that, loath to recognize that the husband's earning power, and therefore his continuing income, is the most important asset of a marriage, judges have not been dividing it fairly at the time of divorce. As Weitzman summarizes the situation, "Under the new divorce laws, ... a woman is now expected to become self-sufficient (and, in many cases, to support her children as well)." Alimony and child support are either not awarded, not adequate, or not paid, in the great majority of cases. For many separated or divorced women, as for most single mothers, the idea of the male provider is nothing but a misleading myth that has negatively affected their own work lives while providing them with nothing at all.[10] [....]

TOWARD A HUMANIST JUSTICE

The family is the linchpin of gender, reproducing it from one generation to the next. As we have seen, family life as typically practiced in our society is not just, either to women or to children. Moreover, it is not conducive to the rearing of citizens with a strong sense of justice. In spite of all the rhetoric about equality between the sexes, the traditional or quasi-traditional division of family labor still prevails. Women are made vulnerable by constructing their lives around the expectation that they will be primary parents; they become more vulnerable within marriages in which they fulfill this expectation, whether or not they also work for wages; and they are most vulnerable in the event of separation or divorce, when they usually take over responsibility for children

---

10. In 2007, 57 percent of custodial mothers and 40 percent of custodial fathers were awarded child support. The average annual child support awarded to women was $5,366, and to men was $5,239. A little over 60 percent of women and men actually received the child support owed them.

without adequate support from their ex-husbands. Since approximately half of all marriages end in divorce, about half of our children are likely to experience its dislocations, often made far more traumatic by the socioeconomic consequences of both gender-structured marriage and divorce settlements that fail to take account of it. I have suggested that, for very important reasons, the family needs to be a just institution, and have shown that contemporary theories of justice neglect women and ignore gender. How can we address this injustice?

This is a complex question. It is particularly so because we place great value on our freedom to live different kinds of lives, there is no current consensus on many aspects of gender, and we have good reason to suspect that many of our beliefs about sexual difference and appropriate sex roles are heavily influenced by the very fact that we grew up in a gender-structured society. All of us have been affected, in our very psychological structures, by the fact of gender in our personal pasts, just as our society has been deeply affected by its strong influence in our collective past. Because of the lack of shared meanings about gender, it constitutes a particularly hard case for those who care deeply about both personal freedom and social justice. The way we divide the labor and responsibilities in our personal lives seems to be one of those things that people should be free to work out for themselves, but because of its vast repercussions it belongs clearly within the scope of things that must be governed by principles of justice. Which is to say, in the language of political and moral theory, that it belongs both to the sphere of "the good" and to that of "the right."

I shall argue here that any just and fair solution to the urgent problem of women's and children's vulnerability must encourage and facilitate the equal sharing by men and women of paid and unpaid work, of productive and reproductive labor. We must work toward a future in which all will be likely to choose this mode of life. A just future would be one without gender. In its social structures and practices, one's sex would have no more relevance than one's eye color or the length of one's toes. No assumptions would be made about "male" and "female" roles; childbearing would be so conceptually separated from child rearing and other family responsibilities that it would be a cause for surprise, and no little concern, if men and women were not equally responsible for domestic life or if children were to spend much more time with one parent than the other. It would be a future in which men and women participated in more or less equal numbers in every sphere of life, from infant care to different kinds of paid work to high-level politics. Thus it would no longer be the case that having no experience of raising children would be the practical prerequisite for attaining positions of the greatest social influence. Decisions about abortion and rape, about divorce settlements and sexual harassment, or about any other crucial social issues would not be made, as they often are now, by legislatures and benches of judges overwhelmingly populated by men whose power is in large part due to their advantaged position in the gender structure. If we are to be at all true to our democratic ideals, moving away from gender is essential. Obviously, the attainment of such a social world requires major changes in a multitude of institutions and social settings outside the home, as well as within it.

Such changes will not happen overnight. Moreover, any present solution to the vulnerability of women and children that is just and respects individual freedom must take into account that most people currently live in ways that are greatly affected by gender, and most still favor many aspects of current, gendered practices. Sociological studies confirm what most of us already infer from our own personal and professional acquaintances: there are no currently shared meanings in this country about the extent to which differences between the sexes are innate or environmental, about the appropriate roles of men and women, and about which family forms and divisions of labor are most beneficial for partners, parents, and children. There are those, at one extreme, for whom the different roles of the two sexes, especially as parents, are deeply held tenets of religious belief. At the other end of the spectrum are those of us for whom the sooner all social differentiation between the sexes vanishes, the better it will be for all of us. And there are a thousand varieties of view in between. Public policies must respect people's views and choices. But they must do so only insofar as it can be ensured that these choices do not result, as they now do, in the vulnerability of women and children. Special protections must be built into our laws and public policies to ensure that, for those who choose it, the division of labor between the sexes does not result in injustice. [. . . .]

First, public policies and laws should generally assume no social differentiation of the sexes. Shared parental responsibility for child care would be both assumed and facilitated. Few people outside of feminist circles seem willing to acknowledge that society does not have to choose between a system of female parenting that renders women and children seriously vulnerable and a system of total reliance on day care provided outside the home. While high-quality day care, subsidized so as to be equally available to all children, certainly constitutes an important part of the response that society should make in order to provide justice for women and children, it is only one part. If we start out with the reasonable assumption that women and men are equally parents of their children, and have equal responsibility for both the unpaid effort that goes into caring for them and their economic support, then we must rethink the demands of work life throughout the period in which a worker of either sex is a parent of a small child. We can no longer cling to the by now largely mythical assumption that every worker has "someone else" at home to raise "his" children.

The facilitation and encouragement of equally shared parenting would require substantial changes. It would mean major changes in the workplace, all of which could be provided on an entirely (and not falsely) gender-neutral basis. Employers must be required by law not only completely to eradicate sex discrimination, including sexual harassment. They should also be required to make positive provision for the fact that most workers, for differing lengths of time in their working lives, are also parents, and are sometimes required to nurture other family members, such as their own aging parents. Because children are borne by women but can (and, I contend, should) be raised by both parents equally, policies relating to pregnancy and birth should be quite distinct from those relating to parenting. Pregnancy and childbirth, to whatever varying extent they require leave from work, should be regarded as temporarily disabling conditions like any others, and employers should be mandated to provide leave for all such conditions. Of course, pregnancy and childbirth are far more than simply "disabling conditions," but they should be treated as such for leave purposes, in part because their disabling effects vary from one woman to another. It seems unfair to mandate, say, eight or more weeks of leave for a condition that disables many women for less time and some for much longer, while not mandating leave for illnesses or other disabling conditions. Surely a society as rich as ours can afford to do both.

Parental leave during the post-birth months must be available to mothers and fathers on the same terms, to facilitate shared parenting; they might take sequential leaves or each might take half-time leave. All workers should have the right, without prejudice to their jobs, seniority, benefits, and so on, to work less than full-time during the first year of a child's life, and to work flexible or somewhat reduced hours at least until the child reaches the age of seven. Correspondingly greater flexibility of hours must be provided for the parents of a child with any health problem or disabling condition. The professions whose greatest demands (such as tenure in academia or the partnership hurdle in law) coincide with the peak period of child rearing must restructure their demands or provide considerable flexibility for those of their workers who are also participating parents. Large-scale employers should also be required to provide high-quality on-site day care for children from infancy up to school age. And to ensure equal quality of day care for all young children, *direct government subsidies* (not tax credits, which benefit the better-off) should make up the difference between the cost of high-quality day care and what less well paid parents could reasonably be expected to pay.

There are a number of things that schools, too, must do to promote the minimization of gender. As Amy Gutmann has recently noted, in their present authority structures (84 percent of elementary school teachers are female, while 99 percent of school superintendents are male), "schools do not simply reflect, they perpetuate the social reality of gender preferences when they educate children in a system in which men rule women and women rule children." She argues that, since such sex stereotyping is "a formidable obstacle" to children's rational deliberation about the lives they wish to lead, sex should be regarded as a relevant qualification in the hiring of both teachers and administrators, until these proportions have become much more equal.

An equally important role of our schools must be to ensure in the course of children's education that they become fully aware of the politics of gender. This does not only mean ensuring that women's experience and women's writing are included in the curriculum, although this in itself is undoubtedly important. Its political significance has become obvious from the amount of protest that it has provoked. Children need also to be taught about the present inequalities, ambiguities, and uncertainties of marriage, the facts of workplace discrimination and segregation, and the likely consequences of making life choices based on assumptions about gender. They should be discouraged from thinking about their futures as *determined* by the sex to which they happen to belong. For many children, of course, personal experience has already "brought home" the devastating effects of the traditional division of labor between the sexes. But they do not necessarily come away from this experience with positive ideas about how to structure their own future family lives differently. As Anita Shreve has recently suggested, "the old home economics courses that used to teach girls how to cook and sew might give way to the new home economics: teaching girls *and boys* how to combine working and parenting." Finally, schools should be required to provide high-quality after-school programs, where children can play safely, do their homework, or participate in creative activities.

The implementation of all these policies would significantly help parents to share the earning and the domestic responsibilities of their families, and children to grow up prepared for a future in which the significance of sex difference is greatly diminished. Men could participate equally in the nurturance of their children, from infancy and throughout childhood, with predictably great effects on themselves, their wives or partners, and their children. And women need not become vulnerable through economic dependence. In addition, such arrangements would alleviate the qualms many people have about the long hours that some children spend in day care. If one parent of a preschooler worked, for example, from eight to four o'clock and the other from ten to six o'clock, a preschool child would be at day care for only six hours (including nap time), and with each one or both of her or his parents the rest of the day. If each parent were able to work a six-hour day, or a four-day week, still less day care would be needed. Moreover, on-site provision of day care would enable mothers to continue to nurse, if they chose, beyond the time of their parental leave.

The situation of single parents and their children is more complicated, but it seems that it too, for a number of reasons, would be much improved in a society in which sex difference was accorded an absolute minimum of social significance. Let us begin by looking at the situation of never-married mothers and their children. First, the occurrence of pregnancy among single teenagers, which is almost entirely unintended, would presumably be reduced if girls grew up more assertive and self-protective, and with less tendency to perceive their futures primarily in terms of motherhood. It could also be significantly reduced by the wide availability of sex education and contraception. Second, the added weight of responsibility given to fatherhood in a gender-free society would surely give young men more incentive than they now have not to incur the results of careless sexual behavior until they were ready to take on the responsibilities of being parents. David Ellwood has outlined a policy for establishing the paternity of all children of single mothers at the time of birth, and for enforcing the requirement that their fathers contribute to their support throughout childhood, with provision for governmental backup support in cases where the father is unable to pay. These proposals seem eminently fair and sensible, although the minimum levels of support suggested ($1,500 to $2,000 per year) are inadequate, especially since the mother is presumed to be either taking care of the child herself or paying for day care (which often costs far more than this) while she works.

Third, never-married mothers would benefit greatly from a work structure that took parenthood seriously into account, as well as from the subsidization of high-quality day care. Women who grew up with the expectation that their work lives would be as important a part of their futures as the work lives of men would be less likely to enter dead-ended, low-skilled occupations, and would be better able to cope economically with parenthood without marriage.

Most single parenthood results, however, not from single mothers giving birth, but from marital separation and divorce. And this too would be significantly altered in a society not structured along the lines of gender. Even if rates of divorce were to remain unchanged (which is impossible to predict), it seems inconceivable that separated and divorced fathers who had shared equally in the nurturance of their children from the outset would be as likely to neglect them, by not seeing them or not contributing to their support, as many do today. It seems reasonable to expect that children after divorce would still have two actively involved parents, and two working adults economically responsible for them. Because these parents had shared equally the paid work and the family work, their incomes would be much more equal than those of most divorcing parents today. Even if they were quite equal, however, the parent without physical custody should be required to contribute to the child's support, *to the point where the standards of living of the two households were the same.* This would be very different from the situation of many children of divorced parents today, dependent for both their nurturance and their economic support solely on mothers whose wage work has been interrupted by primary parenting.

It is impossible to predict all the effects of moving toward a society without gender. Major current injustices to women and children would end. Men would experience both the joys and the responsibilities of far closer and more sustained contact with their children than many have today. Many immensely influential spheres of life—notably politics and the professional occupations—would for the first time be populated more or less equally by men and women, most of whom were also actively participating parents. This would be in great contrast to today, when most of those who rise to influential positions are either men who, if fathers, have minimal contact with their children, or women who have either forgone motherhood altogether or hired others as full-time caretakers for their children because of the demands of their careers. These are the people who make policy at the highest levels—policies not only *about* families and their welfare and about the education of children, but about the Foreign policies, the wars and the weapons that will determine the future or the lack of future for all these families and children. Yet they are almost all people who gain the influence they do in part by never having had the day-to-day experience of nurturing a child. This is probably the most significant aspect of our gendered division of labor, though the least possible to grasp. The effects of changing it could be momentous.

PROTECTING THE VULNERABLE

The pluralism of beliefs and modes of life is fundamental to our society, and the genderless society I have just outlined would certainly not be agreed upon by all as desirable. Thus when we think about constructing relations between the sexes that could be agreed upon in the original position, and are therefore just from all points of view, we must also design institutions and practices acceptable to those with more traditional beliefs about the characteristics of men and women, and the appropriate division of labor between them. It is essential, if men and women are to be allowed to so divide their labor, as they must be if we are to respect the current pluralism of beliefs, that society protect the vulnerable. Without such protection, the marriage contract seriously exacerbates the initial inequalities of those who entered into it, and too many women and children live perilously close to economic disaster and serious social dislocation; too many also live with violence or the continual threat of it. It should be noted here that the rights and obligations that the law would need to promote and mandate in order to protect the vulnerable need not—and should not—be designated in accordance with sex, but in terms of different functions or roles performed. There are only a minute percentage of "househusbands" in this country, and a very small number of men whose work lives take second priority after their wives'. But they can quite readily be protected by the same institutional structures that can protect traditional and quasi-traditional wives, so long as these are designed without reference to sex.

Gender-structured marriage, then, needs to be regarded as a currently necessary institution (because still chosen by some) but one that is socially problematic. It should be subjected to a number of legal requirements, at least when there are children. Most important, there is no need for the division of labor between the sexes to involve the economic dependence, either complete or partial, of one partner on the other. Such dependence can be avoided if both partners have *equal legal entitlement* to all earnings coming into the household. The clearest and simplest way of doing this would be to have employers make out wage checks equally divided between the earner and the partner who provides all or most of his or her unpaid domestic services. In many cases, of course, this would not change the way couples actually manage their finances; it would simply codify what they already agree on—that the household income is rightly shared, because in a real sense jointly earned. Such couples recognize the fact that the wage-earning spouse is no more supporting the homemaking and child-rearing spouse than the latter is supporting the former; the form of support each offers the family is simply different. Such couples might well take both checks, deposit them in a joint account, and really share the income, just as they now do with the earnings that come into the household.

In the case of some couples, however, altering the entitlement of spouses to the earned income of the household as I have suggested *would* make a significant difference. It would make a difference in cases where the earning or higher-earning partner now directly exploits this power, by refusing to make significant spending decisions jointly, by failing to share the income, or by psychologically or physically abusing the nonearning or low-earning partner, reinforced by the notion that she (almost always the wife) has little option but to put up with such abuse or to take herself and her children into a state of destitution. It would make a difference, too, in cases where the higher-earning partner indirectly exploits this earning power in order to perpetuate the existing division of labor in the family. In such instances considerable changes in the balance of power would be likely to result from the legal and societal recognition that the partner who does most of the domestic work of the family contributes to its well-being just as much, and therefore rightly *earns* just as much, as the partner who does most of the workplace work.

What I am suggesting is *not* that the wage-working partner pay the homemaking partner for services rendered. I do not mean to introduce the cash nexus into a personal relationship where it is inappropriate. I have simply suggested that since both partners in a traditional or quasi-traditional marriage work, there is no reason why only one of them should get paid, or why one should be paid far more than the other. The equal splitting of wages would constitute public recognition of the fact that the currently unpaid labor of families is just as important as the paid labor. If we do *not* believe this, then we should insist on the complete and equal sharing of both paid and unpaid labor, as occurs in the genderless model of marriage and parenting described earlier. It is only if we do believe it that society can justly allow couples to distribute the two types of labor so unevenly. But in such cases, given the enormous significance our society attaches to money and earnings, we should insist that the earnings be recognized as equally earned by the two persons. To call on Walzer's language, we should do this in order to help prevent the inequality of family members in the sphere of wage work to invade their domestic sphere.

It is also important to point out that this proposal does not constitute unwarranted invasion of privacy or any more state intervention into the life of families than currently exists. It would involve only the same kind of invasion of privacy as is now required by such things as registration of marriages and births, and the filing of tax returns declaring numbers and names of dependents. And it seems like intervention in families only because it would alter the existing relations of power within them. If a person's capacity to fulfill the terms of his or her work is dependent on having a spouse at home who raises the children and in other ways sustains that worker's day-to-day life, then it is no more interventionist to pay both equally for their contributions than only to pay one.

The same fundamental principle should apply to separation and divorce, to the extent that the division of labor has been practiced within a marriage. Under current divorce laws, as we have seen, the terms of exit from marriage are disadvantageous for almost all women in traditional or quasi-traditional marriages. Regardless of the consensus that existed about the division of the family labor, these women lose most of the income that has supported them and the social status that attached to them because of their husband's income and employment, often at the same time as suddenly becoming single parents, and prospective wage workers for the first time in many years. This combination of prospects would seem to be enough to put most traditional wives off the idea of divorcing even if they had good cause to do so. In addition, since divorce in the great majority of states no longer requires the consent of both spouses, it seems likely that wives for whom divorce would spell economic and social catastrophe would be inhibited in voicing their dissatisfactions or needs within marriage. The terms of exit are very likely to affect the use and the power of voice in the ongoing relationship. At worst, these women may be rendered virtually defenseless in the face of physical or psychological abuse. This is not a system of marriage and divorce that could possibly be agreed to by persons in an original position in which they did not know whether they were to be male or female, traditionalist or not. It is a fraudulent contract, presented as beneficial to all but in fact to the benefit only of the more powerful.

For all these reasons, it seems essential that the terms of divorce be redrawn so as to reflect the gendered or nongendered character of the marriage that is ending, to a far greater extent than they do now. The legal system of a society that allows couples to divide the labor of families in a traditional or quasi-traditional manner must take responsibility for the vulnerable position in which marital breakdown places the partner who has completely or partially lost the capacity to be economically self-supporting. When such a marriage ends, it seems wholly reasonable to expect a person whose career has been largely unencumbered by domestic responsibilities to support financially the partner who undertook these responsibilities. This support, in the form of combined alimony and child support, should be far more substantial than the token levels often ordered by the courts now. Both postdivorce households should enjoy the same standard of living. Alimony should not end after a few years, as the (patronizingly named) "rehabilitative alimony" of today does; it should continue for at least as long as the traditional division of labor in the marriage did and, in the case of short-term marriages that produced children, until the youngest child enters first grade and the custodial parent has a real chance of making his or her own living. After that point, child support should continue at a level that enables the children to enjoy a standard of living equal to that of the noncustodial parent. There can be no reason consistent with principles of justice that some should suffer economically vastly more than others from the breakup of a relationship whose asymmetric division of labor was mutually agreed on. [....]

5

After the Family Wage

Nancy Fraser

The current crisis of the welfare state has many roots—global economic trends, massive movements of refugees and immigrants, popular hostility to taxes, the weakening of trade unions and labor parties, the rise of national and "racial"-ethnic antagonisms, the decline of solidaristic ideologies, and the collapse of state socialism. One absolutely crucial factor, however, is the crumbling of the old gender order. Existing welfare states are premised on assumptions about gender that are increasingly out of phase with many people's lives and self-understandings. They therefore do not provide adequate social protections, especially for women and children.

The gender order that is now disappearing descends from the industrial era of capitalism and reflects the social world of its origin. It was centered on the ideal of *the family wage*. In this world people were supposed to be organized into heterosexual, male-headed nuclear families, which lived principally from the man's labor-market earnings. The male head of the household would be paid a family wage, sufficient to support children and a full-time wife-and-mother, who performed domestic labor without pay. Of course, countless lives never fit this pattern. Still, it provided the normative picture of a proper family.

The family-wage ideal was inscribed in the structure of most industrial-era welfare states. That structure had three tiers, with social-insurance programs occupying the first rank. Designed to protect people from the vagaries of the labor market (and to protect the economy from shortages of demand), these programs replaced the breadwinner's wage in case of sickness, disability, unemployment, or old age. Many countries also featured a second tier of programs, providing direct support for full-time female homemaking and mothering. A third tier served the "residuum." Largely holdover from traditional poor relief, public assistance programs provided paltry, stigmatized, means-tested aid to needy people who had no claim to honorable support because they did not fit the family-wage scenario.

Today, however, the family-wage assumption is no longer tenable—either empirically or normatively. We are currently experiencing the death throes of the old, industrial gender order with the transition to a new, *postindustrial* phase of capitalism. The crisis of the welfare state is bound up with these epochal changes. It is rooted in part in the collapse of the world of the family wage, and of its central assumptions about labor markets and families.

In the labor markets of postindustrial capitalism, few jobs pay wages sufficient to support a family single-handedly; many, in fact, are temporary or part-time and do not carry standard benefits. Women's employment is increasingly common, moreover—although far less well paid than men's. Postindustrial families, meanwhile, are less conventional and more diverse. Heterosexuals are marrying less and later, and divorcing more and sooner. And gays and lesbians are pioneering new kinds of domestic arrangements. Gender norms and family forms are highly contested, finally. Thanks in part to the feminist and gay-and-lesbian liberation movements, many people no longer prefer the male breadwinner/female homemaker model. One result of these trends is a steep increase in solo-mother families: growing numbers of women, both divorced and never married, are struggling to support themselves and their families without access to a male breadwinner's wage. Their families have high rates of poverty.

In short, a new world of economic production and social reproduction is emerging—a world of less stable employment and more diverse families. Though no one can be certain about its ultimate shape, this much seems clear: the emerging world, no less than the world of the family wage, will require a welfare state that effectively insures people against uncertainties. It is clear, too, that the old forms of welfare state, built on assumptions of male-headed families and relatively stable jobs, are no longer suited to providing this protection. We need something new, a postindustrial welfare state suited to radically new conditions of employment and reproduction.

What, then, should a postindustrial welfare state look like? Conservatives have lately had a lot to say about "restructuring the welfare state," but their vision is counterhistorical and contradictory; they seek to reinstate the male breadwinner/female homemaker family for the middle class, while demanding that poor single mothers "work." Neoliberal policies have recently been instituted in the United States but they, too, are inadequate in the current context. Punitive, androcentric, and obsessed with employment despite the absence of good jobs, they are unable to provide security in a postindustrial world. Both these approaches ignore one crucial thing: a postindustrial welfare state, like its industrial predecessor, must support a gender order. But the only kind of gender order that can be acceptable today is one premised on *gender equity*.

Feminists, therefore, are in a good position to generate an emancipatory vision for the coming period. They, more than anyone, appreciate the importance of gender relations to the current crisis of the industrial welfare state and the centrality of gender equity to any satisfactory resolution. Feminists also appreciate the importance of carework for human well-being and the effects of its social organization on women's standing. They are attuned, finally, to potential conflicts of interest within families and to the inadequacy of androcentric definitions of work.

To date, however, feminists have tended to shy away from systematic reconstructive thinking about the welfare state. Nor have we yet developed a satisfactory account of gender equity that can inform an emancipatory vision. We need now to undertake such thinking. We should ask: What new, postindustrial gender order should replace the family wage? And what sort of welfare state can best support such a new gender order? What account of gender equity best captures our highest aspirations? And what vision of social welfare comes closest to embodying it?

Two different sorts of answers are currently conceivable, I think, both of which qualify as feminist. The first I call the Universal Breadwinner model. It is the vision implicit in the current political practice of most US feminists and liberals. It aims to foster gender equity by promoting women's employment; the centerpiece of this model is state provision of employment-enabling services such as day care. The second possible answer I call the Caregiver Parity model. It is the vision implicit in the current political practice of most Western European feminists and social democrats. It aims to promote gender equity chiefly by supporting informal carework; the centerpiece of this model is state provision of caregiver allowances.

Which of these two approaches should command our loyalties in the coming period? Which expresses the most attractive vision of a postindustrial gender order? Which best embodies the ideal of gender equity?

In this chapter, I outline a framework for thinking systematically about these questions. I analyze highly idealized versions of Universal Breadwinner and Caregiver Parity in the manner of a thought experiment. I postulate, contrary to fact, a world in which both these models are feasible in that their economic and political preconditions are in place. Assuming very favorable conditions, then, I assess the respective strengths and weaknesses of each.

The result is not a standard policy analysis, however, for neither Universal Breadwinner nor Caregiver Parity will in fact be realized in the near future; and my discussion is not directed primarily at policy-making elites. My intent, rather, is theoretical and political in a broader sense. I aim, first, to clarify some dilemmas surrounding "equality" and "difference" by reconsidering what is meant by gender equity. In so doing, I also aim to spur increased reflection on feminist strategies and goals by spelling out some assumptions that are implicit in current practice and subjecting them to critical scrutiny.

My discussion proceeds in four parts. In the first section, I propose an analysis of gender equity that generates a set of evaluative standards. Then, in the second and third sections, I apply those standards to Universal Breadwinner and Caregiver Parity, respectively. I conclude, in the fourth section, that neither of those approaches, even in an idealized form, can deliver full gender equity. To have a shot at *that*, I contend, we must develop a new vision of a postindustrial welfare state that effectively dismantles the gender division of labor.

GENDER EQUITY: A COMPLEX CONCEPTION

To evaluate alternative visions of a postindustrial welfare state, we need some normative criteria. Gender equity, I have said, is one indispensable standard. But of what precisely does it consist?

Feminists have so far associated gender equity with either equality or difference, where "equality" means treating women exactly like men, and where "difference" means treating women differently insofar as they differ from men. Theorists have debated the relative merits of these two approaches as if they represented two antithetical poles of an absolute dichotomy. These arguments have generally ended in stalemate. Proponents of "difference" have successfully shown that equality strategies typically presuppose "the male as norm," thereby disadvantaging women and imposing a distorted standard on everyone. Egalitarians have argued just as cogently, however, that difference approaches typically rely on essentialist notions of femininity, thereby reinforcing existing stereotypes and confining women within existing gender divisions. Neither equality nor difference, then, is a workable conception of gender equity.

Feminists have responded to this stalemate in several ways. Some have tried to resolve the dilemma by reconceiving one or another of its horns; they have reinterpreted difference or equality in what they consider a more defensible form. Others have concluded "a plague on both your houses" and sought some third, wholly other, normative principle. Still others have tried to embrace the dilemma as an enabling paradox, a resource to be treasured, not an impasse to be gotten round. Many feminists, finally, have retreated altogether from normative theorizing—into cultural positivism, piecemeal reformism, or postmodern antinomianism.

None of these responses is satisfactory. Normative theorizing remains an indispensable intellectual enterprise for feminism, indeed for all emancipatory social movements. We need a vision or picture of where we are trying to go, and a set of standards for evaluating various proposals as to how we might get there. The equality/difference theoretical impasse is real, moreover; it cannot be simply sidestepped or embraced. Nor is there any "wholly other" third term that can magically catapult us beyond it. What, then, should feminist theorists do?

I propose we conceptualize gender equity as a complex, not a simple, idea. This means breaking with the assumption that gender equity can be identified with any single value or norm, whether it be equality, difference, or something else. Instead, we should treat it as a complex notion comprising a plurality of distinct normative principles. The plurality will include some notions associated with the equality side of the debate, as well as some associated with the difference side. It will also encompass still other normative ideas that neither side has accorded due weight. Wherever they come from, however, the important point is this: each of several distinct norms must be respected simultaneously in order that gender equity be achieved. Failure to satisfy any one of them means failure to realize the full meaning of gender equity.

In what follows, I assume that gender equity is complex in this way. And I propose an account of it that is designed for the specific purpose of evaluating alternative pictures of a postindustrial welfare state. For issues other than welfare, a somewhat different package of norms might be called for. Nevertheless, I believe that the general idea of treating gender equity as a complex conception is widely applicable. The analysis here may serve as a paradigm case demonstrating the usefulness of this approach.

For this particular thought experiment, in any case, I unpack the idea of gender equity as a compound of seven distinct normative principles. Let me enumerate them one by one.

1. The Antipoverty Principle

The first and most obvious objective of social-welfare provision is to prevent poverty. Preventing poverty is crucial to achieving gender equity now, after the family wage, given the high rates of poverty in solo-mother families and the vastly increased likelihood that US women and children will live in such families. If it accomplishes nothing else, a welfare state should at least relieve suffering by meeting otherwise unmet basic needs. Arrangements, such as those in the United States, that leave women, children, and men in poverty, are unacceptable according to this criterion. Any postindustrial welfare state that prevented such poverty would constitute a major advance. So far, however, this does not say enough. The antipoverty principle might be satisfied in a variety of different ways, not all of which are acceptable. Some ways, such as the provision of targeted, isolating, and stigmatized poor relief for solo-mother families, fail to respect several of the following normative principles, which are also essential to gender equity in social welfare.

2. The Antiexploitation Principle

Antipoverty measures are important not only in themselves but also as a means to another basic objective: preventing exploitation of vulnerable people. This principle, too, is central to achieving gender equity after the family wage. Needy women with no other way to feed themselves and their children, for example, are liable to exploitation—by abusive husbands, by sweatshop foremen, and by pimps. In guaranteeing relief of poverty, then, welfare provision should also aim to mitigate exploitable dependency. The availability of an alternative source of income enhances the bargaining position of subordinates in unequal relationships. The nonemployed wife who knows she can support herself and her children outside her marriage has more leverage within it; her "voice" is enhanced as her possibilities of "exit" increase. The same holds for the low-paid nursing-home attendant in relation to her boss. For welfare measures to have this effect, however, support must be provided as a matter of right. When receipt of aid is highly stigmatized or discretionary, the antiexploitation principle is not satisfied. At best the claimant would trade exploitable dependence on a husband or a boss for exploitable dependence on a caseworker's whim. The goal should be to prevent at least three kinds of exploitable dependencies: exploitable dependence on an individual family member, such as a husband or an adult child; exploitable dependence on employers and supervisors; and exploitable dependence on the personal whims of state officials. Rather than shuttle people back and forth among these exploitable dependencies, an adequate approach must prevent all three simultaneously. This principle rules out arrangements that channel a homemaker's benefits through her husband. It is likewise incompatible with arrangements that provide essential goods, such as health insurance, only in forms linked conditionally to scarce employment. Any postindustrial welfare state that satisfied the antiexploitation principle would represent a major improvement over current US arrangements. But even it might not be satisfactory. Some ways of satisfying this principle would fail to respect several of the following normative principles, which are also essential to gender equity in social welfare.

A postindustrial welfare state could prevent women's poverty and exploitation and yet still tolerate severe gender inequality. Such a welfare state is not satisfactory. A further dimension of gender equity in social provision is redistribution, reducing inequality between women and men. Equality, as we saw, has been criticized by some feminists. They have argued that it entails treating women exactly like men according to male-defined standards, and that this necessarily disadvantages women. That argument expresses a legitimate worry, which I shall address under another rubric below, but it does not undermine the ideal of equality per se. The worry pertains only to certain inadequate ways of conceiving equality, which I do not presuppose here. At least three distinct conceptions of equality escape the objection. These are essential to gender equity in social welfare.

3. The Income-Equality Principle

One form of equality that is crucial to gender equity concerns the distribution of real per capita income. This sort of equality is highly pressing now, after the family wage, when US women's earnings are approximately 70 percent of men's, when much of women's labor is not compensated at all, and when many women suffer from "hidden poverty" due to unequal distribution within families. As I interpret it, the principle of income equality does not require absolute level, but it does rule out arrangements that reduce women's incomes after divorce by nearly half, while men's incomes nearly double. It likewise rules out unequal pay for equal work and the wholesale undervaluation of women's labor and skills. The income-equality principle requires a substantial reduction in the vast discrepancy between men's and women's incomes. In so doing, it tends, as well, to help equalize the life-chances of children in that a majority of US children are currently likely to live at some point in solo-mother families.

4. The Leisure-Time-Equality Principle

Another kind of equality that is crucial to gender equity concerns the distribution of leisure time. This sort of equality is highly pressing now, after the family wage, when many women, but only a few men, do both paid work and unpaid primary carework and when women suffer disproportionately from "time poverty." One recent British study found that 52 percent of women surveyed, compared to 21 percent of men, said they "felt tired most of the time." The leisure-time-equality principle rules out welfare arrangements that would equalize incomes while requiring a double shift of work from women but only a single shift from men. It likewise rules out arrangements that would require women, but not men, to do either the "work of claiming" or the time-consuming "patchwork" of piecing together income from several sources and of coordinating services from different agencies and associations.

5. The Equality-of-Respect Principle

Equality of respect is also crucial to gender equity. This kind of equality is especially pressing now, after the family wage, when postindustrial culture routinely represents women as sexual objects for the pleasure of male subjects. The principle of equal respect rules out social arrangements that objectify and deprecate women—even if those arrangements prevent poverty and exploitation, and even if in addition they equalize income and leisure time. It is incompatible with welfare programs that trivialize women's activities and ignore women's contributions—hence with "welfare reforms" in the United States that assume AFDC [Aid to Families with Dependent Children] claimants do not "work." Equality of respect requires recognition of women's personhood and recognition of women's work.

A postindustrial welfare state should promote equality in all three of these dimensions. Such a state would constitute an enormous advance over present arrangements, but even it might not go far enough. Some ways of satisfying the equality principles would fail to respect the following principle, which is also essential to gender equity in social welfare.

6. The Antimarginalization Principle

A welfare state could satisfy all the preceding principles and still function to marginalize women. By limiting support to generous mothers' pensions, for example, it could render women independent, well provided for, well rested, and respected but enslaved in a separate domestic sphere, removed from the life of the larger society. Such a welfare state would be unacceptable. Social policy, should promote women's full participation on a par with men in all areas of social life—in employment, in politics, in the associational life of civil society. The antimarginalization principle requires provision of the necessary conditions for women's participation, including day care, elder care, and provision for breast-feeding in public. It also requires the dismantling of masculinist work cultures and woman-hostile political environments. Any postindustrial welfare state that provided these things would represent a great improvement over current arrangements. Yet even it might leave something to be desired. Some ways of satisfying the antimarginalization principle would fail to respect the last principle, which is also essential to gender equity in social welfare.

7. The Antiandrocentrism Principle

A welfare state that satisfied many of the foregoing principles could still entrench some obnoxious gender norms. It could assume the androcentric view that men's current life patterns represent the human norm and that women ought to assimilate to them. (This is the real issue behind the previously noted worry about equality.) Such a welfare state is unacceptable. Social policy should not require women to become like men nor to fit into institutions designed for men, in order to enjoy comparable levels of well-being. Policy should aim instead to restructure androcentric institutions so as to welcome human beings who can give birth and who often care for relatives and friends, treating them not as exceptions but as ideal-typical participants. The antiandrocentrism principle requires decentering masculinist norms—in part by revaluing practices and traits that are currently undervalued because they are associated with women. It entails changing men as well as changing women.

Here, then, is an account of gender equity in social welfare. On this account, gender equity is a complex idea comprising seven distinct normative principles, each of which is necessary and essential. No postindustrial welfare state can realize gender equity unless it satisfies them all.

How, then, do the principles interrelate? Here everything depends on context. Some institutional arrangements permit simultaneous satisfaction of several principles with a minimum of mutual interference; other arrangements, in contrast, set up zero-sum situations, in which attempts to satisfy one principle interfere with attempts to satisfy another. Promoting gender equity after the family wage, therefore, means attending to multiple aims that are potentially in conflict. The goal should be to find approaches that avoid trade-offs and maximize prospects for satisfying all—or at least most of the seven principles.

In the next sections, I use this approach to assess two alternative models of a postindustrial welfare state. First, however, I want to flag four sets of relevant issues. One concerns the social organization of carework. Precisely how this work is organized is crucial to human well-being in general and to the social standing of women in particular. In the era of the family wage, carework was treated as the private responsibility of individual women. Today, however, it can no longer be treated in that way. Some other way of organizing it is required, but a number of different scenarios are conceivable. In evaluating postindustrial welfare state models, then, we must ask: How is responsibility for carework allocated between such institutions as the family, the market, civil society, and the state? And how is responsibility for this work assigned within such institutions: by gender? by class? by "race"-ethnicity? by age?

A second set of issues concerns the bases of entitlement to provision. Every welfare state assigns its benefits according to a specific mix of distributive principles, which defines its basic moral quality. That mix, in each case, needs to be scrutinized. Usually, it contains varying proportions of three basic principles of entitlement: need, desert, and citizenship. Need-based provision is the most redistributive, but it risks isolating and stigmatizing the needy; it has been the basis of traditional poor relief and of modern public assistance, the least honorable forms of provision. The most honorable, in contrast, is entitlement based on desert, but it tends to be antiegalitarian and exclusionary. Here one receives benefits according to one's "contributions," usually tax payments, work, and service—where "tax payments" means wage deductions paid into a special fund, "work" means primary labor-force employment, and "service" means the military, all interpretations of those terms that disadvantage women. Desert has usually been seen as the primary basis of earnings-linked social insurance in the industrial welfare state. The third principle, citizenship, allocates provision on the basis of membership in society. It is honorable, egalitarian, and universalist, but also expensive, hence hard to sustain at high levels of quality and generosity; some theorists worry, too, that it encourages free-riding, which they define, however, androcentrically. Citizenship-based entitlements are most often found in social-democratic countries, where they may include single-payer universal health insurance systems and universal family or child allowances; they are virtually unknown in the United States—except for public education. In examining models of postindustrial welfare states, then, one must look closely at the construction of entitlement. It makes considerable difference to women's and children's well-being, for example, whether day-care places are distributed as citizenship entitlements or as desert-based entitlements, that is, whether or not they are conditional on prior employment. It likewise matters, to take another example, whether carework is supported on the basis of need, in the form of a means-tested benefit for the poor, or whether it is supported on the basis of desert, as return for "work" or "service," now interpreted nonandrocentrically, or whether, finally, it is supported on the basis of citizenship under a universal Basic Income scheme.

A third set of issues concerns differences among women. Gender is the principal locus of this chapter, to be sure, but it cannot be treated en bloc. The lives of women and men are crosscut by several other salient social divisions, including class, "race"-ethnicity, sexuality, and age. Models of postindustrial welfare states, then, will not affect all women—nor all men—in the same way; they will generate different outcomes for differently situated people. For example, some policies will affect women who have children differently from those who do not; some, likewise, will affect women who have access to a second income differently from those who do not; and some, finally, will affect women employed full-time differently from those employed part-time, and differently yet again from those who are not employed. For each model, then, we must ask: Which groups of women would be advantaged and which groups disadvantaged?

A fourth set of issues concerns desiderata for postindustrial welfare states other than gender equity. Gender equity, after all, is not the only goal of social welfare. Also important are nonequity goals, such as efficiency, community, and individual liberty. In addition there remain other equity goals, such as "racial"-ethnic equity, generational equity, class equity, and equity among nations. All of these issues are necessarily backgrounded here. Some of them, however, such as "racial"-ethnic equity, could be handled by means of parallel thought experiments: one might define "racial"-ethnic equity as a complex idea, analogous to the way gender equity is treated here, and then use it, too, to assess competing visions of a postindustrial welfare state.

With these considerations in mind, let us now examine two strikingly different feminist visions of a postindustrial welfare state. And let us ask: Which comes closer to achieving gender equity in the sense I have elaborated here?

THE UNIVERSAL-BREADWINNER MODEL

In one vision of postindustrial society, the age of the family wage would give way to the age of the Universal Breadwinner. This is the vision implicit in the current political practice of most US feminists and liberals. (It was also assumed in the former communist countries!) It aims to achieve gender equity principally by promoting women's employment. The point is to enable women to support themselves and their families through their own wage-earning. The breadwinner role is to be universalized, in sum, so that women, too, can be citizen-workers.

Universal Breadwinner is a very ambitious postindustrial scenario, requiring major new programs and policies. One crucial element is a set of employment-enabling services, such as day care and elder care, aimed at freeing women from unpaid responsibilities so they could take full-time employment on terms comparable to men. Another essential element is a set of workplace reforms aimed at removing equal-opportunity obstacles, such as sex discrimination and sexual harassment. Reforming the workplace requires reforming the culture, however—eliminating sexist stereotypes and breaking the cultural association of breadwinning with masculinity. Also required are policies to help change socialization, so as, first, to reorient women's aspirations toward employment and away from domesticity, and second, to reorient men's expectations toward acceptance of women's new role. None of this would work, however, without one additional ingredient: macroeconomic policies to create full-time, high-paying, permanent jobs for women. These would have to be true breadwinner jobs in the primary labor force, carrying full, first-class social-insurance entitlements. Social insurance, finally, is central to Universal Breadwinner. The aim here is to bring women up to parity with men in an institution that has traditionally disadvantaged them.

How would this model organize carework? The bulk of such work would be shifted from the family to the market and the state, where it would be performed by employees for pay. Who, then, are these employees likely to be? In many countries today, including the United States, paid institutional carework is poorly remunerated, feminized, and largely racialized and/or performed by immigrants. But such arrangements are precluded in this model. If the model is to succeed in enabling *all* women to be breadwinners, it must upgrade the status and pay attached to carework employment, making it, too, into primary-labor-force work. Universal Breadwinner, then, is necessarily committed to a policy of "comparable worth"; it must redress the widespread undervaluation of skills and jobs currently coded as feminine and/or "nonwhite," and it must remunerate such jobs with breadwinner-level pay.

Universal Breadwinner would link many benefits to employment and distribute them through social insurance, with levels varying according to earnings. In this respect, the model resembles the industrial-era welfare state. The difference is that many more women would be covered on the basis of their own employment records. And many more women's employment records would look considerably more like men's.

Not all adults can be employed, however. Some will be unable to work for medical reasons, including some adults not previously employed. Others will be unable to get jobs. Some, finally, will have carework responsibilities that they are unable or unwilling to shift elsewhere. Most of these last will be women. To provide for these people, Universal Breadwinner must include a residual tier of social welfare that provides need-based, means-tested wage replacements.

Universal Breadwinner is far removed from present realities. It requires massive creation of primary-labor-force jobs—jobs sufficient to support a family single-handedly. That, of course, is wildly askew of current postindustrial trends, which generate jobs not for breadwinners but for "disposable workers." Let us assume for the sake of the thought experiment, however, that its conditions of possibility could be met. And let us consider whether the resulting postindustrial welfare state could claim title to gender equity.

1. Antipoverty

We can acknowledge straight off that Universal Breadwinner would do a good job of preventing poverty. A policy that created secure breadwinner-quality jobs for all employable women and men—while providing the services that would enable women to take such jobs—would keep most families out of poverty. And generous levels of residual support would keep the rest out of poverty through transfers.

2. Antiexploitation

The model should also succeed in preventing exploitable dependency for most women. Women with secure breadwinner jobs are able to exit unsatisfactory relations with men. And those who do not have such jobs but know they can get them will also be less vulnerable to exploitation. Failing that, the residual system of income support provides backup protection against exploitable dependency—assuming that it is generous, nondiscretionary, and honorable.

3. Income Equality

Universal Breadwinner is only fair, however, at achieving income equality. Granted, secure breadwinner jobs for women—plus the services that would enable women to take them—would narrow the gender wage gap. Reduced inequality in earnings, moreover, translates into reduced inequality in social-insurance benefits. And the availability of exit options from marriage should encourage a more equitable distribution of resources within it. But the model is not otherwise egalitarian. It contains a basic social fault line dividing bread-winners from others, to the considerable disadvantage of the others—most of whom would be women. Apart from comparable worth, moreover, it does not reduce pay inequality among breadwinner jobs. To be sure, the model re-duces the weight of gender in assigning individuals to unequally compensated breadwinner jobs, but it thereby increases the weight of other variables, pre-sumably class, education, "race"-ethnicity, and age. Women—and men—who are disadvantaged in relation to those axes of social differentiation will earn less than those who are not.

4. Leisure-Time Equality

The model is quite poor, moreover, with respect to equality of leisure time, as we know from the communist experience. It assumes that all of women's current domestic and carework responsibilities can be shifted to the market and/or the state. But that assumption is patently unrealistic. Some things, such as childbearing, attending to family emergencies, and much parenting work, cannot be shifted—short of universal surrogacy and other presumably undesirable arrangements. Other things, such as cooking and (some) housekeeping, could—provided we were prepared to accept collective living arrangements or high levels of commodification. Even those tasks that are shifted, finally, do not disappear without a trace but give rise to burdensome new tasks of coordination. Women's chances for equal leisure, then, depend on whether men can be induced to do their fair share of this work. On this, the model does not inspire confidence. Not only does it offer no disincentives to free-riding, but in valorizing paid work, it implicitly devalues unpaid work, thereby fueling the motivation to shirk. Women without partners would in any case be on their own. And those in lower-income households would be less able to purchase replacement services. Employed women would have a second shift on this model, then, albeit a less burdensome one than some have now; and there would be many more women employed full-time. Universal Breadwinner, in sum, is not likely to deliver equal leisure. Anyone who does not free-ride in this possible postindustrial world is likely to be harried and tired.

5. Equality of Respect

The model is only fair, moreover, at delivering equality of respect. Because it holds men and women to the single standard of the citizen-worker, its only chance of eliminating the gender respect gap is to admit women to that status on the same terms as men. This, however, is unlikely to occur. A more likely outcome is that women would retain more connection to reproduction and domesticity than men, thus appearing as breadwinners manqué. In addition, the model is likely to generate another kind of respect gap. By putting a high premium on breadwinner status, it invites disrespect for others. Participants in the means-tested residual system will be liable to stigmatization, and most of these will be women. Any employment-centered model, even a feminist one, has a hard time constructing an honorable status for those it defines as "nonworkers."

6. Antimarginalization

This model is also only fair at combating women's marginalization. Granted, it promotes women's participation in employment, but its definition of participation is narrow. Expecting employment of all who are able, the model may actually impede participation in politics and civil society. Certainly, it does nothing to promote women's participation in those arenas. It fights women's marginalization, then, in a one-sided, "workerist" way.

7. Antiandrocentrism

Last, the model performs poorly in overcoming androcentrism. It valorizes men's traditional sphere—employment—and simply tries to help women fit in. Traditionally female carework, in contrast, is treated instrumentally; it is what must be sloughed off in order to become a breadwinner. It is not itself accorded social value. The ideal-typical citizen here is the breadwinner, now nominally gender-neutral. But the content of the status is implicitly masculine; it is the male half of the old breadwinner/homemaker couple, now universalized and required of everyone. The female half of the couple has simply disappeared. None of her distinctive virtues and capacities has been preserved for women, let alone universalized to men. The model is androcentric.

We can summarize the merits of Universal Breadwinner in Table 5.1. Not surprisingly, Universal Breadwinner delivers the best outcomes to women whose lives most closely resemble the male half of the old family-wage ideal couple. It is especially good to childless women and to women without other major domestic responsibilities that cannot easily be shifted to social services. But for those women, as well as for others, it falls short of full gender equity.

Table 5.1

Principle	Universal Breadwinner
Antipoverty	Good
Antiexploitation	Good
Income equality	Fair
Leisure-time equality	Poor
Equality of respect	Fair
Antimarginalization	Fair
Antiandrocentrism	Poor

THE CAREGIVER-PARITY MODEL

In a second vision of postindustrial society, the era of the family wage would give way to the era of Caregiver Parity. This is the picture implicit in the political practice of most Western European feminists and social democrats. It aims to promote gender equity principally by supporting informal carework. The point is to enable women with significant domestic responsibilities to support themselves and their families either through carework alone or through carework plus part-time employment. (Women without significant domestic responsibilities would presumably support themselves through employment.) The aim is not to make women's lives the same as men's but, rather, to "make difference costless." Thus, childbearing, child rearing, and informal domestic labor are to be elevated to parity with formal paid labor. The caregiver role is to be put on a par with the breadwinner role—so that women and men can enjoy equivalent levels of dignity and well-being.

Caregiver Parity is also extremely ambitious. On this model, many (though not all) women will follow the current US female practice of alternating spells of full-time employment, spells of full-time carework, and spells that combine part-time carework with part-time employment. The aim is to make such a life-pattern costless. To this end, several major new programs are necessary. One is a program of caregiver allowances to compensate childbearing, child rearing, housework, and other forms of socially necessary domestic labor; the allowances must be sufficiently generous at the full-time rate to support a family—hence equivalent to a breadwinner wage. Also required is a program of workplace reforms. These must facilitate the possibility of combining supported carework with part-time employment and of making transitions between different life-states. The key here is flexibility. One obvious necessity is a generous program of mandated pregnancy and family leaves so that caregivers can exit and enter employment without losing security or seniority. Another is a program of retraining and job search for those not returning to old jobs. Also essential is mandated flextime so that caregivers can shift their hours to accommodate their carework responsibilities, including shifts between full- and part-time employment. Finally, in the wake of all this flexibility, there must be programs to ensure continuity of all the basic social-welfare benefits, including health, unemployment, disability, and retirement insurance.

This model organizes carework very differently from Universal Bread-winner. Whereas that approach shifted carework to the market and the state, this one keeps the bulk of such work in the household and supports it with public funds. Caregiver Parity's social-insurance system also differs sharply. To assure continuous coverage for people alternating between carework and employment, benefits attached to both must be integrated in a single system. In this system, part-time jobs and supported carework must be covered on the same basis as full-time jobs. Thus, a woman finishing a spell of supported carework would be eligible for unemployment insurance benefits on the same basis as a recently laid off employee in the event she could not find a suitable job. And a supported careworker who became disabled would receive disability payments on the same basis as a disabled employee. Years of supported care-work would count on a par with years of employment toward eligibility for retirement pensions. Benefit levels would be fixed in ways that treat carework and employment equivalently.

Caregiver Parity also requires another, residual tier of social welfare. Some adults will be unable to do either carework or waged work, including some adults without prior work records of either type. Most of these people will probably be men. To provide for them, the model must offer means-tested wage-and-allowance replacements. Caregiver Parity's residual tier should be smaller than Universal Breadwinner's, however; nearly all adults should be covered in the integrated breadwinner-caregiver system of social insurance.

Caregiver Parity, too, is far removed from current US arrangements. It requires large outlays of public funds to pay caregiver allowances, hence major structural tax reform and a sea change in political culture. Let us assume for the sake of the thought experiment, however, that its conditions of possibility could be met. And let us consider whether the resulting postindustrial welfare state could claim title to gender equity.

1. Antipoverty

Caregiver Parity would do a good job of preventing poverty—including for those women and children who are currently most vulnerable. Sufficiently generous allowances would keep solo-mother families out of poverty during spells of full-time carework. And a combination of allowances and wages would do the same during spells of part-time supported carework and part-time employment. Since each of these options would carry the basic social-insurance package, moreover, women with "feminine" work patterns would have considerable security.

2. Antiexploitation

Caregiver Parity should also succeed in preventing exploitation for most women, including for those who are most vulnerable today. By providing income directly to nonemployed wives, it reduces their economic dependence on husbands. It also provides economic security to single women with children, reducing their liability to exploitation by employers. Insofar as caregiver allowances are honorable and nondiscretionary, finally, recipients are not subject to caseworkers' whims.

3. Income Equality

Caregiver Parity performs quite poorly, however, with respect to income equality, as we know from the Nordic experience. Although the system of allowances-plus-wages provides the equivalent of a basic minimum breadwinner wage, it also institutes a "mommy track" in employment—a market in flexible, noncontinuous full- and/or part-time jobs. Most of these jobs will pay considerably less even at the full-time rate than comparable breadwinner-track jobs. Two-partner families will have an economic incentive to keep one partner on the breadwinner track rather than to share spells of carework between them, and given current labor markets, making the breadwinner the man will be most advantageous for heterosexual couples. Given current culture and socialization, moreover, men are generally unlikely to choose the mommy track in the same proportions as women. So the two employment tracks will carry traditional gender associations. Those associations are likely in turn to produce discrimination against women in the breadwinner track.

Caregiver Parity may make difference cost less, then, but it will not make difference costless.

4. Leisure-Time Equality

Caregiver Parity does somewhat better, however, with respect to equality of leisure time. It makes it possible for all women to avoid the double shift, if they choose, by opting for full- or part-time supported carework at various stages in their lives. (Currently, this choice is available only to a small percentage of privileged US women.) We just saw, however, that this choice is not truly costless. Some women with families will not want to forego the benefits of breadwinner-track employment and will try to combine it with carework. Those not partnered with someone on the caregiver track will be significantly disadvantaged with respect to leisure time, and probably in their employment as well. Men, in contrast, will largely be insulated from this dilemma. On leisure time, then, the model is only fair.

5. Equality of Respect

Caregiver Parity is also only fair at promoting equality of respect. Unlike Universal Breadwinner, it offers two different routes to that end. Theoretically, citizen-workers and citizen-caregivers are statuses of equivalent dignity. But are they really on a par with each other? Caregiving is certainly treated more respectfully in this model than in current US society, but it remains associated with femininity. Breadwinning likewise remains associated with masculinity. Given those traditional gender associations, plus the economic differential between the two lifestyles, caregiving is unlikely to attain true parity with breadwinning. In general, it is hard to imagine how "separate but equal" gender roles could provide genuine equality of respect today.

6. Antimarginalization

Caregiver Parity performs poorly, moreover, in preventing women's marginalization. By supporting women's informal carework, it reinforces the view of such work as women's work and consolidates the gender division of domestic labor. By consolidating dual labor markets for breadwinners and caregivers, moreover, the model marginalizes women within the employment sector. By reinforcing the association of caregiving with femininity, finally, it may also impede women's participation in other spheres of life, such as politics and civil society.

7. Antiandrocentrism

Yet Caregiver Parity is better than Universal Breadwinner at combating androcentrism. It treats caregiving as intrinsically valuable, not as a mere obstacle to employment, thus challenging the view that only men's traditional activities are fully human. It also accommodates "feminine" life-patterns, thereby rejecting the demand that women assimilate to "masculine" patterns. But the model still leaves something to be desired. Caregiver Parity stops short of affirming the universal value of activities and life-patterns associated with women. It does not value caregiving enough to demand that men do it, too; it does not ask men to change. Thus, Caregiver Parity represents only one-half of a full-scale challenge to androcentrism. Here, too, its performance is only fair.

Caregiver Parity's strengths and weaknesses are summarized in Table 5.2. In general, Caregiver Parity improves the lot of women with significant carework responsibilities, but for those women, as well as for others, it fails to deliver full gender equity.

Table 5.2

Principle	Caregiver Parity
Antipoverty	Good
Antiexploitation	Good
Income equality	Poor
Leisure-time equality	Fair
Equality of respect	Fair
Antimarginalization	Poor
Antiandrocentrism	Fair

TOWARD A UNIVERSAL CAREGIVER MODEL

Both Universal Breadwinner and Caregiver Parity are highly utopian visions of a postindustrial welfare state. Either would represent a major improvement over current US arrangements, yet neither is likely to be realized soon. Both models assume background preconditions that are strikingly absent today. Both presuppose major political-economic restructuring, including significant public control over corporations, the capacity to direct investment to create high-quality permanent jobs, and the ability to tax profits *and wealth* at rates sufficient to fund expanded high-quality social programs. Both models also assume broad popular support for a postindustrial welfare state that is committed to gender equity.

If both models are utopian in this sense, neither is utopian enough. Neither Universal Breadwinner nor Caregiver Parity can actually make good on its promise of gender equity—even under very favorable conditions. Although both are good at preventing women's poverty and exploitation, both are only fair at redressing inequality of respect: Universal Breadwinner holds women to the same standard as men, while constructing arrangements that prevent them from meeting it fully; Caregiver Parity, in contrast, sets up a double standard to accommodate gender difference, while institutionalizing policies that fail to assure equivalent respect for "feminine" activities and life-patterns. When we turn to the remaining principles, moreover, the two models' strengths and weaknesses diverge. Universal Breadwinner fails especially to promote equality of leisure time and to combat androcentrism, while Caregiver Parity fails especially to promote income equality and to prevent women's marginalization. Neither model, in addition, promotes women's full participation on a par with men in politics and civil society. And neither values female-associated practices enough to ask men to do them too; neither asks men to change. (The relative merits of Universal Breadwinner and Caregiver Parity are summarized in Table 5.3.) Neither model, in sum, provides everything feminists want. Even in a highly idealized form neither delivers full gender equity.

Table 5.3

Principle	Universal Breadwinner	Caregiver Parity
Antipoverty	Good	Good
Antiexploitation	Good	Good
Income equality	Fair	Poor
Leisure-time equality	Poor	Fair
Equality of respect	Fair	Fair
Antimarginalization	Fair	Poor
Antiandrocentrism	Poor	Fair

If these were the only possibilities, we would face a very difficult set of trade-offs. Suppose, however, we reject this Hobson's choice and try to develop a third alternative. The trick is to envision a postindustrial welfare state that combines the best of Universal Breadwinner with the best of Caregiver Parity, while jettisoning the worst features of each. What third alternative is possible?

So far we have examined—and found wanting—two initially plausible approaches: one aiming to make women more like men are now; the other leaving men and women pretty much unchanged, while aiming to make women's difference costless. A third possibility is to *induce men to become more like most women are now*, namely, people who do primary carework.

Consider the effects of this one change on the models we have just examined. If men were to do their fair share of carework, Universal Breadwinner would come much closer to equalizing leisure time and eliminating androcentrism, and Caregiver Parity would do a much better job of equalizing income and reducing women's marginalization. Both models, in addition, would tend to promote equality of respect. If men were to become more like women are now, in sum, both models would begin to approach gender equity.

The key to achieving gender equity in a postindustrial welfare state, then, is to make women's current life-patterns the norm for everyone. Women today often combine breadwinning and caregiving, albeit with great difficulty and strain. A postindustrial welfare state must ensure that men do the same, while redesigning institutions so as to eliminate the difficulty and strain. We might call this vision *Universal Caregiver*.

What, then, might such a welfare state look like? Unlike Caregiver Parity, its employment sector would not be divided into two different tracks; all jobs would be designed for workers who are caregivers, too; all would have a shorter workweek than full-time jobs have now; and all would have the support of employment-enabling services. Unlike Universal Breadwinner, however, employees would not be assumed to shift all carework to social services. Some informal carework would be publicly supported and integrated on a par with paid work in a single social-insurance system. Some would be performed in households by relatives and friends, but such households would not necessarily be heterosexual nuclear families. Other supported carework would be located outside households altogether—in civil society. In state-funded but locally organized institutions, childless adults, older people, and others without kin-based responsibilities would join parents and others in democratic, self-managed carework activities.

A Universal Caregiver welfare state would promote gender equity by effectively dismantling the gendered opposition between breadwinning and caregiving. It would integrate activities that are currently separated from one another, eliminate their gender-coding, and encourage men to perform them too. This, however, is tantamount to a wholesale restructuring of the institution of gender. The construction of breadwinning and caregiving as separate roles, coded masculine and feminine, respectively, is a principal undergirding of the current gender order. To dismantle those roles and their cultural coding is in effect to overturn that order. It means subverting the existing gender division of labor and reducing the salience of gender as a structural principle of social organization. At the limit, it suggests deconstructing gender. By deconstructing the opposition between breadwinning and caregiving, moreover, Universal Caregiver would simultaneously deconstruct the associated opposition between bureaucratized public institutional settings and intimate private domestic settings. Treating civil society as an additional site for carework, it would overcome both the "workerism" of Universal Breadwinner and the domestic privatism of Caregiver Parity. Thus, Universal Caregiver promises expansive new possibilities for enriching the substance of social life and for promoting equal participation.

Only by embracing the Universal Caregiver vision, moreover, can we mitigate potential conflicts among our seven component principles of gender equity and minimize the need for trade-offs. Rejecting this approach, in contrast, makes such conflicts, and hence trade-offs, more likely. *Achieving gender equity in a postindustrial welfare state, then, requires deconstructing gender.*

Much more work needs to be done to develop this third—Universal Caregiver—vision of a postindustrial welfare state. A key is to develop policies that discourage free-riding. *Contra* conservatives, the real free-riders in the current system are not poor solo mothers who shirk employment. Instead, they are men of all classes who shirk carework and domestic labor, as well as corporations who free-ride on the labor of working people, both underpaid and unpaid.

A good statement of the Universal Caregiver vision comes from the Swedish Ministry of Labor: "To make it possible for both men and women to combine parenthood and gainful employment, a new view of the male role and a radical change in the organization of working life are required." The trick is to imagine a social world in which citizens' lives integrate wage earning, caregiving, community activism, political participation, and involvement in the associational life of civil society—while also leaving time for some fun. This world is not likely to come into being in the immediate future, but it is the only imaginable postindustrial world that promises true gender equity. And unless we are guided by this vision now, we will never get any closer to achieving it.

Suggested Further Readings for Part II

Ann Crittenden, *The Price of Motherhood: Why the Most Important Job in the World Is Still the Least Valued* (New York: Metropolitan Books, 2001).

Francine Deutsch, *Halving It All: How Equally Shared Parenting Works* (Cambridge, MA: Harvard University Press, 1999).

Nancy Folbre, *The Invisible Heart: Economics and Family Values* (New York: The New Press, 2001).

Janet Gornick and Marcia Meyers et al., *Gender Equality: Transforming Family Divisions of Labor* (London: Verso, 2009).

Mona Harrington, *Care and Equality: Inventing a New Family Politics* (New York: Routledge, 2000).

Jerry Jacobs and Kathleen Gerson, *The Time Divide: Work, Family, and Gender Inequality* (Cambridge, MA: Harvard University Press, 2004).

Hilde Lindemann Nelson, ed., *Feminism and Families* (New York: Routledge, 1997).

Liza Mundy, *The Richer Sex: How the New Majority of Female Breadwinners Is Transforming Sex, Love, and Family* (New York: Simon and Schuster, 2012).

Joan Williams, *Reshaping the Work-Family Debate: Why Men and Class Matter* (Cambridge, MA: Harvard University Press, 2010).

See also the Suggested Further Readings for the Introduction and Part IV.

Parents and Children

Introduction to Part III

Western societies have traditionally given parents great leeway in raising their children. Whether this arrangement is just, however, is far from clear. Family privacy often hides child abuse and neglect; subpar parenting practices can significantly limit educational achievement and negatively impact children's future career and relational opportunities. Even at their best, private family arrangements represent a major barrier to equal opportunity. At least in the United States, for example, children who grow up in low-income families are much more likely to be poor as adults than children who grow up in middle- or upper-income families.

Reflecting on these facts, Véronique Munoz-Dardé asks in the first reading in this section a question as old as Plato: "Is the family to be abolished then?" Drawing on Rawls's social contract theory, Munoz-Dardé engages this question with a thought experiment. If individuals were placed in an imaginary pre-social condition and given the opportunity to design the institutions of a just society from scratch, she asks, would they choose to retain the private family as the primary institution for raising children, or would they instead choose well-run orphanages or boarding schools (assuming the individuals who make this choice would be raised in the manner they choose)? Echoing Aristotle's response to Plato, she argues that, given the tendency of public institutions to treat individuals as means rather than ends, individuals would choose families over orphanages, thus providing a rational justification for private family arrangements. Nonetheless, she concludes that individuals in the

111

original position would also demand basic reforms to family life—including stronger individual legal protections and better welfare support—to ensure the physical well-being of children and enhance equal opportunities among them.

In "The Place of Parenting within a Liberal Theory of Justice," Daniel Engster discusses an alternative proposal for promoting children's well-being. A number of theorists have argued in recent years that individuals should be required to obtain a parenting license from the state before being allowed to raise children. If potential parents were required to demonstrate an aptitude for parenting and the financial means necessary for child rearing, advocates argue that children would be better cared for and the state would not be left to subsidize poor people's children. Engster takes on this argument point by point. He first argues that there are good reasons rooted in justice for the state to subsidize child rearing. He then argues that parental licensing proposals would likely generate numerous negative consequences for women and children and, ultimately, would do more harm than good. Bringing these two arguments together, Engster concludes that the best approach to supporting children's well-being and fostering liberal justice is public support for parenting in the form of paid parenting leaves, child care subsidies, and other government subsidies.

Joel Feinberg's "The Child's Right to an Open Future" explores another dimension of state responsibilities toward children: the responsibility to ensure that they enjoy an open future. According to Feinberg, children have the right to grow up to be self-determining over their choice of careers, religions, hobbies, and other goods. As such, the state has a duty to protect children from child rearing practices that unduly limit their free and open development. This position raises some important riddles, however, such as how child rearing can ever be justifiable given that parents invariably close some potential futures to their children. Overall, Feinberg's chapter raises deep questions about the responsibilities of parents and the state toward children and the nature of children's rights. It also points ahead to Part V of this book where dilemmas of child rearing and multiculturalism are further explored.

6

Is the Family to Be Abolished Then?

Véronique Munoz-Dardé

1

The family is one of the main causes of morally arbitrary inequality. Moreover, it is not an inequality that makes everyone better off. And it is not inevitable that we should have the family. Would everyone, and, in particular, the worst off, prefer the family to a generalized well-run orphanage? In this chapter, I want to examine this issue by addressing a question that I borrow from John Rawls: "Is the family to be abolished then?" (1971, p. 511).

It may be useful to define the domain of inquiry more precisely. The question asked is not whether the family is to be abolished *tout court*. The narrower inquiry I conduct here concerns whether from *the point of view of justice* the family should be abolished. The question arises because the effects of the family are so profound that its mere existence may severely impede the access of individuals to equal life chances. Moreover, this institution induces inequalities that are not beneficial to the badly off, and that are not the effect of a choice for which they can be held responsible. It would therefore seem natural for justice theorists to inquire into the justice of the family, especially if concerned either by the position of the worst off in society, or by the distinction between brute luck and choices for which we are responsible. Theorists of distributive justice are, however, inclined to treat the family as inevitable, or at least as obviously necessary. To the extent that they discuss it at all, they tend either to promptly dismiss the issue or to diffuse it by focusing on the autonomy of families, rather than on the liberty and autonomy of individuals within them.

The dissatisfaction with such theorists does not stem, obviously, from their refusing to recommend the abolition of the family. It is to do, rather, with the fact that by failing to inquire into the exact reasons for preserving the family in some form and by not identifying what, if anything, we ought to prioritize *over* the principle of equality of life chances, they are led to accept too readily unjust arrangements. In other words: by assuming what they should seek to prove—that families have to be treated as entities of value such that laws which harm them for the sake of equality cannot be part of a just society—their theories might have to pay the cost of leaving the less fortunate in society in a worse position than they might have been as a result of a proper inquiry into this issue.

In looking at the justice of the family from the point of view of the worst off, the perspective I will adopt throughout this chapter is broadly Rawlsian. More specifically, I adopt here, but do not argue for, Rawls's claim that utilitarianism is not individualistic enough. My aim is confined to exploring the *consequences* of this claim for reflection on the family. From this standpoint, two aspects are instantly apparent. Firstly, that justice requires us not to be concerned with family welfare or autonomy, but with each family member's demands for respect and well-being. Secondly, that the deprivations or sufferings of the worst off are not compensated for by the total of individual well-being. So whether or not a great many individuals are better off because of the existence of the family is irrelevant in settling whether the family would be one of the institutions of a just society. What matters is whether the existence of the family ensures that the least advantaged members of society are better off than they would be with its abolition.

The following two sections will be devoted to exploring some of the respective merits of the family, and of what I shall describe as a generalized and well-run orphanage. I shall then turn to some of the policy implications of this discussion. I will argue for the strict removal of aggregate conceptions of family members in matters of rights and of access to advantage. My contention is that if we really want political institutions which guarantee that every person is cared for, then these should not enforce, nor assume, communal or family attachments. A second, perhaps more surprising concluding thought is that there should be no such thing as marriage by the state.

I shall begin with a sketch of what I take the elements of the problem to be.

2

Let me concede an initial difficulty with the question of justice of the family. The difficulty concerns the definition of the institution of the family itself: for there are many possible understandings of what constitutes a family. For the purpose of this chapter, however, I shall concentrate on a fairly precise aspect, namely the family as a small intimate group where elders are responsible for raising and caring for children, and have authority over them, irrespective of the children's wishes.

The family in some form is the most accepted solution given to the fact that some must take responsibility for young dependents. (And other forms of dependents: people who are temporarily or permanently in the same situation as infants with regard to capacity for taking decisions on matters that affect them, such as some handicapped or some elderly.) State legislation operates on the basis of the additional assumption that the biological family is the most acceptable form for this institution, and accepts other forms only when they are judged successfully to mimic the biological one.

From the perspective of justice, the family thus understood poses at least two sorts of concern. The first of these is constituted by serious and reiterated doubts about the possibility of successfully implementing justice *within* this institution. There are frequently expressed areas of skepticism that it will ever be possible to achieve a just division of labor and, more generally, a thorough application of principles of rights and justice within the family. In turn, these produce injustices in society at large, for example because sexism in the family is then responsible for the enduring sexism in society, and the reproduction of gender inequalities. (This has been the focus of attention for many feminist political theorists, whether they hold that justice in the family can and should be achieved, or not.)

But whether or not this is possible, whether the question of justice in the family can be given a satisfactory answer or not, considerations of justice arise anyhow. A second area of concern, noticed by several justice theorists, is that as long as the institution of the family exists, there will be severe constraints on meeting fair equality of opportunity, or life chances, between people raised in different families (e.g., Rawls 1971, pp. 74, 301, and 511). A way of presenting this view is that as long as there are families, and hence deep inequalities between people's initial circumstances as regard class, social condition, cultivated attitudes to effort, to self-sacrifice, to autonomy, and so on, the ideal of equal realization of people's natural capacities and moral powers, including their capability to form, revise and pursue their own conception of the good, shall not be delivered.

Hence from at least two different perspectives, strong suspicions are expressed that the existence of the family is only compatible with a diminished justice.

The reason justice theorists who point towards these negative effects of the existence of the family, both for gender equality and for fair equality of life chances, do not however wish to pursue this problem much further is that they treat the family as a given, in two different ways. Some simply take their lead from Rousseau and consider the family to be a brute natural fact, the only institution not based on conventions (1761, Book 1, 2). From this perspective it may be true that family circumstances deeply affect our prospects in life, but since there will always be families, the only duty of political institutions is to compensate those who have been particularly unlucky, in the same way that they may concede some extra benefits to counterbalance the misfortune of somebody born with no legs. However, the family is hardly a brute fact in this sense: the brute fact is that we are born as helpless infants, and that for some time decisions which regard us are entirely or overwhelmingly taken by others (decisions that affect not only our opportunities in life, but the kind of person we become). But it is not a brute fact that children should be educated and cared for by parents, within families.

So, a second, more refined, position—famously adopted by Rawls—consists in claiming that the existence of the family is not inevitable, and that it does lead to unequal chances between individuals, but that it is nevertheless necessary for moral development, and hence for citizens to have a sense of justice (Rawls 1971, § 70–76; Okin adopts a similar view on moral development).

Notice that this conception of moral development may coincide with common sense, but that it rests on fairly strong empirical assumptions. Whether the natural capacities and moral powers may be more developed within families than within a well-run orphanage, with devoted teachers (something like a good boarding school for all) is an empirical matter difficult to settle.

Psychological research on this empirical link between families and moral development may not be conclusive, but luckily it is something we may not need to pursue. For even if it is conceivable that some would flourish more fully morally within families than within a well-run orphanage, the case is wholly implausible from the perspective of the least well off. A related problem is that justifying the necessity of the family in this way constitutes in any case an intriguing strategy. For this second approach to the family concedes that it is not inevitable that we should have the family, and that the family does constitute an obstacle for fair equality of life chances, but proposes an instrumental defense of it. The problem with this defense is that the value sacrificed and the value this sacrifice is used as a means for seem to be the same. It is mystifying that the family should be maintained for citizens to develop a sense of justice, at the cost of diminished justice. More precisely, it is odd that the explicit price to pay for securing *presumed* optimal conditions for the moral development of some should be a *verified* unequal realization of people's potential, including unequal realization of their moral powers. (This is especially so given the great improbability that the least well off raised in a well-run orphanage would develop their potential less than the least well off in the family.)

Some may however think that I am exaggerating, and that a more pragmatic view is called for. In fact, several justice theorists tend to adopt a third fallback position: that whether we find a justification for its necessity or not, there is no need to radically question the shared assumption that the family is the adequate locus for rearing children. They maintain that the severe limitations and constraints imposed by the family on the reach of principles of justice can readily be accepted by the least well off, provided two main types of guarantees are in place. The first is that some later redistribution occurs, for example, according to Rawls's difference principle. The second is that the family should not be placed in an alleged "private sphere," beyond the reach of the principles of justice. They therefore insist that family matters should not be treated as private or internal matters, and that each family member should be guaranteed individual privacy, and rights and liberties.

If these guarantees are secured then, so it is claimed, those with lesser life chances can accept a diminished justice. An immediate problem is: how diminished? Egalitarians and feminists (these are not exclusive categories) have both insisted that quite a lot of injustice will follow. Not only the pattern of burdens and benefits, but people's attitudes, their capacity to form, revise and pursue a conception of the good, are affected by early socialization in the family in such a way that the redistribution and regulation, whilst necessary and important, will only marginally affect the enduring effects of this initial inequality in peoples' circumstances. On the other hand, on pains of allowing abhorrent state interference, early equalization cannot be secured by imposing on each family the duty to socialize their children in just the same way. (One of the reasons many people do intensely desire to have children is their being able to bring them up as they see fit, with the values and practices they believe are good, and it would take intense and perhaps futile coercion to prevent them to do so.)

So the worst off in the distribution of benefits and burdens, those who have fewer opportunities for realizing their capacities and for forming and pursuing their own conception of the good life, may have a reasonable complaint against the existence of the family, even when the suggested guarantees are in place. A more robust defense of the family seems therefore called for, against the idea of its abolition. Perhaps the only way to be able to decide whether or not justice would require us to abolish families, is to inquire whether the severe constraints their existence imposes on the reach of the principle of fair equality of life chances is justified by another, prior principle.

In the next section, I will turn to examine whether the family should be deemed necessary by a prior and independent principle of justice in this way.

3

What are then the compelling reasons, if any, for *not* abolishing the family?

It is a familiar thought experiment for political philosophers to imagine what things would be without a state, to reflect whether we need a state, and which form, if any, it should take. In a similar disguise, we could imagine parties in a sort of Rawlsian original position carrying out this thought-experiment with respect to the family, to decide whether the family is justified, if at all, and what form, if any, it should have. Admittedly this is not a thought experiment envisaged by Rawls himself, but it need not strike us as anti-Rawlsian. The question parties would examine is how the major social institutions within the overall society fit together, so that the principles of justice independently arrived at in a prior stage of inquiry are effective. It is in this context that the existence of the family and its permissible form, or forms, if any may be envisaged.

Let us add that setting up such a thought-experiment means that parties would neither be heads of families (or parents), nor have the special ties of sentiment that in families parents often have toward their offspring. Again, although Rawls does not explicitly stipulate these conditions, they nevertheless do not contravene the main aspects of his theory. The parties in the original position are not making agreements embedded within the institutions of the basic structure, such as the family, because their agreements concern those institutions themselves. The appeal of the deduction of principles of political justice behind the veil of ignorance is precisely that bargaining advantages that arise within institutions of the basic structure, such as the family, are removed. The point of view of the parties therefore actually needs to be disassociated from, and not affected by, families as we know and experience them.

The parties could then envisage a set of possible social worlds, and in particular contrast two of them. In the first model, the family in some form would exist. No difference needs to be made at this stage between different forms be it, say, the biological mum-dad model, homosexual adoptive lines, or small communities such as those formed by kibbutzim. A family is thus any social unit in which a group of elders are primarily responsible and have primary authority over a *particular* group of children. The distinctive feature of a society in which children are raised in families is thus that children are looked after by different groups of elders, with different criteria and resources in each instance.

The second model would be constituted by a generalized, well-run orphanage. The adjective "well-run" may produce some disconcert. The extent to which the orphanage is to be considered well-run is the following: since the state has overall control, it is able to equally guarantee to all children whichever conditions and principles are considered optimum for their upbringing, *as long as* these conditions are compatible with such an overall control. It could be imagined as a generalized boarding school, with a comfortable material environment, and well-qualified teachers, able to devote individualized attention to children. These teachers could take pride in the achievements of their pupils, but would probably not have the sort of personal investments that parents generally have. To the extent that they do not see their pupils as a prolongation of their own person in the same way as parents tend to do, they would probably have less fixed ideas, for example, as regards the orientation they should take professionally. (Often parents try to attempt to live an additional life through their children.) Teachers would also be explicitly bound by a principle of impartiality, or at least fairness, between their pupils. You may disagree with my idealization of boarding-schools—imagination and tastes differ here—but the idea of the well-run state institution for the upbringing of children should by now be sufficiently distinct from, say, a Dickensian home, to be able to proceed.

So would the parties choose the former model, would they prefer the family? Rawls himself seems to think so. ("The family in some form is just.") But we have seen that the instrumental justification he gives, that is that the family is necessary for moral development, does not by itself seem sufficient, especially from the perspective of the least well off. For what this justification shows is at best that the utilitarian sum of the interests of all human beings counted equally will best be served by the persistence of the family. The reason this argument is generally not challenged, even by critics of utilitarianism, is because we tend naturally to support the family on the basis of consequential considerations of just the same sort. One such consideration invoked at least since Aristotle is that we are naturally attached to our offspring, and therefore on average take better care of them. Notice that, since it is impossible to discern whether people care for their offspring because of societal moral and legal expectations, the argument is again inconclusive.

Here is precisely where the advantages of situating the question in a broadly Rawlsian context become apparent. Firstly, the heuristic device of the veil of ignorance generates less contingent reasoning. Secondly, the priority of principles of justice focuses the diffuse problem of the desirability or otherwise of the family on its compatibility with principles of justice, such as the above considered principle of fair equality of life chances. (The precise question then becomes whether the family can fit together with other major social institutions within the basic structure of society, so that prior and independent principles of justice would still be operative.) And thirdly, the lexical order in which principles are placed allows us to consider whether trying to eradicate the family in order to deliver equality would threaten a prior principle of liberty.

The third characteristic is the one that matters particularly now, given the constraints the family poses on meeting the principle of equality of life chances that were explored in previous sections. For if we hold that liberty should not be sacrificed for the sake of greater equality, and if it can further be shown that abolition of families would pose an unavoidable threat to the equal liberty of citizens, then we would have found a reason for *not* abolishing families, regardless of their effects on equality of life chances. If on the other hand no such compelling reason can be found, then the case for a state well-run orphanage could look strong.

Here is one way of trying to make the family-cum-priority of liberty argument. People desire to bring up their own kids as they see fit. It would therefore not be legitimate to constrain them into not doing so. But this is clearly insufficient. Surely, that people are constrained into not realizing some of their aspirations does not by itself constitute a violation of the principle of equal liberty. If these constraints are necessary for protecting the equal liberty of others, then they are clearly legitimate. In fact, extensive limitations on authority of parents over children already exist, just for this reason.

A second, more plausible, line of argumentation would be a revised version of the role of the family for moral development. The claim would be that in the orphanage, children would not be able to develop their moral powers even to the *minimum* degree for them to ever make full use of their equal liberties as citizens. If children in the orphanage never reach this minimum level, then even if the least well off in it are better off than the least well off in the family, forcing everyone below an adequate threshold of moral development for citizens to be free would hardly make sense.

Why would the family do better at this (if unequally so)? Well, probably because in most cases children in families are treated as ends in themselves, they are cared for as the special person they are, intimate relationships and the language of affection connected with it constituting a force of individuation. (Interestingly, this would make the family a necessary locus of cultivation of the modern value of individuality.) The thought would be that children need to be treated partially, as the singular person they are, in order to flourish and fully acquire "a lively sense of their own worth as persons, to be able to develop and exercise their moral powers and to advance their aims and ends with self-confidence." This seems persuasive enough but then, why would an orphanage, *if well-run*, fail to provide this to a minimally adequate degree?

Clearly, we are here again touching matters that can perhaps only be settled by empirical research. But there is yet a third line of argument that partly stems from this, and that need not be so contingent on empirical knowledge. For I have assumed until now that the orphanage should be *well-run*. The question is: how probable is that, were the family to entirely disappear? Would not my fantasy of a generalized boarding school with teachers devoted to the individuality of each child vanish, were the state to have the *sole* control of the upbringing of children? Wouldn't it be the case that children would then be brought up not as ends in themselves, but as mere means for a collective purpose?

Bertrand Russell, the only modern philosopher I have found who contrasts advantages of entirely state-run institutions for the upbringing of children with the family, suggests precisely this argument. Teachers may, says Russell, retain something of the personal feeling that parents have, but the power belongs to administrators who are likely to "regard human beings, not as ends in themselves, but as material for some kind of construction. Moreover, the administrator invariably likes uniformity.... Children handed over to the mercy of institutions will therefore tend to be all alike, while the few who cannot conform to the recognised pattern will suffer persecution." It is not necessary to adopt the particular distaste Russell displays for administrators to see the force of his argument: if the state had, generation after generation, the *sole* control of education and care of children these would be less likely to be treated as ends in themselves, they would be forced into occupations, whether they find them worthy or not, and the development of their individuality would be threatened. This would interfere with their capacity to form their own conception of the good, and with their liberty to conduct their life as they wish.

Note that this need not commit us to a romantic view of the family: pressures for uniformity, and threats to individuality and individual privacy can and do occur within it. Rather, what we have seen is that the entire dependency of infants makes them extremely vulnerable to domination. If submitted to the absolute authority of any single institution, be it the family or the state, the coercive power of that institution becomes far too great to be compatible with liberty. Hence it seems that the best protection of individuality against domination is the *respective* restrictions that state and family impose on each other. (So if this is a defense of the existence of the family, it is also an argument for not allowing it all the power over children.)

There is an additional and complementary aspect in Russell's observation. Implicitly, he is suggesting that the diversity of families makes it possible for the worth of different ways of life to be available as options, and hence creates the conditions necessary for pluralism. By implication, the idea is that in societies where there are families the variety of these is creating conditions of pluralism *even* for people who do not live in families. For there is a fundamental difference between the generalized orphanage and the current "mixed economy" between orphanages and families. Even for people brought up within orphanages, the existence of families creates conditions such that the diversity of forms of life is available in society, and that individuality is to some extent valued and cultivated. But these conditions might not obtain if administrators were themselves brought up within the generalized orphanage, over many generations.

I believe that these two aspects combine into an argument in favor of allowing the perpetuation of the family, one that seems enough for not adopting the second model. For it is possible that *if generalized over many generations* an orphanage could not be well-run; that denial of individuality, lack of respect of individual self-determination, and pressure for uniformization would combine in such a way that children could not develop their moral powers even to the minimum degree for them to make full use of their equal liberties.

To summarize. There is a tentative but strong enough reason for thinking that the family should not be abolished. This reason is that the complete abolition of this institution would probably pose such extreme threats to individual liberty and capacity for self-determination, that it would defeat the very purpose that made us envisage its substitution by a well-run orphanage. For this purpose was to deliver greater equal opportunity for all to make their own judgment about what constitutes a good life, and to live accordingly.

In the next section I will explore what I take to be the main theoretical consequences of holding that the family should not be abolished for this particular reason.

4

The first thing to notice is that the above defense of the persistence of the family is a very limited one. It is justified by the greater evils that would (possibly) be created by forcing its disappearance.

Observe that whilst thin, this defense of the justice of the family has immediate and powerful effects on the conception of justice *within* the family. For it works only insofar as the family does not threaten the very value its persistence is deemed to protect, namely the enabling of each person to develop her individuality and to make her own decisions about how to conduct her life. So it commits us to thinking that it is not the family, or to be more precise family autonomy, which should be protected by legal institutions, but the conditions for the autonomy and private life of each of the individuals within it.

But some may think that this does not obtain, for they will disagree with the instrumental defense. They will protest "This is hardly why we value families." And surely, something rings true about this complaint. We do not have children so that they enjoy greater liberty. Nor do we think that the main important effect of the affection that we devote to them is their greater autonomy. We think that we are united to them by intimate, unique and precious ties of sentiments. I therefore agree with this intrinsic defense, but I think that if meant as an objection, then it misconstrues the point of the discussion so far. For the question initially posed was not "What, if anything, is valuable about the family?" but rather "Is the family to be abolished?" Since it is asked from the perspective of justice, the question concerns primarily the extent and content of just state coercion, as well as its effects. A more extensive version of it would be: "Given the unjust effects of the existence of the family, would justice imply using the legal and coercive apparatus of the state to discourage people from forming families, and to substitute families by a generalized well-run orphanage?" The answer is no, because the risk of harming the principle of equal liberty is too great. So while this answer only works if one accepts the *independent* priority of liberty, it says nothing about whether liberty and autonomy are values that we prioritize *within* families.

Hence, while forceful, the intrinsic defense of the family is irrelevant here. Or rather, if it has any relevance at all, it is to reinforce the idea that state coercion is not permissible to enforce family ties at the cost of individual liberty. Let me explain. Since the answer to the abolition of the family is that it should not take place, then the question becomes: "From the perspective of justice, what if anything can and should the state enforce regarding the family?" We may regard ties of sentiments as fundamentally valuable, but the reason they are so is that they are freely exchanged between people. Not only is it futile to try to foster love or friendship; even if it were possible, doing so might decrease their value. I might not value your friendship if I knew it to be the result of coercion. So a state in which sentimental ties are valued is a state in which there is no other legal intervention than to create the adequate conditions so that citizens can form and develop them freely when they so feel. Some may think that family ties are not quite like that, that state coercion is needed to encourage people to maintain them. But then, they distrust precisely the strength of these ties, and with it the intensity of their value and importance for many people.

I claimed earlier that from the perspective of justice, the laws that can be coercively enforced cannot be concerned with protecting the autonomy of the family as a corporate person, but only the autonomy and private life of each of the individuals within it. And I have added that while capturing something fundamental about the family, the sentimental view does nothing to weaken this claim.

What this claim amounts to, is that corporate persons such as the family should be of no concern for state legal institutions, other than their effect on actual persons. Does this mean that there is nothing that the state should do with respect to the two problems I described at the outset, namely the reproduction of a gendered division of burdens and benefits in the family, and the absence of equality of life chances between people raised in different families?

I will devote the next section of this chapter to outlining why I think that this is not the case. There are, of course, general consequences of my argument for egalitarian debates (to the extent to which the unavoidable existence of the family in a just society blurs the distinction between brute luck and choices for which we are responsible). I shall however leave this question to another inquiry. What I want to do here, rather, is to focus more specifically on consequences of the argument delineated so far for policies that affect the family. My claim in the concluding section will be that rejecting a tradition-bound conception of the family as a corporate person helps making some concrete improvements in an egalitarian direction. This will take a little detour through the institution of marriage.

5

I have delayed until now to say anything about the form of the family, from the perspective of justice. I want to suggest that it is the rigidity and the fusional character of the particular form or definition of the family with which state legislation operates which is partly responsible for the mentioned areas of injustice. The way it happens is the following: the assumption made, and enforced, is that the biological family is the only truly acceptable form. Other forms are very slowly and reluctantly accepted, but only when and to the extent that they are considered to successfully mimic the biological one. This in turn has several effects.

Firstly, the family is seen as a natural unit, a body in which legislative action can only very diffidently intrude (analogously to a surgeon loath to operate unless there is a serious disease that obliges her to do so). As a result, work within the family is considered to be of a special type, which cannot be the object of legislation and restrictions which apply to any other association within society. This has traditionally particularly penalized women.

The second effect is that, because they are considered as an inseparable part of a special unit that is supposed to automatically take good care of them and protect them against hardship or misfortune, family members are not sufficiently individually protected by legal rights. This lack of protection is apparent with regard to ill-treatment or prejudice within the family, but also conversely with respect to poverty by absence or withdrawal of family support. Hence the least well off in the distribution of burdens and benefits see their vulnerability increased rather than moderated by the existence of this legal conception of the family.

Finally, the traditional biological form of the family sanctioned by the state excludes other forms of association between adults from the legitimate exercise of parenting. For the cornerstone of this biology-bound legal conception of the family as a corporate person, with its anti-egalitarian and ostracizing effects, is marriage. Through legal marriage, links of affection are formalized in a contract restricted only to some, on no other basis than the fact that they are two adults of the opposite sex. A series of assumptions are then made: that the partners joined in this contract are well-suited to look after each other *and* after their biological children, and also that the resulting family forms a corporate person, with no serious conflict of interest between its members.

To summarize: What we have seen is that the coercive apparatus of the state is at fault with regard to the family in two directions. Firstly it legislates by effectively imposing a license for parenting which is not based on any relevant test, which has ostracizing effects, and which upholds and reproduces a gendered-biological conception of the proper family. Secondly, the absence of full individualized legal protection within the family leaves the most vulnerable subject to abuse, coercion and/or poverty.

Three main legal moves are therefore called for. The first is not to treat the family as a corporate person, but as a nonmandatory association. As such, the family could take several forms, but rights, including rights to primary goods considered necessary for a person to form, revise and pursue her conception of the good, would in any case be granted to individuals, regardless of their family status.

The second, related move is not to treat the family as an implicit provider for the supply of welfare, and to institutionalize instead impartial and individualized care by the state (this includes welfare rights, but could also take the form of a universal basic income). This approach seems to me to have an important positive effect, namely that there is then no urge to impose on all families a comprehensive liberal conception of just relations within it. If the family is based on affection rather than on transfer of goods and resources, and if work within it is submitted to no more and no less legal constraints than in any other free association, then any form, traditional or otherwise, is legitimate, as long as it is compatible with the above mentioned individual rights.

A third and complementary move is to abolish marriage *by the state* (not any other form of marriage). For either state marriage has the effect of aggregating family members in matters of rights and access to advantage, with greater resulting vulnerability of the worst off, or it is a mere ritual, with segregating effects. Where it conditions access to advantage, state marriage creates inequalities that are not beneficial to the worst off. As for the ritual, there does not seem any reason for public funding to be spent on it, nor for the state to have a say on who takes part in it. For some, this ritual has considerable meaning, for example for religions or sentimental reasons, and they will continue to organize public occasions in which they will declare their union. But state institutions should have no more intervention in it than it has at present in, say, choosing the dress of the bride and paying for it.

The conclusion of my argument is therefore that if principles of rights are elaborated with the interests of the worst off at heart, the family should not be abolished, but that state marriage should.

You may now say: "Look, you have taken the typical route Kantians are so apt to go down, by always wanting to privilege impartial values and individual rights. This is going to lead us to an estrangement from and a devaluation of our most intimate emotions regarding those we most care for; this will further lead to a society in which people will be encouraged to act towards everyone out of duty, and not on such natural humane feelings as sympathy or compassion."

But as I tried to show earlier in this chapter, assuming that removing a legally enforced family bond is going to weaken the fondness family members have for each other, to result in estrangement, and in the sterilization of humane feelings shows remarkably little confidence in the strength of those sentiments. This said, perhaps a last clarification is called for. Ultimately, my claim in this chapter is that we should displace most of the *expectations* for securing material impartial care for the needs of individuals to the state. The aim is for affection not to be enforced (which is futile), nor assumed (for it fails). If political institutions fulfill their impartial role, the family can then be the realm of the genuinely affectional, not a fallible refuge which increases the vulnerability of the worst off.

6

Maybe all I have said will strike some as a way of announcing the death of the family, at least in effect if not in intention. The family may change so significantly that we may not recognize it. But isn't that probable anyway? Innovative family practices happen all the time. The family strikes us as an immutable institution *because* it changes constantly. Contrary to what is commonly assumed, it is the instability of social understanding of what constitutes a proper family, and proper family relations, which has allowed for the persistence of the family as a strong and meaningful institution over time. From the perspective of justice though, some of its more interesting mutations are still to come.

7

The Place of Parenting within a Liberal Theory of Justice

Daniel Engster

Parenting has an ambiguous place within the liberal tradition. On the one hand, liberal theorists have traditionally portrayed parenting as a private activity. According to this view, parents should not only be allowed to raise their children as they wish but also have responsibility for meeting the costs of childrearing through their own resources. On the other hand, liberal theorists have also generally acknowledged an important public dimension to parenting. From John Locke onward, writers have generally portrayed parents as the stewards of their children with moral responsibility for ensuring their survival and preparing them for citizenship in a liberal society. If parents are unable to fulfill these responsibilities, liberal thinkers have generally maintained that the state should step in to provide family support and, in extreme cases, take over the care of children directly.

These two different conceptions of parenting stand in some tension. If the state treats parenting primarily as a private activity, some children will inevitably fail to receive the protection and resources they need to survive and develop into competent liberal citizens. If the state provides special support for parents and children, however, it unfairly favors parenting projects over other private pursuits in apparent violation of liberal neutrality. Liberal states generally attempt to mediate this conflict by striking a balance of sorts between these positions. The standard liberal position holds that states should intervene into families only as a last resort when necessary to protect children against abuse or neglect, and provide only means-tested resources to the poorest families. This intermediate position usually draws criticisms from all sides. People complain on the one side that the state is not doing enough to protect and support the health and development of children, and on the other side that it is unfairly favoring parents over non-parents and not holding poor individuals sufficiently responsible for their parenting choices.

Robert Taylor suggests that this liberal antinomy regarding parenting can be resolved through the implementation of a parental licensing scheme. Taylor's parental licensing scheme would limit parenting opportunities solely to those individuals who can demonstrate the moral, intellectual, emotional, and financial capacities to raise children without public support. Aside from issuing and enforcing licenses, the liberal state would have no responsibility under this plan for supporting childrearing. As a result, the state could remain neutral among private conceptions of the good life while still ensuring children's healthy development and well-being. [. . . .]

In this chapter, I argue that Taylor's and other theorists' parental licensing plans are incompatible with some basic liberal values. Although these plans would address some of the problems associated with the private parenting model, they would generate new problems that are at least equally as bad. In particular, these plans would create special burdens for women, expose many children to harm, and potentially undermine basic liberal freedoms. Ultimately, they would fail on their own terms, making the lives of many children worse. In order to arrive at a more tenable parenting policy, I outline an alternative public parenting model. In the public parenting model, individuals would remain free to decide whether or not they wish to have children and retain a large degree of discretion over how to raise them, but the costs of childrearing would be publicly shared. Parenting would thus be recast as a distributed general duty or assigned responsibility within a general regime of public support for children. While this model might appear unfair since it lends public support to the private choices that individuals make about having and raising children, as I argue below, the underlying assumption of this position—that parenting is a private pursuit—is misguided. There are good liberal grounds for providing state support for parenting such that state parenting support does not violate liberal neutrality. In the final analysis, the public parenting model is more consistent with liberal values than either the private parenting model or parental licensing plans.

My argument has three steps. In the first section, I challenge the idea that parenting can be sensibly understood as a private project. I focus here on Taylor's argument, but my aim is more general. The purpose is to demonstrate that the first half of the liberal parenting antinomy is false. This argument is important because it addresses two common arguments against public parenting support: that it is unfair to non-parents and a violation of liberal neutrality. In the second section, I explore Taylor's and other theorists' parental licensing proposals. I argue here that the attempt to implement a parental licensing plan would generate numerous undesirable consequences. Since my criticisms are mostly speculative, so are my conclusions. If it were possible to implement a parental licensing plan without generating significant negative consequences, it might be desirable to do so. As I attempt to show, however, this seems very unlikely. In the third section, I draw together the various strands of my argument in order to justify a public parenting model. My claim here is that state subsidies and support for parenting represent the most coherent approach within a liberal framework to the care of children. More contentiously, I argue that the public parenting model is an essential component of any coherent liberal theory of justice.

PARENTING AS A PRIVATE PROJECT

"Suppose I said that I had a project, one that required a major investment of time, money, and energy (e.g., climbing Mt. Everest), and that this entitled me to a bigger than usual share of social resources, whether in the form of money (travel grants) or leisure (paid leave from work)." So begins Robert Taylor's discussion of parenting. As Taylor observes, most liberals do not believe that individuals should receive special public subsidies to help them pursue their private projects, whether mountain climbing, stamp collecting, or yachting. Yet, many liberals do endorse public support for parenting projects. This apparent inconsistency is partially understandable, Taylor admits, given "children's nature as (emergent) persons: Kantians, for example, would argue that children are incipient finite rational beings whom parents and other citizens have an important obligation to prepare for cosmopolitan citizenship and moral agency more broadly." Nonetheless, Taylor observes that there is a deep tension here. Parenting can be understood at least in part as a private project: while some people may embrace it, others avoid it for the sake of pursuing other projects. To allocate special resources to parenting but not other private projects thus violates liberal principles of fairness and neutrality: "if special state support is provided for parenting projects but not for other kinds of projects (such as mountain climbing) that can be just as demanding and all-consuming, then a case can surely be made that such support is nonneutral with respect to '(justice-respecting) conceptions of the good life' and therefore prima facie inconsistent with liberal principles of distributive justice."

While Taylor's logic is valid, his premise is false: parenting is significantly different from other private projects in at least three important ways. First, parenting is often much less voluntary than other projects and almost always imposes unequal burdens on women. In this regard, it raises questions about fairness and equality that do not arise in relation to most private projects. While many individuals do, of course, voluntarily decide to have children and pursue this goal as if it were a mountain to climb, parenting is just as often something that happens to individuals without their fully wanting it or planning for it.

Women, in particular, are often subject to various legal regulations that can limit their reproductive autonomy. In nearly all societies, women are further expected to take on primary responsibility for the care of children. Although many women do seemingly choose to stay at home to care for their children of their own free will, there are good reasons for thinking that many women's parenting choices are strongly influenced by social factors. Unequal earnings between women and men, social expectations about who should care for children, and gender socialization all push women to take on the majority of the childrearing tasks, especially among very young children. Few other personal pursuits, aside perhaps from other activities that are similarly gendered, are subject to such deep and pervasive social pressures. Treating women's parenting choices as simply another personal preference akin to choosing whether or not to climb a mountain is thus problematic: it ignores the pervasive and strong role of social institutions and norms in shaping these choices.

Women who take on the primary care of children, in turn, suffer a number of social penalties and generally enjoy less equality in society at large. As Susan Okin argues, one of the main reasons that women generally earn less money and have lower status positions than men is because they take more time off from work to care for children. If women's parenting choices are constrained and influenced by social forces, and if they suffer social penalties because of these choices, there exists at least one good reason for liberal states to subsidize parenting activities but not other private projects. Women enjoy less social equality in liberal societies at least in part because they are held wholly personally responsible when they choose to take on primary care of children. Since social institutions and norms encourage women to make this choice, however, it would seem that they ought not to be held wholly personally responsible for it. Society, via the state, should at least partially compensate them, or at very least not penalize them, for fulfilling parenting roles that it encourages them to assume. Public parenting subsidies and services represent one way that states can do so.

A second way that parenting is different from other personal projects is that it produces a necessary public good. As numerous commentators have noted, parents who raise happy, healthy, and successful children generate numerous positive externalities for others throughout society. Well-raised children are more likely to be competent, reliable, productive citizens and workers than poorly raised children. Even more basically, individuals who have and raise children help to sustain and reproduce society: if no one gave birth to and cared for children, society would cease to exist within a few generations. Taylor considers this challenge to his argument but rejects it. Why, he asks, should existing individuals "take an interest in political society's continuation (and its procreative preconditions) after they have had their hour upon the stage"? "Many individuals, after all, may care little or not at all for the preservation of political society after their deaths." Taylor does have a point. Not all human beings have an interest in the continuation of society after their death or even in the propagation of the species. Yet, Taylor incorrectly assumes that the main interest existing human beings have in the propagation of new human beings pertains only to the distant future. In fact, we all depend upon the propagation of new human beings more directly to sustain us during our own lives.

Taylor briefly acknowledges this alternative understanding of human beings' procreative interests. He notes that a serious decrease in birth rates might undermine "pay-as-you-go" pension schemes or the ability of a nation to defend itself militarily. While he finds this approach "more promising" as a basis for justifying public parenting subsidies, he nonetheless contends that our "obligations to our contemporaries could be met in some way other than supporting procreation (e.g., transitioning to a fully-funded pension scheme or a more capital-intensive military)." Taylor discounts these arguments much too quickly, however, and fails to consider the numerous ways in which the well-being of present generations of human beings depends on the existence of younger ones.

Existing generations of human beings depend upon younger generations not just for pension support and military protection but also to provide medical care, produce and deliver food, maintain water supplies and roads, build and repair homes, make and sell clothes, and so forth. Imagine, for example, what life would be like for the last generation of human beings in a world where human procreation had stopped. As this group moved from childhood to early adulthood, schools would close, neighborhoods would be abandoned, and the production of goods would markedly decrease. Even if old age pensions or health care plans were funded, there would be fewer and fewer people to administer these programs over time, and fewer and fewer doctors, nurses, and other care providers to look after the sick and needy. Indeed, as this last generation became aged and feeble, it is not clear how they would find food or maintain access to clean water and other public goods. Taylor overlooks these points because he fails to appreciate the deep interdependency between generations of human beings. Our interest in procreation is not wholly future oriented but relates to our present survival and well-being. If no one gave birth to and cared for children, our own lives would be greatly shortened and impoverished. In this respect, parenting is significantly different from gardening and other private projects that might also generate positive externalities. As distinct from these other activities, parenting is necessary to sustain human life and society.

Once it is acknowledged that we have an interest in the generation of new children, it is but a short step to further acknowledging that we also have an interest in making sure that all children are raised in a reasonably good manner. In order to benefit from the existence of younger generations, older generations must see to it that children grow up in circumstances that are likely to nurture their reason, imagination, emotion, and sociability. Otherwise, children may be unable or unwilling to support the survival and flourishing of their elders. Admittedly, the argument here falls short of justifying public support for all children. From a narrowly self-interested perspective, existing generations might wish to support the generation and care only of that number of children necessary to sustain their lives and well-being. Nonetheless, since the number of children necessary to sustain the survival and well-being of older generations is likely to be substantial, this argument does offer broad justification for the public support of children. By contrast, mountain climbing, yachting, and other private and personal projects do not command a similar public interest.

The third way that parenting is different from other personal projects is the most important. Unlike most other personal projects, parenting is centrally concerned with fostering the survival and development of other human beings. Taylor does acknowledge the "special status" of parenting projects based on "children's nature as (emergent) persons." However, he does not grasp the significance of this admission. If children are recognized even as emergent persons, they presumably can make some justifiable claims on others regarding their treatment and care. In particular, as emergent persons, it would seem that children should at least be able to claim the resources and care necessary for their survival and development, or welfare rights.

In most liberal societies, parents are given primary responsibility for meeting their children's welfare rights. Insofar as children have welfare rights, however, parents cannot be solely responsible for guaranteeing these rights. Rights claims overflow particular relations and generate obligations among all others who are capable of meeting them. If it were possible to meet children's welfare rights without involving their parents, we might fulfill our moral responsibilities to children directly. In most cases, however, this is not possible given existing parenting arrangements. We usually must work through parents to help children. There are at least two ways of doing so. We can either limit parenting opportunities strictly to those individuals who have the private capacities and resources to meet their children's needs (parental licensing), or we can provide public services and subsidies to parents as a means to support their children (the public parenting model). These two options will be discussed in more detail below. In either case, though, the claim that parenting can be plausibly understood as a personal project much like mountain climbing is refuted. We all bear at least a residual moral responsibility for ensuring the survival and development of other parents' children. Parenting is not a personal project just like any other.

Is public parenting support unfair to non-parents? Is it a violation of liberal neutrality? The upshot of the preceding arguments is that it is not. Public parenting support may or may not be the best way to support the survival and development of children (more on this below), but it is at the very least not inconsistent with liberal values. Parenting has important gender implications for social justice, produces a necessary social good, and involves the moral rights of children. As such, we all have an interest (both pragmatic and moral) in supporting parenting activities. There is nothing unfair or biased about liberal states giving public support to parenting but not, say, to mountain climbing because the former activity is a public concern in the way that the latter is not. The first part of the liberal antinomy regarding parenting is thus incorrect. Parenting is not just another private project. The important question, then, is not whether the state is ever justified in regulating or supporting parenting but how it can best do so. For Taylor and others, the answer lies with parental licensing schemes.

PARENTAL LICENSING SCHEMES

Most advocates of parental licensing schemes justify their plans as a means to better protect children's welfare rights. In particular, they reject the first element of the private parenting model: that individuals should be free to decide whether or not they wish to have and raise children without public regulation. Without some sort of check on who can parent, parental licensing proponents point out that violent, potentially abusive, psychologically imma-ture, and financially insecure individuals can all become parents with primary responsibility for the survival and development of a young human being. The usual outcome is harm to the child as well as public welfare expenditures. From parental licensing proponents' perspective, such individuals ought not to be allowed ever to become parents in the first place. By attempting to regulate individuals' parenting choices, however, parental licensing plans would likely generate numerous undesirable consequences, violate basic liberal freedoms, and cause more harm than good to many children. This last point is particu-larly important since it indicates that parental licensing plans would likely fail on their own terms.

Hugh LaFollette has outlined the most influential and widely discussed philosophical argument for a parental licensing scheme. LaFollette asserts most generally that if (1) an activity is potentially harmful to others, (2) the activity requires a certain level of competence for its safe performance, and (3) there exists a reliable procedure for determining whether an individual is competent to perform the activity safely, then the state should regulate it. We require individuals to obtain automobile licenses because driving is potentially harmful to others and requires a certain level of competence for its safe performance, and we have a fairly reliable procedure for determining driving competence. According to LaFollette, parenting shares all these same characteristics. Parents can harm their children through abuse or neglect or by providing inadequate care. In order to raise children without harm, par-ents must possess at least a minimal competence, including requisite levels of knowledge, energy, temperament, and stability. Finally, while it might be difficult to design tests to pick out the best potential parents, we can develop tests that would at least identify the worst potential parents. Relatively accurate tests already exist for picking out individuals who are "violence-prone, easily frustrated, or unduly self-centered," and LaFollette suggests that these tests along with relevant biographical information about an applicant's upbringing might serve as the basis for parental screening. From LaFollette's perspective, parenting is thus a paradigm case of an activity that is rightfully subject to state regulation and licensing.

Taylor supplements LaFollette's parental licensing plan with financial requirements. LaFollette focuses on the psychological and moral prerequisites of parental competency, but financial capacities are equally important. Parents without adequate financial resources will not be able to meet their children's basic biological needs or provide them with an adequate education. Taylor also worries that the children of the poor "will become a burden on the state, forcing it to violate project-neutrality." Hence, Taylor suggests that the state ought to subject prospective parents not only to psychological tests (along the lines proposed by LaFollette) but also financial tests. Since prospective parents' economic fortunes may change after the birth of their child, Taylor adds that they should further be required to purchase performance bonds to ensure that their children will be adequately cared for into adulthood.

There are surprisingly few critiques of parental licensing schemes, and the critiques that do exist are not particularly strong. The most fundamental objection to parental licensing schemes is that they violate the right of individuals to have and rear children. Yet, as LaFollette notes, most liberal rights are subject to some restrictions. All liberal states place limits on free speech, religion, and assembly for the sake of protecting innocent people from harm. Similarly, then, LaFollette argues that the right of individuals to raise children might be justifiably limited for the sake of protecting children and others from harm. Some critics have also argued that parenting tests are unlikely to be able to distinguish between good and bad parents or significantly reduce child abuse and neglect. Yet, there already exist at least two tests, the Child Abuse Potential Inventory and Family Stress Checklist, that can predict abusive or neglectful parents at 85–90 percent accuracy levels. Lawrence Frisch criticizes parental licensing schemes on the grounds that they prevent individuals from rearing children on the mere suspicion of potential future wrongdoing. LaFollette retorts, however, that most types of licensing schemes work in this way, that is, by preventing individuals from lawfully engaging in some activity until they can demonstrate their competence to do so safely. Unless we want to do away with all licensing, LaFollette argues that this objection has little force. Michael Austin charges parental licensing advocates with inconsistency on the grounds that they call for licenses for parenting but not other activities that can similarly cause harm such as athletics. Licensing advocates might address this criticism, however, either by accepting that activities such as athletics should also be subject to licensing requirements or by arguing that parenting should be specially subject to licensing because of the relatively greater and deeper harm that unfit parents can cause their children.

While licensing advocates can thus offer convincing responses to most existing criticisms, there are nonetheless other problems with parental licensing plans that are not so easily resolved. Most proponents of parental licensing schemes do not go into great detail about the specific provisions of their plans, but instead focus on their general theoretical justifiability. When one begins to consider the specific provisions of these plans, however, a number of problems come to the surface. Consider, first, the timing of licensure applications. There are three general time frames when individuals might apply for parenting licenses: (1) sometime prior to conception, (2) sometime during pregnancy, or (3) at the birth of a child. Each of these time frames presents problems for a licensing plan. Ideally, all women would apply for licenses prior to becoming pregnant, but this does not seem practical. Since many pregnancies are unplanned, some women might accidentally become pregnant before seeking a license and other women might accidently become pregnant after their license had expired. The possibility of giving all women a blanket licensing test at age eighteen or twenty-one would greatly diminish the value of licensing, since people change over time and some women who passed the test at age eighteen might not pass the test at age thirty, and vice versa.

Because of these difficulties, it would be far more practical for states to require all women and their partners to obtain parenting licenses during pregnancy. Yet, this raises other concerns. First, some women might try to hide their pregnancies from the state for fear of having their children taken away from them. Indeed, it is not inconceivable that an extensive underworld of unlicensed pregnancies and births might develop among individuals who feared or opposed (for religious, moral, political, or other reasons) parental licensing requirements. None of this would be good for the health of women or their children. In an effort to avoid detection, pregnant women might avoid seeking prenatal care lest their doctors should report them to public officials. For similar reasons, some women might avoid the help of doctors or licensed midwives in giving birth, or avoid professional health care for themselves and their newborns after the birth of their child.

Even supposing all women did comply with parental licensing requirements during pregnancy, it is far from clear that this would be a good thing for them or their children. If a pregnant woman were to fail the parenting test, she would presumably be offered, and perhaps encouraged to have, an abortion. Advocates of parenting licensing schemes regularly emphasize that they in no way favor forced abortions. Yet, if a woman were told by the state that she was unfit to be a mother and informed that her child would be taken away from her at birth if she chose to remain pregnant, the state would be treading very close to de facto forced abortions. If a woman nonetheless did decide to carry her pregnancy to term, one must wonder what effect the denial of a parenting license might have on her treatment of the fetus. Would the woman make great efforts to eat a healthy diet, avoid alcohol, and not smoke after having already been stigmatized as an unfit mother by the state and told that her child would be taken away from her at birth? It seems possible that some pregnant women might come to harbor deep resentments against their fetuses under these circumstances and provide them with less-than-adequate care.

Probably the best time to license parents would be at the birth of a child. Licensing parents at the birth of a child would provide the most accurate estimate of their present parenting abilities and also avoid some of the negative consequences that might arise if women were tested during pregnancy. However, waiting until birth to test for parenting competency would be unfair to women. Women who give birth have already invested a great deal of themselves into their child. Even the easiest pregnancies usually involve numerous personal and financial sacrifices. Most women, too, form a relationship with their child during pregnancy, especially when they are planning to raise the child themselves. Testing women for competency after birth would therefore place unfair burdens on women. If women are going to be denied the opportunity to raise their children, it seems only fair that they should be notified of this outcome prior to undergoing their pregnancy and labor and forming an attachment with their child. Yet, as argued above, earlier testing periods are beset by a number of other problems. Women who feared—perhaps even irrationally—that their child might be taken from them at birth might further avoid giving birth in hospitals or under the care of registered medical professionals, which once again would threaten their own health and the health of their children. In short, then, there really is no good time to administer a parental licensing test. All time frames have serious drawbacks.

A second important objection to parental licensing schemes is their unequal impact on women. Quite surprisingly, LaFollette, Taylor, or other proponents of parental licensing plans never even consider the gender implications of their proposals. All of these writers seem to assume that parental licensing schemes would weigh equally on men and women, never acknowledging that it is only women who can bear children and usually women who take on primary responsibility for rearing them. Some of the ways in which a parental licensing plan would differentially affect women were mentioned above. If a pregnant woman *or her partner* were found to be unfit for parenting prior to the birth of a child, it would fall to the woman either to have an abortion or to carry the pregnancy to term in full knowledge that she would not be able to raise the child. Men would not have to endure either of these burdens. If a woman's partner were found to be unfit for parenting but the woman still wanted to raise her child, the woman might leave her partner, but this would expose her to personal, financial, and other forms of hardship. Special provisions might be made in this case to help the partner obtain a license, but if these measures were unsuccessful, the woman would once again bear the burden of raising the child on her own or putting it up for adoption. If a pregnant woman were to pass a parental licensing test but her partner did not (perhaps because he was found to have a tendency toward violent behavior), the woman would also be placed in a very vulnerable position. The woman would seemingly have to choose between her partner and her child. The woman's partner might force the woman to have an abortion or threaten her with abuse if she wanted to keep her child. A violent or abusive individual surely is not well-suited to raise a child. The suggestion here is not that a violent parent should be given a license to parent. Rather the point is to highlight some of the ways in which a parental licensing plan might increase the stress and conflicts within relationships and make at least some women more vulnerable to harm. If other policy strategies exist for protecting children from potentially violent or abusive parents that do not increase the stress and conflict within relationships (as discussed below), they should be preferred.

This raises a related concern not considered by advocates of parental licensing plans. Because women are much more likely to raise children than men, their personal and relational lives would also be subject to much greater scrutiny. Under a parental licensing plan, state officials would presumably monitor households with children in order to verify that the parents were licensed. If these plans were to be effective, all adults living in a household with a child would seemingly have to obtain parental licenses. If parental licensing were to be effective, then, the ability of single parents (the overwhelming majority of whom are women) to form relationships with other adults would be subject to great scrutiny. Single parents would presumably only be able to live in households with other adults who possessed a parenting license. If their living situation changed in any way, they would presumably have to notify state officials or face legal penalties. The relational lives of most men would not be subject to such close scrutiny.

A final objection to parental licensing schemes relates to the well-being of the children who are removed from their biological parents. Proponents of parental licensing schemes assume that children who were removed from unfit parents would be quickly adopted by better, wealthier, and more responsible parents. Yet, it is doubtful that this would be the case for many children. In 2006, 4,266,000 children were born in the United States. Jack Westman estimates that roughly 4 percent of these children were born to unfit parents. The Family Stress Checklist places the number much higher, identifying 17.6 percent of adults as potential abusers. If parents were subject to income tests, perhaps as many as 25 percent would have their children taken away from them at birth—or over one million children per year in the United States. Under a parental licensing scheme, one would expect, of course, that fewer unfit mothers would give birth to children. But suppose that even half of the 4 percent of children whom Westman estimates are born each year to unfit parents were born under a parental licensing scheme in the United States. That would amount to an additional 85,000 children (roughly 2 percent of 4.2 million) available for adoption each year. Since 1987, the number of adoptions annually in the United States has remained fairly constant, ranging from 118,000 to 127,000. Perhaps as many as 40 percent of these adoptions regularly occur within families (e.g., step-parents adopting stepchildren), indicating that approximately 75,000 thousand children are adopted outside families each year. If a parental licensing scheme were implemented, the number of non-kin related adoptions that occurred each year would therefore at least need to double in order to place all the extra children. Some increase in adoptions could be expected since nearly all the newly available children would be infants. Adoption costs might also be lowered (though the screening process would presumably remain rigorous) to facilitate more adoptions. Even so, there are a couple of reasons for thinking that some significant number of children would remain unadopted each year. First, the adoption rate and total number of adoptions has been declining since 1970. For whatever reason, people appear to be more interested today in having their own children or not having children at all. Secondly, the increased availability of in vitro fertilization and other new reproductive technologies is likely to depress the number of adoptions in coming years, as infertile couples turn in greater numbers to these new technologies in order to have biologically related children rather than opting for adoption. Under a parental licensing plan, it therefore seems likely that some number of children would linger for months or years in state institutions or foster care without permanent parents. Except in the most extreme situations, these arrangements are usually worse for the development and well-being of children than even suboptimal parental home care. A higher number of children in foster care in the United States are subject to physical and sexual abuse and neglect each year, for example, than the national average. Far from improving the well-being of children, a parental licensing plan thus might actually make the lives of many children worse. In this regard, parental licensing plans would likely fail to achieve their primary purpose, which means their primarily justification would be undermined.

Most of the above criticisms could be overcome through a mandatory universal reversible sterilization program. The idea for such a plan was originally discussed by Roger McIntire in the 1970s and has recently been endorsed by Michael McFall. Under this scheme, the state would administer a reversible contraceptive drug to all children at birth and then require adults to obtain a parenting licence before allowing them to have access to the fertility antidote. This solution would avoid the timing difficulties described above, lessen the differential impact of parental licensing on women, and virtually eliminate the possibility that unfit parents might bear children. Such a plan, however, raises some obvious concerns. Even if minimal requirements were initially established for obtaining the fertility antidote, the government might later impose additional religious, moral, or political requirements on parents—declaring, for example, that only regular Church-goers were fit to bear and rear children. The state might also subtly discriminate against certain racial or ethnic groups by requiring financial, educational, and language requirements that would effectively disqualify large numbers of individuals from these groups from obtaining parenting licenses. However, the main objection to a mandatory universal reversible sterilization program is not so much that state officials might abuse this program (after all, this threat exists with all state programs) as that it represents an illegitimate exercise of state power in itself. Reproduction has long been recognized as one of the most basic human capabilities. As LaFollette notes, some limitations on the right to reproduction (via less intrusive parental licensing plans) are at least theoretically consistent with liberal principles. Mandatory universal reversible sterilization plans, however, coercively intervene into innocent people's bodies in order to suppress this capability, and make reproduction wholly dependent upon state authorization. These programs thus represent a violation of individuals' bodily integrity and self-ownership rights, and violate the most basic liberal freedoms.

Another solution to the problems listed above would be to lower the requirements for obtaining a parenting license. Jack Westman argues, for example, that the requirements for obtaining a parenting license should be "simple and straightforward so that they could be easily met." In his plan, potential parents would be required to be at least eighteen years old and asked to sign a form agreeing "to care for and nurture the child and to refrain from abusing and neglecting the child." A "third, possibly optional, criterion would be completion of a parenting course or its equivalent." The first of these criteria might still generate some of the problems listed above insofar as underage women who wanted to have children but could not obtain their parents' consent might try to hide their pregnancies from state officials. In general, though, Westman's proposal would likely meet with broad compliance. Its main shortcoming is that it would not do very much to improve children's well-being. Since nearly everyone would be able easily to obtain a license, the main purpose behind parental licensing schemes—to prevent unfit individuals from raising children—would be unfulfilled. Westman argues that his licensing plan would nonetheless have symbolic value by helping to foster greater public awareness of the moral and social value of parenting, but this goal can be achieved by other means, such as public support for parenting or a public media campaign. Moreover, it is far from clear that a simple and easy licensing procedure that made parenting readily available to nearly everyone would greatly increase appreciation for the value of childrearing. Many individuals would likely come to regard a parental license as little more than a pro forma certificate and some might even see it as a nuisance.

Westman's proposal highlights the central paradox at the heart of parental licensing proposals. If parental licensing schemes use stringent criteria to select potential parents, they will likely meet with widespread non-compliance and generate harmful unintended consequences for women and children. If parental licensing schemes use weak criteria to select potential parents, they will likely enjoy higher levels of compliance but have little effect on children's well-being. Intermediate proposals such as fines for non-compliant parents would likely enjoy medium to high levels of compliance but deprive parents, especially in low-income families, of the resources needed to care adequately for their children.

Parental licensing proponents usually raise one last argument in defense of their plans. Most liberal states require prospective parents to meet various criteria before they can adopt a child. According to parental licensing advocates, screening potential adoptive parents but not potential biological parents establishes an unfair double standard. Either all parents should be screened and licensed or none should be. LaFollette writes, "If we continue our practice of regulating the adoption of children, and certainly we should, we are rationally compelled to establish a licensing program for all parents." There are, however, several important differences between adoptive and biological parental screening programs. David Archard argues that a higher standard should be set for adoptive parents because adopted children "may present particular and possibly serious difficulties ... arising from the fact that they have been rejected or abused by their natural parents." The higher standard for adoptive parents can also be justified on the grounds that the state has a special responsibility to assure the biological parents of an adoptive child that their child is placed with parents who will provide him or her with at least as high a level of care as they would have provided. Above all, the main reason for supporting a screening and licensing program for adoptive parents but not for biological parents is because of the greater viability of the former. Adoptive screening programs do not face the timing difficulties discussed above, do not weigh more heavily on women than men, and do not generate extra children without permanent homes (though they may prevent some existing children from finding permanent homes). If it were possible to screen all biological parents without any negative effects, then widespread parental licensing might be desirable. Since this does not seem possible, screening is best used only for adoptions.

A PUBLIC PARENTING MODEL

In the first section, I demonstrated that parenting projects are different from other private projects in a number of ways, and that, consequently, public parenting support does not violate liberal principles of fairness or neutrality. In the second section, I showed that parental licensing plans would likely generate numerous serious problems and are therefore not a good strategy for enhancing children's well-being. In this final section, I briefly sketch the details of a public parenting model that can resolve most of the ambiguities and tensions within liberalism regarding childrearing without generating significant negative outcomes.

Rather than attempting to regulate individual parenting choices, as parental licensing plans attempt to do, the public parenting model aims to relieve parents of exclusive private responsibility for the financial, temporal, and other costs of childrearing. The theoretical assumptions behind the public parenting model were outlined above in section one. A public parenting model rests on the recognition that we all have an interest in and bear some responsibility for the good care of children. Since children need to form stable attachments with particular caregivers for their normal psychological and emotional development, and are more likely to receive good care when particular adults are assigned to look after them, the public parenting model still supports assigning particular adults personal responsibility for looking after particular children. However, it distributes the costs of childrearing broadly among all individuals who are capable of paying taxes rather than expecting parents to bear all the costs of childrearing themselves.

The public parenting model particularly supports all policies that have been found to contribute significantly to children's health and development. Under a public parenting model, for example, the state would make affordable prenatal care accessible to all pregnant women, since prenatal care has been found to promote women's and children's health. All new parents would likewise be guaranteed paid parenting leaves from work lasting ideally up to a year in length. Paid parental leaves have been found to correlate strongly with lower infant and child mortality rates, and can also contribute to children's early cognitive and emotional development. The state would also sponsor home care visits from medical and child care specialists during the first year of a child's life to provide new parents with useful information about caring for their infant and to check up on the child's health and development. These home care visits could serve as parenting tutorials without requiring new parents to attend mandatory classes. Under a public parenting model, all children would likewise be guaranteed access to quality and affordable childcare until they begin primary school. Quality public childcare can help to ensure that children receive good care while their parents are at work, compensate for sub-optimal parenting practices at home, and stimulate the cognitive, emotional, social, and linguistic development of children. The state would further provide all parents with public subsidies or tax breaks to help defray the costs of childrearing. Family cash and tax benefits have been found to play a significant role in reducing child poverty that impedes children's health and development. Finally, the state would encourage labor market reforms such as flexible scheduling in order to facilitate parents' ability to care for their children

The public parenting model and the policies associated with it would resolve most of the tensions that exist within liberalism regarding family life and renders the need for parental licenses unnecessary. In the first place, it would resolve the tension between parental autonomy and child well-being. As opposed to parental licensing plans, the public parenting model would not attempt to regulate individual choices about reproduction and childrearing but grant individuals a high degree of autonomy in choosing whether or not they wished to have and raise children. Moreover, none of the policies listed above would seriously intrude upon the intimacy of family life. In fact, many of these policies would actually provide parents more time to spend with their children. As long as parents provided their children with at least a threshold level of adequate care, the public parenting model further offers no objection to their raising their children however they see fit. Parents would still have discretion in determining the particular forms of food, clothing, and shelter they provided to their children and the activities and traditions they promoted in their homes.

The public parenting model would also protect children's welfare rights. The family policies listed above would lift most children out of poverty and promote their survival and health. Those countries that most generously support these parenting policies (the Nordic countries), for example, have some of the lowest child poverty and child mortality rates in the Western world. In all likelihood, these policies would also greatly reduce child abuse and neglect. While an individual's family history and psychological disposition certainly play some role in determining his or her proclivity to abuse, numerous other factors, including poverty, socioeconomic status, and family stress, are also important. Poverty and stress are, in fact, the two factors that most closely and consistently correlate with child abuse and neglect across Western countries. The family policies outlined above would greatly reduce these social and economic triggers for child abuse and neglect, and consequently, promote better functioning families. Existing child protection agencies would further continue to investigate suspected cases of abuse and neglect and intervene into families when necessary to protect children's interests.

Where the goal is to improve children's well-being, the public parenting model thus seems a better strategy than a parental licensing scheme. Under a public parenting model, low-income parents would be provided with subsidies and support so that they could better care for their children. Short-tempered and harried parents would be relieved of some of the central factors that contribute to abuse and neglect. Health providers and childcare workers would have ample opportunities to monitor children's development and identify potential cases of abuse or neglect. By comparison, subjecting potential parents to a psychological and financial test prior to the birth of a child seems a rather limited means for securing children's survival and growth. Of course, one might combine the public parenting model with a parental licensing scheme. However, a parental licensing scheme might actually undermine some of the central benefits of the public parenting model for all the reasons discussed above. The public parenting model shares with parental licensing schemes the commitment to ensuring that parents understand and fulfill their responsibilities to their children. It simply adopts a more supportive approach to achieving this goal.

In addition to better supporting children's well-being, the public parenting model would also help to mitigate the unfair gender inequalities associated with parenting. Paid parenting leaves and affordable quality child care have both been found to increase women's labor market attachment. By supporting women's employment, the public parenting model would lessen, albeit not entirely eliminate, the gender inequalities associated with parenting. At the very least, women would be under less pressure to give up their careers in order to care for their children and would suffer fewer job-related penalties related to parenting.

Finally, the public parenting model would help to decrease the unequal opportunities that children experience because of their different family up-bringings. Research shows that the economic class and social status of children's parents has important long-term effects on their educational achievement, health, and economic success. The children of more economically and socially privileged parents tend to stay in school longer, perform better on standardized tests, enjoy better health, and earn higher incomes than the children of less privileged parents. The family thus represents an important obstacle to the liberal value of equal opportunity. The public parenting model would greatly reduce this tension between families and equal opportunity. By providing all parents with family support and services, the differential advantages enjoyed by the children of privileged parents would be decreased. In the Nordic countries, for example, where family support is widely available, researchers have found that class differences generally have far less impact on students' performance on standardized reading and math tests than in countries without these family policies. Quality childcare, in particular, has been found to have significant long-term effects in improving the educational achievement, employment, and income of disadvantaged children.

Altogether, then, the public parenting model better conforms to liberal values than other models. While still granting individuals the freedom to decide whether or not to have or raise children and a wide degree of discretion over the care of their children, it does a much better job of protecting children against abuse and neglect and ensuring that they receive the care they need to survive and develop. It likewise better supports gender equality and equality of opportunity for children. The public parenting model does, of course, break decisively with the traditional liberal view of parenting as a private responsibility, but this view is itself inconsistent with core liberal values. A careful consideration of the place of the family within liberal thought points to a public parenting model as a necessary element of any coherent liberal theory of justice.

Significantly, most liberals already support the public parenting model in selective public policy domains. Public education is the most obvious example. Even libertarians such as Milton Friedman defend universal public funding of education based on a general social duty to care for children and the positive externalities that education generates for individuals outside the parent-child relationship. While most people today tend not to think of education as a family policy, it clearly is one. Prior to the development of public education systems in the nineteenth and twentieth centuries, parents were primarily responsible for providing education to their children just as they are responsible today (in liberal countries such as the United States) for arranging and paying for their childcare. Yet, if education is a public good, then surely so is childcare. The care and education of children prior to age six is, if anything, more important than their care and education after age six. Many people nonetheless seem blind to this inconsistency. The public parenting model simply extends widely held beliefs about the importance of public education to other areas of family life.

One lingering concern may remain. Even if it is accepted that some public support for parenting is justified, it might be argued that individuals who choose to have and raise children should still bear some responsibility for their choices. The public parenting model supports this intuition. While the public parenting model subsidizes the costs of parenting, it hardly gives parents a free ride. Parents would still be expected to make significant sacrifices for their children, including devoting a large portion of their income, time, and energy to caring for them. Under a public parenting model, individuals who chose to have and raise children would likely also have to forego the pursuit of some other personal goods, such as mountain climbing. The public parenting model does not, then, give parents a free pass. It merely helps to ensure that children receive the basic care they need to survive and develop into productive citizens.

8

The Child's Right to an Open Future

Joel Feinberg

1

How do children's rights raise special philosophical problems? Not all rights of children, of course, do have a distinctive character. Many whole classes of rights are common to adults and children; many are exclusive possessions of adults; perhaps none at all are necessarily peculiar to children. In the common category are rights not to be mistreated directly, for example the right not to be punched in the nose or to be stolen from. When a stranger slaps a child and forcibly takes away his candy in order to eat it himself, he has interfered wrongfully with the child's bodily and property interests and violated his or her rights just as surely as if the aggressor had punched an adult and forcibly helped himself to her purse. Rights that are common to adults and children in this way we can call "A-C-rights."

Among the rights thought to belong only to adults ("A-rights") are the legal rights to vote, to imbibe, to stay out all night, and so on. An interesting subspecies of these are those autonomy-rights (protected liberties of choice) that could hardly apply to small children, the free exercise of one's religion, for example, which presupposes that one has religious convictions or preferences in the first place. When parents choose to take their child to religious observances and to enroll him in a Sunday school, they are exercising *their* religious rights, not (or not yet) those of the child.

The rights that I shall call "C-rights," while not strictly peculiar to children, are generally characteristic of them, and possessed by adults only

145

in unusual or abnormal circumstances. Two subclasses can be distinguished, and I mention the first only to dismiss it as not part of the subject matter of this essay, namely those rights that derive from the child's dependence upon others for the basic instrumental goods of life—food, shelter, protection. Dependency-rights are common to all children, but not exclusive to them, of course, since some of them belong also to handicapped adults who are incapable of supporting themselves and must therefore be "treated as children" for the whole of their lives.

Another class of C-rights, those I shall call "rights-in-trust," look like adult autonomy rights of class A, except that the child cannot very well exercise his free choice until later when he is more fully formed and capable. When sophisticated autonomy rights are attributed to children who are clearly not yet capable of exercising them, their names refer to rights that are to be *saved* for the child until he is an adult, but which can be violated "in advance," so to speak, before the child is even in a position to exercise them. The violating conduct guarantees now that when the child is an autonomous adult, certain key options will already be closed to him. His right while he is still a child is to have these future options kept open until he is a fully formed self-determining adult capable of deciding among them. These "anticipatory autonomy rights" in class C are the children's rights in which I am most interested, since they raise the most interesting philosophical questions. They are, in effect, autonomy rights in the shape they must assume when held "prematurely" by children.

Put very generally, rights-in-trust can be summed up as the single "right to an open future," but of course that vague formula simply describes the form of the particular rights in question and not their specific content. It is plausible to ascribe to children a right to an open future only in some, not all, respects, and the simple formula leaves those respects unspecified. The advantage of the general formula, however, is that it removes temptation to refer to certain rights of children by names that also apply to rights of adults that are quite different animals. The adult's right to exercise his religious beliefs, for example, is a class A right, but the right of the same name when applied to a small child is a right-in-trust, squarely in class C. One can avoid confusing the two by referring to the latter simply as part of the child's right to an open future (in respect to religious affiliation). In that general category it sits side by side with the right to walk freely down the public sidewalk as held by an infant of two months, still incapable of self-locomotion. One would violate that right in trust *now*, before it can even be exercised, by cutting off the child's legs. Some rights with general names are rather more difficult to classify, especially when attributed to older, only partly grown, children. Some of these appear to have one foot in class A and the other in the rights-in-trust subclass of the C category. For example, the right of free speech, interpreted as the freedom to express political opinions, when ascribed to a ten-year-old is perhaps mainly an actual A-right, but it is still partly a C-right-in-trust, at least in respect to those opinions which the child might one day come to form but which are presently beyond his ken.

People often speak of a child's "welfare" or his "interests." The interests protected by children's A-C-rights are those interests the child actually has *now*. Their advancement is, in a manner of speaking, a constituent of the child's good qua child right now. On the other hand the interests he might come to have as he grows up are the ones protected by his rights-in-trust of class C. While he is still a child these "future interests" include those that he will in fact come to have in the future and also those he will never acquire, depending on the directions of his growth.

It is a truism among philosophers that interests are not the same things as present desires, with which they can, and often do, clash. Thus if the violation of a child's autonomy right-in-trust can not always be established by checking the child's *present* interests, a fortiori it cannot be established by determining the child's present *desires* or *preferences*. It is the adult he is to become who must exercise the choice, more exactly, the adult he will become if his basic options are kept open and his growth kept "natural" or unforced. In any case, that adult does not exist yet, and perhaps he never will. But the child is potentially that adult, and it is that adult who is the person whose autonomy must be protected now (in advance).

When a mature adult has a conflict between getting what he wants now and having his options left open in the future, we are bound by our respect for his autonomy not to force his present choice in order to protect his future "liberty." His present autonomy takes precedence even over his probable future good, and he may use it as he will, even at the expense of the future self he will one day become. Children are different. Respect for the child's future autonomy, as an adult, often requires preventing his free choice now. Thus the future self does not have as much moral weight in our treatment of adults as it does with children. Perhaps it should weigh as much with adults pondering their *own* decisions as it does with adults governing their own children. In the self-regarding case, the future self exerts its weight in the form of a claim to prudence, but prudence cannot rightly be imposed from the outside on an autonomous adult.

2

[....]

Children are not legally capable of defending their own future interests against present infringement by their parents, so that task must be performed for them, usually by the state in its role of *parens patriae*. American courts have long held that the state has a "sovereign power of guardianship" over minors and other legally incompetent persons that confers upon it the right, or perhaps even the duty, to look after the interests of those who are incapable of protecting themselves. Mentally disordered adults, for example, who are so deranged as to be unable to seek treatment for themselves, are entitled, under the doctrine of *parens patriae,* to psychiatric care under the auspices of the state. Many "mentally ill" persons, however, are not cognitively deranged, and some of these do not wish to be confined and treated in mental hospitals. The government has no right to impose treatment on these persons, for the doctrine of *parens patriae* extends only to those unfortunates who are rendered literally incapable of deciding whether to seek medical treatment themselves; and even in these cases, the doctrine as liberally interpreted grants power to the state only to "decide for a man as we assume he would decide for himself if he were of sound mind." When the courts must decide for *children,* however, as they presume the children themselves would (or will) when they are adults, their problems are vastly more difficult. As a general rule, the courts will not be so presumptuous as to speak now in the name of the future adult; but, on the other hand, there are sometimes ways of interfering with parents so as to postpone the making of serious and final commitments until the child grows to maturity and is legally capable of making them himself.

In 1944 in the case of *Prince v. Massachusetts* the US Supreme Court upheld a Massachusetts statute that had been applied to prevent Jehovah's Witnesses' children from distributing religious pamphlets on the public streets in what their parents claimed was the free exercise of their religion. The decision in this case has been severely criticized (and I think rightly) as a misapplication of the *parens patriae* doctrine, but the court's statement of that doctrine is unusually clear and trenchant. The state is concerned, said the court, not only with the immediate health and welfare of children but also with—

> the healthy, well-rounded growth of young people into full maturity as citizens with all that implies [in a democracy].... Parents may be free to become martyrs themselves. But it does not follow that they are free in identical circumstances to make martyrs of their children before they have reached the age of full and legal discretion when they can make that decision for themselves.

It was no doubt an overstatement to describe the exposure of children to the apathy or scorn of the passersby in the streets as "martyrdom," but the court's well-stated but misapplied principle suggests other cases where religious liberty must retreat before the claims of children that they be permitted to reach maturity with as many open options, opportunities, and advantages as possible.

Twenty years later, in a quite different sort of case, the religious rights of parents were upheld in a Long Island court at the expense of their three small children. The twenty-four-year-old mother, injured in an automobile collision, was allowed to die when her husband refused on religious grounds to allow doctors to give her a blood transfusion. The husband, like his wife a member of Jehovah's Witnesses, remained adamant despite the pleadings of doctors. Finally the hospital administrator appealed to State Supreme Court Judge William Sullivan, who refused to order the transfusion. [....]

Another close case, I think, but one where the interests of children do seem prior to the religious interests of their parents, was that in which the Kansas courts refused to permit an exemption for Amish communities from the requirement that all children be sent to state-accredited schools. The Amish are descended from eighteenth-century immigrants of strong Protestant conviction who settled in this country in order to organize self-sufficient farming communities along religious principles, free of interference from unsympathetic outsiders. There is perhaps no purer example of religious faith expressed in a whole way of life, of social organization infused and saturated with religious principle. The aim of Amish education is to prepare the young for a life of industry and piety by transmitting to them the unchanged farming and household methods of their ancestors and a thorough distrust of modern techniques and styles that can only make life more complicated, soften character, and corrupt with "worldliness." Accordingly, the Amish have always tried their best to insulate their communities from external influences, including the influence of state-operated schools. [....]

The case against the exemption for the Amish must rest entirely on the rights of Amish *children*, which the state as *parens patriae* is sworn to protect. An education that renders a child fit for only one way of life forecloses irrevocably his other options. He may become a pious Amish farmer, but it will be difficult to the point of practical impossibility for him to become an engineer, a physician, a research scientist, a lawyer, or a business executive. The chances are good that inherited propensities will be stymied in a large number of cases, and in nearly all cases, critical life-decisions will have been made irreversibly for a person well before he reaches the age of full discretion when he should be expected, in a free society, to make them himself. To be prepared for anything, including the worst, in this complex and uncertain world would seem to require as much knowledge as a child can absorb throughout his minority. These considerations have led many to speak of the American child's birth-right to as much education as may be available to him, a right no more "valid" than the religious rights of parents, but one which must be given reluctant priority in cases of unavoidable conflict. [....]

The legal setback to the Amish at the hands of the Kansas Supreme Court was only temporary, however, and six years later in the case of *Wisconsin v. Yoder* they won a resounding victory in the Supreme Court of the United States. The Amish litigants in that case had been convicted of violating Wisconsin's compulsory school attendance law (which requires attendance until the age of sixteen) by refusing to send their children to public or accredited private school after they had graduated from the eighth grade. The US Supreme Court upheld the Wisconsin Supreme Court's ruling that application of the compulsory school-attendance law to the Amish violated their rights under the Free Exercise of Religion Clause of the First Amendment. The Court acknowledged that the case required a balancing of legitimate interests but concluded that the interest of the parents in determining the religious upbringing of their children outweighed the claim of the state in its role as *parens patriae* "to extend the benefit of secondary education to children regardless of the wishes of their parents."

Mr. Chief Justice Burger delivered the opinion of the Court, which showed a commendable sensitivity to the parental interests and the ways they are threatened by secular public education:

> The concept of a life aloof from the world and its values is central to their faith. High school attendance with teachers who are not of the Amish faith, and may even be hostile to it, interposes a serious barrier to integration of the Amish child into the Amish religious community ... compulsory school attendance to the age of sixteen for Amish children carries with it a very real threat of undermining Amish community and religious practice as they exist today; they must either abandon belief and be assimilated into society at large, or be forced to migrate to some other and more tolerant region.

[....]

I am more sympathetic to the separate concurring opinion in the *Yoder* case, written by Mr. Justice White and endorsed by justices Brennan and Stuart, than to the official majority opinion written by the chief justice, and I should like to underline its emphasis. [....]

White gives eloquent answer to Burger's claim that compulsory education of Amish youth in large modern high schools is in effect a kind of indoctrination in secular values. Education can be compulsory, he argues, only because, or only when, it is neutral:

> the State is not concerned with the maintenance of an educational system as an end in itself; it is rather attempting to nurture and develop the human potential of its children, whether Amish or non-Amish: to expand their knowledge, broaden their sensibilities, kindle their imagination, foster a spirit of free inquiry, and increase their human understanding and tolerance. It is possible that most Amish children will wish to continue living the rural life of their parents, in which case their training at home will adequately equip them for their future role. Others, however, may wish to become nuclear physicists, ballet dancers, computer programmers, or historians, and for these occupations, formal training will be necessary.... A State has a legitimate interest not only in seeking to develop the latent talents of its children but also in seeking to prepare them for the life style that they may later choose, or at least to provide them with an option other than the life they have led in the past.

The corrective emphasis of the White concurring opinion then is on the danger of using *Yoder* uncritically as a precedent for finding against Children's C-rights when they are clearly in conflict with the supervisory rights of their parents. A quite different case, involving a child custody decision, will illustrate the equal and opposite danger, of overruling parental rights for the supposititious future interests of a child interpreted in a flagrantly "non-neutral" manner. This horror story is an example of a court taking far too seriously its right under *parens patriae* by enforcing on a child its own special and partisan conception of the way of life that is truly best for it. I refer to the case of six-year-old Mark Painter of Ames, Iowa. An automobile accident took the lives of his mother and sister. His father then left him temporarily with his prosperous maternal grandparents on a large Iowa farm, and went himself to a suburb of San Francisco to begin a new career. A year later, having remarried, he went back to Iowa to pick up his son and return with him to his new home. The grandparents refused to give up the boy, however, and the case went to court. A lower court decision returning the boy to the custody of his natural father was eventually overturned by a state Supreme Court decision favoring the grandparents. The US Supreme Court refused to review that decision, and thus a father was legally deprived of the custody of his own son.

The opinion of the Iowa Supreme Court is a melancholy document. Mr. Painter's new home, it concluded, would not satisfy the child's right to well-rounded growth into full maturity:

> Our conclusion as to the type of home Mr. Painter would offer is based upon his Bohemian approach to finances and life in general. . . . He is either an agnostic or an atheist and has no concern for formal religious training. . . . He has read a lot of Zen Buddhism . . . [his new wife] Mrs. Painter is Roman Catholic. . . . He is a political liberal and got into difficulty in a job at the University of Washington for his support of the activities of the American Civil Liberties Union. . . . We believe the Painter household would be unstable, unconventional, arty, Bohemian, and probably intellectually stimulating.

The home of Mark's Protestant Sunday-school-teaching grandparents, on the other hand, was spacious and commodious, and sure to provide him "with a stable, dependable, conventional, middle-class, Middle West background."

If a parent, as such, has a legally recognized right to the custody of his own child (and surely this must be the case) then we should expect courts to infringe that right only with the greatest reluctance and only for the most compelling reasons. One such reason would be conflict with an even more important right of the child himself. Parents who beat, torture, or mutilate their children, or who willfully refuse to permit them to be educated, can expect the state as *parens patriae* to intervene and assign the children to the custody of court-appointed trustees. Given satisfaction of reasonable moral standards of care and education, however, no court has the right to impose its own conception of the good life on a child over its natural parents' objections. The state can't properly select the influences that are best for a child; it can only insist that all public influences be kept open, that all children through accredited schools become acquainted with a great variety of facts and diversified accounts and evaluations of the myriad human arrangements in the world and in history. This is what it means for parents to "take their chances" with external influences. But apart from that, every parent is free to provide any kind of religious upbringing he chooses, or none at all; to send his child to public or accredited private schools, sectarian or nonsectarian; to attempt to transmit his own ideals, moral and political, whatever they may be, to his child; in short, to create whatever environment of influence he can for his child, subject to the state's important but minimal standards of humanity, health, and education. For a child to be exposed mainly and directly to unconventional values is still, after all, a long way from "martyrdom."

As to the content of the values of any particular parents, there the liberal state is and must be *neutral*. Indeed, the state must be as neutral between atheism and theism in the private households of citizens as it is between Protestantism and Catholicism. The wretched decision in the Painter case, therefore, can be construed in part as a violation of a citizen's right to the free "non-exercise" of religion, for reasons that include no weighable interest or right of his child. It sounds innocuous enough to say that a child's welfare has priority even over a parent's right of custody; but this is no more than an empty platitude when the child's welfare is not objectively and unarguably at issue.

3

The coherence of the above account of the child's right to an open future is threatened by a number of philosophical riddles. The existence of such a right, as we have seen, sets limits to the ways in which parents may raise their own children, and even imposes duties on the state, in its role as *parens patriae*, to enforce those limits. The full statement of the grounds for these protective duties will invoke the interrelated ideals of autonomy (or self-determination) and self-fulfillment, and these concepts are notoriously likely to generate philosophical confusion. Moreover, both friends and enemies of the child's right to an open future are likely to use the obscure and emotionally charged epithet "paternalism," the one side accusingly, the other apologetically, a practice that can only detract further from conceptual clarity. [....]

The word "autonomy," which plays such an essential role in the discussion of children's rights, has at least two relevant senses. It can refer either to the *capacity* to govern oneself, which of course is a matter of degree, or (on the analogy to a political state) to the *sovereign authority* to govern oneself, which is absolute within one's own moral boundaries (one's "territory," "realm," "sphere," or "business"). Note that there are two parallel senses of the term "independent," the first of which refers to self-sufficiency, the de facto capacity to support oneself, direct one's own life, and be finally responsible for one's own decisions, and the second of which, applied mainly to political states, refers to de jure sovereignty and the right of self-determination. In a nutshell, one sense of "autonomy" (and also of "independence") refers to the capacity and the other to the right of self-determination. When the state justifies its interference with parental liberty by reference to the eventual autonomy of the protected child, it argues that the mature adult that the child will become, like all free citizens, has a *right of self-determination*, and that that right is violated in advance if certain crucial and irrevocable decisions determining the course of his life are made by anyone else before he has the *capacity of self-determination* himself.

The child's own good is not necessarily promoted by the policy of protecting his budding right of self-determination. There is no unanimity among philosophers, of course, about that in which a human being's own good consists, but a majority view that seems to me highly plausible would identify a person's good ultimately with his *self-fulfillment*—a notion that is not identical with that of autonomy or the right of self-determination. Self-fulfillment is variously interpreted, but it surely involves as necessary elements the development of one's chief aptitudes into genuine talents in a life that gives them scope, an unfolding of all basic tendencies and inclinations, both those that are common to the species and those that are peculiar to the individual, and an active realization of the universal human propensities to plan, design, and make order. Self-fulfillment, so construed, is not the same as achievement and not to be confused with pleasure or contentment, though achievement is often highly fulfilling, and fulfillment is usually highly gratifying.

One standard way of deriving the right of self-determination is to base it solidly on the good of self-fulfillment. A given normal adult is much more likely to know his own interests, talents, and natural dispositions (the stuff of which his good is composed) than is any other party, and much more capable therefore of directing his own affairs to the end of his own good than is a government official, or a parent at an earlier stage who might preempt his choices for him. The individual's advantages in this regard are so great that for all practical purposes we can hold that recognition and enforcement of the right of self-determination (autonomy) is a causally necessary condition for the achievement of self-fulfillment (the individual's own good). This is the view of John Stuart Mill who argued in *On Liberty* that the attempt even of a genuinely benevolent state to impose upon an adult an external conception of his own good is almost certain to be self-defeating, and that an adult's own good is "best provided for by allowing him to take his own means of pursuing it." Promotion of human well-being and the prevention of harms are primary in Mill's system, so that even so basic a right as that of self-determination must be derived from its conducibility to them. In those rare cases where we can know that free exercise of a person's autonomy will be against his own interests, as for example when he freely negotiates his own slavery in exchange for some other good, there we are justified in interfering with his liberty in order to protect him from harm.

The second standard interpretation of the right of self-determination holds that it is entirely *underivative*, as morally basic as the good of self-fulfillment itself. There is no necessity, on this view, that free exercise of a person's autonomy will promote his own good, but even where self-determination is likely, on objective evidence, to lead to the person's own harm, others do not have a right to intervene coercively "for his own good." By and large, a person will be better able to achieve his own good by making his own decisions, but even where the opposite is true, others may not intervene, for autonomy is even more important a thing than personal well-being. The life that a person threatens by his own rashness is after all *his* life; it *belongs* to him and to no one else. For that reason alone, he must be the one to decide—for better or worse—what is to be done with it in that private realm where the interests of others are not directly involved. [....]

[...] In any case, the two distinct ideals of sovereign autonomy (self-determination) and personal well-being (self-fulfillment) are both likely to enter, indeed to dominate, the discussion of the grounding of the child's right to an open future. That right (or class of rights) must be held in trust *either* out of respect for the sovereign independence of the emerging adult (and derivatively in large part for his own good) or for the sake of the life-long well-being of the person who is still a child (a well-being from which the need of self-government "by and large" can be derived), or from both. In such ways the good (self-fulfillment) and the right (self-determination) of the child enter the justificatory discussion. And both can breed paradox from the start, unless handled with care.

The paradoxes I have in mind both have the form, *prima facie*, of vicious circles. Consider first the self-determination circle. If we have any coherent conception of the fully self-determined adult, he is a person who has determined both his own life-circumstances and his own character. The former consists of his career-type (doctor, lawyer, merchant, chief), his life-style (swinger, hermit, jogger, scholar), and his religious affiliation and attitude (piety, hypocrisy, indifference, total absorption), among other things. The latter is that set of habitual traits that we create by our own actions and cultivated feelings in given types of circumstances, our characteristic habits of response to life's basic kinds of situations. Aristotle analyzed these as deeply rooted *dispositions* to act or feel in certain ways in certain kinds of circumstances, and since his time it has become a philosophical truism that we are, in large part, the products of our own making, since each time we act or feel in a given way in a given kind of circumstance, we strengthen the disposition to act or feel in that (brave or cowardly, kind or cruel, warm or cold) way in similar circumstances in the future. Now, whatever policy is adopted by a child's parents, and whatever laws are passed and enforced by the state, the child's options in respect to life circumstances and character will be substantially narrowed well before he is an adult. He will have to be socialized and educated, and these processes will inevitably influence the development of his own values, tastes, and standards, which will in turn determine in part how he acts, feels, and chooses. That in turn will reinforce his tendencies to act, feel, and choose in similar ways in the future, until his character is set. If the parents and the state try to evade the responsibility for character and career formation by an early policy of drift, that will have consequences on the child too, for which they shall have to answer. And in any case, simply by living their own lives as they choose, the parents will be forming an environment around the child that will tend to shape his budding loyalties and habits, and they will be providing in their own selves ready models for emulation. This inevitable narrowing of options can yet be done without violation of the child's *C-right* of self-determination provided it is somehow in accordance with the child's actual or presumptive, explicit or tacit *consent*. But we can hardly ask the child's actual explicit consent to our formative decisions because at the point when these processes start—where the "twig begins to be bent"—he is not developed enough to give his consent. But neither has he values and preferences of his own for the parents to consult and treat as clues to what his disposition to give or withhold consent would be. At the early stage the parents cannot even ask in any helpful way what the child *will* be like, apart from the parental policies under consideration, when he *does* have relevant preferences, values, and the capacity to consent. That outcome will depend on the character the child will have then, which in part depends, in turn, on how his parents raise him now. They are now shaping the him who is to decide later and whose presumptive later decision cannot be divined. As Henley puts it: "Whether a certain sort of life would please a child often depends upon how he has been socialized, and so we cannot decide to socialize him for that life by asking whether that kind of life would please him."

The paradox of self-determination can be put even more forcefully as an infinite regress. If the grown-up offspring is to determine his own life, and be at least in large part the product of his own "self-determination," he must already have a self fully formed and capable of doing the determining. But he cannot very well have determined *that* self on his own, because he would have to have been already a formed self to do that, and so on, ad infinitum. The vicious circle is avoided only by positing an infinite series of prior selves, each the product of an earlier self.

The paradoxes of self-fulfillment present much the same sort of appearance as the paradoxes of self-determination and can be expressed in quite parallel language. These arise, however, not when we ask what a child will come to prefer, choose, or consent to later in the exercise of his matured autonomy, but rather, simply, what would be good for him, his presumptive choice notwithstanding. To answer this question we must seek to learn his governing propensities, his skills and aptitudes, his highest "potential." We must gauge how his nature is "wound up" and in what direction he is faced, in order to determine what would fulfill his most basic tendencies. We stumble into the vicious circle when we note that if a person's own good is to be understood as self-fulfillment, we cannot fully know the small child's long-term future good until its "nature" is fully formed, but equally we cannot determine how best to shape its nature until we know what will be for its own good. We cannot just leave the child's entire future open for him to decide later according to his settled adult values, because he must begin to acquire those values now in childhood, and he will in fact acquire his governing dispositions now, whatever we do. And in closing his future options in some ways now by our educating, our socializing, our choice of influential environments, we cannot be guided entirely by what accords with the child's own future character, because that character will in large part be a product of the self we are molding now. In a nutshell: the parents help create some of the interests whose fulfillment will constitute the child's own good. They cannot aim at an independent conception of the child's own good in deciding how to do this, because to some extent, the child's own good (self-fulfillment) depends on which interests the parents decide to create. The circle is thus closed.

4

Closed, but not closed tight. The plausible-sounding propositions that seem to lock us into paradox in reality are only approximate generalizations, merely partial truths whose soft spots make viable escape-hatches. The "paradoxes" stem from a failure to appreciate how various judgments used in their for-mulation are only partly true, and how certain central distinctions are matters of degree. It is an overstatement, for example, that there is any early stage at which a child's character is *wholly* unformed and his talents and temperament *entirely* plastic, without latent bias or limit, and another that there can be no "self-determination" unless the self that does the determining is already *fully* formed. Moreover, it is a distortion to represent the distinction between child and adult in the rigid manner presupposed by the "paradoxes."

There is no sharp line between the two stages of human life; they are really only useful abstractions from a continuous process of development every phase of which differs only in degree from that preceding it. Many or most of a child's C-rights-in-trust have already become A-rights by the time he is ten or twelve. Any "mere child" beyond the stage of infancy is only a child in some respects, and already an adult in others. Such dividing lines as the eighteenth or twenty-first birthday are simply approximations (plausible guesses) for the point where *all* the natural rights-in-trust have become actual A-rights. In the continuous development of the relative-adult out of the relative-child there is no point before which the child himself has no part in his own shaping, and after which he is the sole responsible maker of his own character and life plan. The extent of the child's role in his own shaping is again a process of constant and continuous growth already begun at birth, as indeed is the "size" of his self, that is the degree to which it is already formed and fixed.

Right from the beginning the newborn infant has a kind of rudimentary character consisting of temperamental proclivities and a genetically fixed potential for the acquisition of various talents and skills. The standard sort of loving upbringing and a human social environment in the earliest years will be like water added to dehydrated food, filling it out and actualizing its stored-in tendencies. Then the child's earliest models for imitation will make an ineluctable mark on him. He will learn one language rather than another, for instance, and learn it with a particular accent and inflection. His own adult linguistic style will be in the making virtually from the beginning. For the first year or two he will have no settled dispositions of action and feeling of the kind Aristotle called virtues and vices (excellences and defects of character), but as Aristotle said, he is born with the capacity to acquire such dispositions, and the process is under way very early as his basic habits of response are formed and reinforced.

At a time so early that the questions of how to socialize and educate the child have not even arisen yet, the twig will be bent in a certain definite direction. From then on, the parents in promoting the child's eventual autonomy and well-being will have to respect that initial bias from heredity and early environment. Thus from the beginning the child must—inevitably *will*—have some "input" in its own shaping, the extent of which will grow continuously even as the child's character itself does. I think that we can avoid, or at least weaken, the paradoxes if we remember that the child can contribute towards the making of his own self and circumstances in ever-increasing degree. Always the self that contributes to the making of the new self is itself the product both of outside influences and an earlier self that was not quite as fully formed. That earlier self, in turn, was the product both of outside influences and a still earlier self that was still less fully formed and fixed, and so on, all the way back to infancy. At every subsequent stage the immature child plays an ever-greater role in the creation of his own life, until at the arbitrarily fixed point of full maturity or adulthood, he is at last fully and properly in charge of himself, sovereign within his terrain, his more or less finished character the product of a complicated interaction of external influences and ever-increasing contributions from his own earlier self. At least that is how growth proceeds when parents and other authorities raise a child with maximal regard for the autonomy of the adult he will one day be. That is the most sense that we can make of the ideal of the "self-made person," but it is an intelligible idea, I think, with no paradox in it.

Similarly, the parents who raise their child in such a way as to promote his self-fulfillment most effectively will at every stage try to strengthen the basic tendencies of the child as manifested at that stage. They will give him opportunities to develop his strongest talents, for instance, after having enjoyed opportunities to discover by various experiments just what those talents are. And they will steer the child toward the type of career that requires the kind of temperament the child already has rather than a temperament that is alien to him by his very nature. There can be no self-fulfillment for a child prone to sedentary activity by his native body type and endowed with fine motor control over his sensitive fingers if he is inescapably led into a job calling for a large muscled, energetic person with high gross motor control but no patience for small painstaking tasks, or vice versa. The child will even have very basic tendencies toward various kinds of attitudes from an early stage, at least insofar as they grow naturally out of his inherited temperamental propensities. He may be the naturally gregarious, outgoing sort, or the kind of person who will naturally come to treasure his privacy and to keep his own counsels; he may appreciate order and structure more or less than spontaneity and freedom; he may be inclined, *ceteris paribus*, to respect or to challenge authority. Such attitudes grow from basic dispositions of temperament and are the germ, in turn, of fundamental convictions and styles of life that the child will still be working out and trying to understand and justify when he is an adult. The discerning parent will see all of these things ever more clearly as the child grows older, and insofar as he steers the child at all, it will be in the child's own preferred directions. At the very least he will not try to turn him upstream and make him struggle against his own deepest currents. Then if the child's future is left open as much as possible for his own finished self to determine, the fortunate adult that emerges will already have achieved, without paradox, a certain amount of self-fulfillment, a consequence in large part of his own already autonomous choices in promotion of his own natural preferences.

Suggested Further Readings for Part III

Harry Adams, *Justice for Children: Autonomy, Development, and the State* (Albany: State University of New York Press, 2008).

Anne Alstott, *No Exit: What Parents Owe Their Children and What Society Owes Parents* (Oxford: Oxford University Press, 2005).

David Archard, *Children: Rights and Childhood* (New York: Routledge, 1993).

David Archard, *Children, Family, and the State* (Aldershot: Ashgate, 2003).

David Archard and Colin MacLeod, eds., *The Moral and Political Status of Children* (Oxford: Oxford University Press, 2002).

Harry Brighouse and Adam Swift, "Legitimate Parental Partiality," *Philosophy and Public Affairs* 37, no. 1 (2009): 43–80.

Matthew Clayton, *Justice and Legitimacy in Upbringing* (Oxford: Oxford University Press, 2006).

Howard Cohen, *Equal Rights for Children* (Totowa, NJ: Rowman and Littlefield, 1980).

Daniel Engster and Ramiro Gonzales, "Children and Justice: A Proposal for National Parent Training Classes," *Public Affairs Quarterly* 26, no. 3 (2012): 221–241.

Nancy Folbre, *Valuing Children: Rethinking the Economics of the Family* (Cambridge, MA: Harvard University Press, 2008).

Hugh LaFollette, "Licensing Parents," *Philosophy and Public Affairs* 9, no. 2 (1980): 182–196.

Dorothy Roberts, *Shattered Bonds: The Color of Child Welfare* (New York: Basic Civitas Books, 2002).

Robert Taylor, "Children as Projects and Persons: A Liberal Antinomy," *Social Theory and Practice* 35, no. 4 (2009): 555–576.

Barbara Woodhouse, "Children's Rights," in *Handbook of Youth and Justice*, ed. Susan White (New York: Plenum Publishers, 2001), 377–410.

IV

Families and the State

Introduction to Part IV

The connections between familial and political life have always been of interest to Western political philosophers. The invention of the modern liberal state in the early seventeenth century complicated the relationship: Most theorists of that period portrayed the family as a natural entity existing prior to and separate from the state. And yet marriage—widely conceived of as a union between man and woman for the sake of procreation, in which men rule over women and children—is an institution over which church and state fought long and hard for control. Debates about the proper relationship between the state and families continue today in a number of forms, but perhaps most contentiously in arguments about family privacy and marriage.

This section opens with a now-classic discussion of family privacy. In "The Myth of State Intervention in the Family," Frances E. Olsen challenges the idea that families do, could, or should exist outside of the state's influence. Policies of the modern state, she contends, are pervasive. Even when it moves to protect families from outside intrusion, the state effectively constructs them. Whether upholding parental rights, enforcing marriage contracts, or defining kin, the state is deeply implicated in the form and functioning of families. Thus, Olsen argues, it is nonsense to talk about *whether* the state intervenes in the family. The real question is *how* the government should be involved in families. Rather than assuming that families should enjoy a natural sphere of privacy, Olsen challenges us to consider whether there is any justifiable reason for exempting any family relations from the same level of state regulation applied to citizens in the public realm.

The second and third readings in this part challenge now-traditional views about marriage. Owing largely to space limitations, we do not include readings defending traditional views. The Suggested Further Readings section at the end of this part includes many references to these views (see especially Blankenhorn 2007; Corvino and Gallagher 2012; George and Elshtain 2006; Rauch 2004; Shell 2004; Sullivan 1997; and Warner 1999).

In the first reading on marriage, Mary Lyndon Shanley argues that justice, equality, and protecting the vulnerable, especially children, demand that we expand the legal institution of marriage to include same-sex couples. The state has an interest in promoting and stabilizing relationships among adults, particularly when children are involved. It must do so in ways that treat diverse citizens fairly. To achieve these ends, Shanley argues, marriage should be extended (e.g., to same-sex couples) so that it better supports values of equality and care but not so far (e.g., on her account, to traditional polygamous relationships) that it begins to undermine these values. Against those who advocate replacing marriage with a system of privately designed contracts, she warns that the most valuable features of family relations would be threatened by such arrangements.

In the final selection in this part, "The Liberal Case for Disestablishing Marriage," Tamara Metz questions the assumption that the state should be involved in marriage at all. Although she shares Shanley's commitments to justice, equality, and care, she rejects the view that they are met when the state defines and controls marriage. Recent debates about legalizing gay marriage and curtailing divorce, she argues, point to unresolved tensions within liberalism about the role that the state should play in marriage. In fact, she claims that the current regime represents an overextension of legitimate state power and a violation of individual freedom. Drawing a comparison with religion, Metz argues that the most coherent approach to marriage from a liberal perspective is disestablishment, that is, the state should neither sanction nor lend support to marriage as such. Instead, in an argument complementary to Levy's views, Metz contends that the state should promote the legitimate public goals that it currently aims to achieve through marriage by shifting support to intimate caregiving unions. In this way, it could better ensure equality, fairness, and care than current marriage laws do.

9

The Myth of State Intervention in the Family

Frances E. Olsen

Most people concede that there are times when state officials should intervene in the private family. Doctrines of family privacy are no longer thought to justify societal neglect of beaten wives or abused children. Yet society continues to use the ideal of the private family to orient policy. It seems important therefore to examine the concept of state intervention in the private family. In this essay, I argue that the private family is an incoherent ideal and that the rhetoric of nonintervention is more harmful than helpful.

Although most people accept in general the assertion that the state should not intervene in the family, they qualify the assertion with the caveat that the state should sometimes intervene in order to correct inequality or prevent abuse. I refer to this widely accepted caveat as the "protective intervention argument" against nonintervention in the family.

This essay presents a different argument against the policy of nonintervention in the family. It suggests that the terms "intervention" and "nonintervention" are largely meaningless. The terms do not accurately describe any set of policies, and as general principles, "intervention" and "nonintervention" are indeterminate. I refer to this argument as the "incoherence argument."

A useful comparison can be drawn between arguments against a policy of nonintervention in the private family and arguments against a policy of nonintervention in the free market. The policy of nonintervention in the free market, often referred to as laissez faire, was pursued by many American courts in the nineteenth and early twentieth centuries. The group of scholars known as legal realists played an important role in discrediting the legal theories that supported laissez faire. Their arguments form a useful contrast and resource for the arguments I present in this chapter.

The protective intervention argument applies in a similar manner to both laissez faire and nonintervention in the family: whenever either the market or the family misfunctions, the state should intervene to correct inequality and protect the defenseless. The most common and easily accepted argument against laissez faire is that the free market sometimes breaks down or works to the serious disadvantage of particular individuals or groups; state intervention is then necessary to protect the interests of the weaker economic actors and of society in general. This parallels the protective intervention argument regarding the family. Sometimes the family misfunctions; instead of being a haven that protects and nurtures family members, the family may become a center of oppression and exploitation. When this happens the state should step in to prevent abuse and to protect the rights of the individual family members. Both the market version and the family version of this protective intervention argument presuppose that it would be possible for the state to remain neutral, but present reasons that the state should not do so.

The incoherence argument against nonintervention in the family parallels the legal realists' argument against laissez faire. Both laissez faire and nonintervention in the family are false ideals. As long as a state exists and enforces any laws at all, it makes political choices. The state cannot be neutral or remain uninvolved, nor would anyone want the state to do so. The staunchest supporters of laissez faire always insisted that the state protect their property interests and that courts enforce contracts and adjudicate torts. They took this state action for granted and chose not to consider such protection a form of state intervention. Yet the so-called free market does not function except for such laws; the free market could not exist independently of the state. The enforcement of property, tort, and contract law requires constant political choices that may benefit one economic actor, usually at the expense of another. As Robert Hale pointed out more than a half century ago, these legal decisions "are bound to affect the distribution of income and the direction of economic activities." Any choice the courts make will affect the market, and there is seldom any meaningful way to label one choice intervention and the other laissez faire. When the state enforces any of these laws it must make political decisions that affect society.

Similarly, the staunchest opponents of state intervention in the family will insist that the state reinforce parents' authority over their children. Familiar examples of this reinforcement include state officials returning runaway children and courts ordering incorrigible children to obey their parents or face incarceration in juvenile facilities. These state actions are not only widely supported, they are generally not considered state intervention in the family. Another category of state policies is even less likely to be thought of as intervention. Supporters of nonintervention insist that the state protect families from third-party interference. Imagine their reaction if the state stood idly by while doctors performed non-emergency surgery without the knowledge or permission of a ten-year-old patient's parents, or if neighbors prepared to take the child on their vacation against the wishes of the parents, or if the child decided to go live with his fourth grade teacher. Once the state undertakes to prevent such third-party action, the state must make numerous policy choices, such as what human grouping constitutes a family and what happens if parents disagree. These choices are bound to affect the decisions people make about forming families, the distribution of power within the family, and the assignment of tasks and roles among family members. The state is responsible for the background rules that affect people's domestic behaviors. Because the state is deeply implicated in the formation and functioning of families, it is nonsense to talk about whether the state does or does not intervene in the family. Neither "intervention" nor "nonintervention" is an accurate description of any particular set of policies, and the terms obscure rather than clarify the policy choices that society makes.

THE PROTECTIVE INTERVENTION ARGUMENT

To understand the incoherence argument, it is useful to examine in more detail the protective intervention argument—the argument that nonintervention would be possible but is not always a good idea. The protective intervention argument is an argument in favor of selective intervention. In exceptional situations, the state should intervene in the family to protect the interests of society and of the family members who may be at risk; aside from such exceptional situations, state intervention should ordinarily be limited to routine matters such as setting formal requirements for marriage licenses and providing public schooling for children.

According to the usual version of the protective intervention argument, state intervention beyond routine matters should be carefully limited. Excessive or unnecessary intervention jeopardizes people's freedom and interferes with family intimacy. Because of the risks inherent in state intervention, say proponents of protective intervention, safeguards should be devised to protect against government abuse and to prevent unnecessary expansion of state intervention. As long as proper safeguards exist, however, state intervention can be useful—an important force for good.

FAMILIES CAN MALFUNCTION

The argument in favor of selective state intervention is based on the notion that although families ought to be safe, supportive, and loving, some families at some times are not. The family is supposed to be a warm, nurturant enclave governed by an ethic of altruism and caring—a haven protecting its members from the dangers of an authoritarian state and from the anarchistic intrusions of private third parties. Proponents of protective intervention recognize that in some unfortunate situations, the family can cease to be a haven and become instead, "a center of oppression, raw will and authority, violence and brutality, where the powerful economically and sexually subordinate and exploit the powerless."

STATE PROTECTION OF INDIVIDUALS

When a family malfunctions it may be important for the state to protect an individual from the private oppression that members of families sometimes inflict on each other. The protective intervention argument justifies state intervention in the family to protect children from abuse or serious neglect. State officials can remove children from their families if the children have been physically or sexually abused. In cases of child neglect, the state may send social workers into the children's homes or remove the children, temporarily or permanently, for their protection. Such state protection can include ordering medical care, even against the parents' religious scruples. These policies are generally considered to be a form of state intervention in the family, but accepted as intervention that is justified, indeed necessary.

Until recent years, state protection for battered wives was also considered state intervention in the family—again, perhaps justified intervention, but intervention nonetheless. The protective intervention argument characterizes such state protection as a beneficial and necessary form of intervention into a family that has problems. Few people today would openly oppose state enforcement of rape and battery laws against spouses. If providing shelter houses and legal aid to battered wives constitutes state intervention, many argue that such intervention is fully justified to protect individual wives from being oppressed by their husbands. In the exceptional cases in which families misfunction, the state should step in to protect the powerless.

This protective intervention argument begins to blend into the incoherence argument when people dispute whether such protection should be considered intervention at all. Some people would assert that when the family relationship has broken down, so has any justifiable claim to family privacy, and that state protection of the individual no longer constitutes intervention into the family. Indeed, proponents of this view might argue that it would be state intervention to try to keep the family together—for example, not to allow estranged spouses to get a divorce. In such arguments, the idea that the privacy of the family unit should be protected from state intervention begins to be replaced by the notion that what merits protection is the privacy of the individual regarding sexuality, procreation, and the formation of intimate, family-like relationships. I consider this concept of individual privacy to be part of the protective intervention argument—that state intervention is sometimes justified—because although the privacy argument redefines state intervention, it still considers intervention and nonintervention coherent, meaningful concepts.

SAFEGUARDS AGAINST EXCESSIVE INTERVENTION

The protective intervention argument usually treats nonintervention as the norm and intervention as an exception. As one jurist put it: "The normal behavior of husband and wife or parents and children towards each other is beyond the law—as long as the family is 'healthy.' The law comes in when things go wrong."

People who support selective state intervention often assert that safeguards are necessary to protect families from excessive state intervention— attempts by the state to offer protection when it is not really necessary. Child abuse and neglect statutes typically provide that until behaviors pass some threshold, the family is to remain private and the state should not intrude. The Constitution has been held to supply additional protection to family privacy by requiring a clear and convincing showing of abuse or neglect before parental rights may be severed. Physical or sexual abuse or serious neglect is usually necessary to trigger state intervention. This possibility of state intervention, even if it actually occurs only in rare exceptional cases, can play a significant role in keeping family behavior within reasonable bounds of decency.

Divorce or legal separation may also be considered a sufficient trigger to justify state intervention that would otherwise not be allowed. For example, many people who would oppose such policies in an ongoing family believe that if parents separate, the state should order the noncustodial parent to provide financial support for his or her child in case the parent would not do so without a court order. As long as they see safeguards, such as thresholds of family misbehavior or breakdown, to protect against excessive intervention, most people today support a certain level of protective intervention by the state.

THE INCOHERENCE ARGUMENT

The incoherence argument goes further and I believe is more fundamental than the protective intervention argument. The protective intervention argument treats nonintervention as a fully possible but sometimes unwise choice; the incoherence argument questions the basic coherence of the concepts intervention and nonintervention. The state defines the family and sets roles within the family; it is meaningless to talk about intervention or nonintervention, because the state constantly defines and redefines the family and adjusts and readjusts family roles. Nonintervention is a false ideal because it has no coherent meaning.

For example, suppose a good-natured, intelligent sovereign were to ascend the throne with a commitment to end state intervention in the family. Rather than being obvious, the policies she should pursue would be hopelessly ambiguous. Is she intervening if she makes divorces difficult, or intervening if she makes them easy? Does it constitute intervention or nonintervention to grant divorce at all? If a child runs away from her parents to go live with her aunt, would nonintervention require the sovereign to grant or to deny the parents' request for legal assistance to reclaim their child? Because complete agreement on family roles does not exist, and because these roles undergo change over time, the state cannot be said simply to ratify preexisting family roles. The state is continuously affecting the family by influencing the distribution of power among individuals.

The incoherence argument is more complex with regard to the family than with regard to the market. Because nonintervention in the family has been understood as a variety of things, demonstrating its incoherence becomes more complicated than demonstrating that laissez faire is incoherent with respect to the market. Laissez faire is incoherent because no apolitical or neutral way exists to enforce property, contract, or tort law; once the state undertakes to enforce any of these laws, courts are forced to make political choices that cannot help but have important effects on the market and on the direction of economic activities. The alternative of not enforcing any property, contract, and tort law—creating a "state of nature"—is unacceptable in the marketplace. Once one rules out a state of nature, the government can no longer keep "hands off" the market; the question becomes simply which particular policies the government shall support.

The greater complexity of the incoherence argument with respect to the family than with respect to the market makes it initially easier to see that the state is not a neutral arbiter when it deals with the family. Historically, the state bolstered the power of the father over his family. A policy-based refusal to bolster this power might well be considered "intervention"—whether justified under the protective intervention argument or considered obtrusive and unjustified. Even today the state is often expected to enforce parents' authority over their children. To many who endorse hierarchical family relations, "nonintervention" seems to mean simply state support for the family member with power. "Nonintervention" loses much of its appeal if one thinks of it as mere reinforcement of the status quo. Moreover, because the status quo undergoes continual change, nonintervention in the hierarchical family cannot be coherent. Even if state officials attempted simply to support the status quo they would still be forced to make political choices that have important effects on the distribution of roles and power within a family.

In recent years, the state has been expected to treat the members of the family—especially the husband and wife—more as equals. With increasing juridical equality within the family, the parallel between laissez faire with respect to the market and nonintervention with respect to the family becomes closer. Complete juridical equality would require a new concept of state intervention and nonintervention. At least two radically different concepts are possible, though neither would be acceptable to most people and, as I will demonstrate, neither is coherent. One possibility, which I refer to as the Market Model, is based on enforcement of all laws, just as they are enforced in the market. Under this model, all rights and obligations would be enforced between family members the same way laws are enforced between strangers. In this manner the state could avoid direct support for family hierarchy. Nonintervention under the Market Model would be incoherent for the same reasons laissez faire is incoherent: enforcement of any property, tort, or contract law, whether between family members or strangers, requires political choices that necessarily affect the power of the individuals and groups involved and the direction of both their intimate and their commercial relations.

A second possible model of state "nonintervention" in a juridically equal family is non-enforcement or delegalization—no rights or obligations to be enforced between family members. I refer to this construct as the State of Nature Model. Unlike the situation regarding the market, something approaching this model is acceptable to many as a form of "nonintervention" in the family. It can be demonstrated, however, that nonintervention under the State of Nature Model is also incoherent. First, because the "state of nature" would exist only within the family, the state would have to decide the boundaries of family. In addition, if the state of nature within the family were partial instead of complete, the state would have to decide which rights and obligations it would enforce within the family. These decisions require political choices that necessarily affect the roles and power within a family. Once the state undertakes to enforce some but not all rights and obligations, the state cannot avoid policy choices that will affect family life. No logical basis exists for identifying these state choices as either intervention or nonintervention.

INTRODUCTION: LAISSEZ FAIRE
AND NONINTERVENTION

As I have suggested, the incoherence argument against nonintervention in the family is both simpler and more complex than the corresponding argument against laissez faire in the market. An important claim of laissez faire was that the state could and should treat market actors as juridical equals and enforce evenhandedly uncontroversial neutral ground rules that would ensure the protection of all. The incoherence argument against laissez faire demonstrated that the ground rules were not and could not be made neutral and that they could not be enforced evenhandedly. Opponents of laissez faire showed that policy issues arose constantly within every aspect of tort and contract law doctrine—that the kind of apolitical legal system that laissez faire envisioned and depended upon was a myth.

In the case of the market, laissez faire seemed at least to produce a kind of state neutrality, because courts treated people as juridical equals. Workers and bosses were said to have identical rights to freedom of contract. Legal formalism or conceptualism presupposed that it was possible for a legal system to be rational, objective, and principled—scientific rather than political. The failure of legal formalism or conceptualism rendered laissez faire incoherent. Had it really been true that law could be apolitical, that contract law could simply enforce the will of the parties, and tort law simply require those at fault to compensate their victims, laissez faire might well have been coherent. No one has come up with any plausible method for removing the need for political choice from law, however, and I consider it highly unlikely that any such method exists or could be devised.

NONINTERVENTION AND THE HIERARCHICAL FAMILY

The notion of nonintervention in the family is in a sense less plausible than laissez faire in the market. The ideal laissez-faire state would treat market actors as juridical equals; the state does not treat members of a family as juridical equals. Further, the constitutive role of law in creating the market is less obvious than law's constitutive role in creating and defining the family. Laws establish who is married to whom and who shall be considered the child of whom.

The existence of this "legal-positivist" view of the family should not, however, obscure the coexisting and competing "natural law" belief that the family exists as a natural human formation, not created but merely recognized (or not recognized) by the state. Such a notion is implicit in the sense shared by most of us that some families exist that are not legally recognized. In fact, a great deal of family law doctrine can be seen as a response to the problems caused by the disjunction between legally recognized or de jure families and "natural" or de facto families—the gap between the legal definition of family and the sense people have of what a family really is.

Although the state defines and reinforces specific roles and a particular hierarchy within the family, these policies are often considered nonintervention; indeed, a refusal to bolster family hierarchy has sometimes been considered state intervention in the family. The idea that the state can intervene or not intervene in the family, and particularly that the state practices a policy of nonintervention when it bolsters family hierarchy, would seem to depend upon the belief that a natural family exists separate from legal regulations, and that the hierarchy the state enforces is a natural hierarchy, created by God or by nature, not by law.

The Concept of a Natural Family

Last century the idea that wives were naturally dependent upon their husbands was believed by some people as firmly as the idea that children are naturally dependent upon their parents is believed now. The state was expected to bolster the husband's power over his wife whenever it was threatened. The husband chose the family domicile and the wife was essentially forced to live there, just as children are today. As expressed in a nineteenth-century treatise on domestic relations: "The domicile of the wife follows that of the husband; the domicile of the infant may be changed by the parent. Thus does the law of domicile conform to the law of nature." Natural law or "Divine Providence" was thought to be the origin of our laws regarding the family. "Positive law but enforces the mandates of the law of nature, and develops rather than creates a system." Although there have been changes in what is considered natural within the family, the basic notion that family relations are natural relations has not changed that much. Today women may no longer be considered naturally dependent on their husbands, but children are still considered naturally dependent on their parents.

A similar concept of a natural family finds expression in constitutional law. At least since 1944, the Supreme Court has recognized a constitutionally protected right of family privacy—a "private realm of family life which the state cannot enter." The source of this family privacy has recently been said to be "not in state law, but in intrinsic human rights." The Supreme Court clearly envisions a concept of family relationship that is not dependent upon state law: "Nor has the [Constitution] refused to recognize those family relationships unlegitimized by a marriage ceremony." The family has its "origins entirely apart from the power of the State." Thus, for purposes of constitutional adjudication, "the legal status of families has never been regarded as controlling." The nineteenth-century concept of a natural family has continued into the twentieth century. We now recognize law's important role in creating the nineteenth-century family. I would hope we will not have to wait until the twenty-first century to recognize the constitutive role of law in the twentieth-century family.

State Enforced Hierarchy: Not Intervention?

Nonintervention would seem to have meaning against a backdrop of preexisting prescribed social roles within the family. State-created background rules shape and reinforce these social roles by assigning power and responsibility within the family. These background rules are not usually thought of as state intervention, but they implicate the state in the prescribed family roles and undermine claims of nonintervention. The setting of the roles requires political choices that can hardly be considered nonintervention. The state whose policy choices have had such a great effect upon these family roles certainly cannot be considered neutral, nor should the label "nonintervention" be used to conceal or confuse the political nature of the choices society makes.

Moreover, the enforcement of these family roles, which is what many people mean by "nonintervention," requires the state to make continual policy choices about the scope and meaning of the roles it is enforcing. The content of family roles has changed over the years and there has never been complete agreement about the authority husbands and parents have over wives and children or about the responsibilities that go along with the authority. State officials must determine borderline questions about the nature and extent of family hierarchy on a case-by-case basis, and pursuing a policy of "nonintervention" cannot relieve state officials from having to make ad hoc political decisions about the family.

The Family Head Model: Direct Empowerment of Superior

Last century some people believed that by empowering the head of the family—the husband and father—to act for the family and to settle intrafamily disputes, the state could avoid intervening in the family. I refer to this policy as the Family Head Model. In theory, this model would relieve the state of making case-by-case decisions regarding the family.

During the early nineteenth century, the husband was the juridical head of the family, entitled to control the wife and children. He was also the financial head of the family. The common law, enforced by the state, provided that a wife's property belonged to her husband. Any personal property to which the wife held legal title was transferred automatically, by operation of law, to her husband; and the husband was given a life estate in her real property. He was entitled to the services of his wife and children. If they received wages, these wages belonged to him; even if they worked without pay, the father could recover the value of services they provided to third parties. Although he could not legally sell the sexual services of his wife and minor daughters, he could recover money from any man who had sexual intercourse with them without his permission. Some people objected to these policies, but there is no evidence that anyone considered the policies state intervention.

Moreover, the nineteenth-century concept of nonintervention might require the state to bolster the authority of the father. If the wife were to leave and take the children with her, the courts would ordinarily be expected to grant a habeas corpus writ ordering her to return them to him. For courts to refuse to issue such a writ would be considered state intervention in the family.

Today courts are less expected to bolster the power of the husband over the wife, but they are still expected to reinforce parents' authority over children. Many states have a procedure whereby courts can label a child "incorrigible" or "in need of supervision" and order the child to obey the parents or be locked up in the functional equivalent of jail. Parents also have considerable power over whether their child will be institutionalized as mentally defective or troubled. My point is not that such situations are very common, but that these state policies that empower parents are not considered state intervention in the family.

In more subtle ways, also, the state directly authorizes parents to act on behalf of the child. The parents are empowered by the state, as well as by custom, to name the child and to change its name if they wish. They determine the state of which the child shall be a legal citizen. They enroll the child in school. These powers are established by state regulations, regulations that define family roles but are hardly noticed and certainly not considered state intervention.

Creating Economic Dependence

The social interaction within a family can be significantly affected by the economic dependence of wives on husbands and of children on parents. It is obvious to us today that laws and regulations in force early last century made the wife economically dependent upon the husband, and an adolescent economically dependent on his father, typically until age twenty-one. Neither married women nor minors could carry on a trade or business except under the authority of the husband and father; their services belonged to him and he could collect any wages they might earn. Last century this dependency seemed natural to many people.

Today the state's role in reinforcing economic dependency is less obvious but it is still significant. Although state laws no longer require women to perform unpaid work for their husbands as part of the marriage contract, as in previous centuries, federal tax laws still provide a significant economic incentive for domestic labor to remain unpaid. An additional basis for women's economic dependency is low pay; statistically, women's wages are only 61 percent of men's. Although state laws that in the past encouraged or required sex discrimination in employment have been preempted by federal antidiscrimination laws, a number of government agencies save many thousands of dollars by paying lower salaries for jobs held mainly by women than for jobs of comparable worth that men perform.

A child's economic dependence on her parent reinforces and increases the parent's power over the child. Although young children might not be capable of independence, as children grow older, their dependence is increasingly attributable to state regulations. Child labor laws, however wise as policy, are state regulations that make it difficult for children to gain economic independence. And the state goes further. State laws not only limit a child's opportunity for paid employment, they also require her to attend school—work for which she receives no pay. Finally, when a state pays welfare benefits for a child or orders one parent to pay support for a child, the money does not go to the child herself, but to a custodian, usually the other parent. This maintains the child's economic dependency on her custodian. If we are concerned about the state intervening in the family if it provides free contraceptives to girls without telling their parents, we should not overlook the fact that state policies have made it difficult for girls to pay for contraceptives or to get them any other way.

Eliminating Alternative Sources of Support or Nurturance

Last century a woman was required to live in the home of her husband. He could choose to live anywhere, and she was obliged to follow him. One method of enforcing this requirement was to eliminate alternative living possibilities. Anyone who offered lodging to a runaway wife could be charged with harboring her. Although her father might, as a practical matter, get by with this infraction, it would be difficult for anyone else to do so. Most women would be unable to help her and most men ill-advised to do so. If a runaway wife formed a close relationship with a man, they could be suspected of adultery and treated very harshly. If she actually had sexual relations with another man, she could be recaptured and forced home by her husband. The husband could bring a civil suit and recover money damages from the man for "criminal conversation." The husband would continue to own his wife's property and to be entitled to her services, but he would no longer have to support her. In many cases he could take their children away from her and perhaps even bar her from visiting them.

Today the state will ordinarily not penalize third parties who offer lodging or friendship to a woman without the permission of her husband, but laws continue to penalize those who offer the same to children without the permission of their parents. The state is implicated in the power and role distribution within the family when its laws prevent children from looking to third parties for support. Yet the state is not accused of intervening in the family when it forces children to live with their parents or when it prohibits doctors from treating minors without the parents' knowledge and approval. The child may be required to associate or forbidden from associating with people, at the whim of the parents. Statutes permitting courts to issue grandparent visitation orders that may limit this parental prerogative in certain egregious cases are themselves sometimes criticized as state "intervention" in the family. The state gives parents considerable coercive power over children and then characterizes its refusal to monitor this power as "nonintervention."

Limiting State Protection

Last century the father was permitted to discipline his wife and children, and this permission often extended to corporal punishment. Behavior that would constitute a criminal offense if directed at a stranger was fully legal against one's children and mere grounds for separation or divorce if directed against one's spouse. Doctrines of intrafamily tort immunity protected the husband and father from civil suits by his beaten wife or children.

Today, intrafamily tort immunity has been widely abolished, but a great deal of behavior that would be criminal or tortious between strangers may still be done with impunity within a family. In many states, the husband may legally force sexual intercourse upon his wife. In most states, spouse abuse is treated differently from other forms of personal violence—sometimes better, often worse. Children are offered limited state protection against their parents. Usually, crimes and torts will be recognized only if a child is badly abused; and even this occasional enforcement is often thought to constitute state intervention—justified, but intervention nonetheless. In theory, parents can be prosecuted for homicide, sexual abuse, serious physical assaults, and child neglect. In practice, however, a child's dependency is so extensive that many crimes, including assault and sexual abuse, often go unprosecuted.

Changes in Family Hierarchy over Time

The nature and degree of power that the state allows one family member to exercise over another has changed over time and is regularly contested. Reforms that have claimed to provide for juridical equality between men and women have tended to modify the legal role expectations placed on husbands and wives. The role relationship between parent and child has also undergone considerable change over time. Because parents' power over their children is incomplete, the state must adjudicate borderline cases and in doing so necessarily influences the family. At one extreme, state prosecution of a father for intentionally killing his child is universally approved and is unlikely to be considered state intervention in the family; at the other extreme, charging a father with kidnapping for sending a child to her room as a form of punishment would strike most people as serious state intervention in the family. Courts must frequently draw a line between protecting the individual family member and promoting family authority, and different courts would draw the line closer to one or the other of these extremes. Exactly where a court draws the line, or where it would be expected to draw the line, will affect power relations within the family. The choices that courts make will be based on policy considerations and the state cannot avoid making decisions that will influence family relations.

Moreover, when parents disagree, the state has to decide which of the two to empower or to refuse to empower. This choice will in turn influence relations between the parents. Thus, what is frequently referred to as "nonintervention" involves an initial policy choice regarding family roles, followed by further policy choices regarding the details of those roles.

Because nonintervention is understood with reference to specific family roles and the state is expected to take these roles into account in settling disputes, courts must make one choice after another regarding the content and nature of these roles. As long as they do not ratify and enforce all assertions of authority by a husband or parent—for example, they prosecute intrafamily murder—courts must decide which behavior they will sanction and which they will not. These decisions require courts to take a stand on complex issues of intergenerational conflict and gender politics. The simple claim that the state should not intervene in the family tends to obscure the genuine problems of ethics and policy that continually arise.

NONINTERVENTION AND THE EGALITARIAN FAMILY

In theory it would be possible for the state to avoid taking a stand in favor of juridical hierarchy within the family. There are at least two ways the state could settle lawsuits involving families that would avoid ratifying family hierarchy. One would be to treat the family as a miniature state of nature by refusing to enforce any lawsuits between family members; the other would be to treat marriage as nothing more than an express contract and parentage as irrelevant, and enforce all lawsuits between family members just as though the litigants were not related. A consideration of these two contrasting extremes will further illustrate the difficulty with the concept of "nonintervention."

State of Nature Model

The state might seem to be able to remain neutral among family members by steadfastly refusing to enforce any tort, contract, or criminal law between members of a family. This approach, if carried to the extreme, would create a "state of nature" within the family, and could be said to take seriously the notion that families should work out their own problems. If a wife were being beaten, it would be up to her to deal with the problem; the state would not "intervene." If she dealt with the problem by shooting her husband, the state would be expected to continue its policy of "nonintervention." If a person were indicted for murder, it would be a sufficient defense to prove that the defendant and the victim were members of the same family. The killing would then be considered a family matter into which the state should not intrude.

As in any imagined state of nature, this approach would seem to benefit the stronger and prejudice the weaker members of a family. In fact, though, it might disempower the physically weak less than the system that seems to operate in some communities—a system that treats intrafamily battery as private, but leaves homicide fully outlawed. Such a system is especially disempowering to wives if spouse abuse is not recognized as a justification for or defense to homicide.

The State of Nature Model would not really enable the state to remain neutral or uninvolved in the family. Even if the state of nature were complete within the family, the state would still have to decide who constituted a family and how to deal with lawsuits involving third parties and members of the family. Also, a complete state of nature would not fit contemporary views of nonintervention in the family. A partial state of nature within the family might be acceptable to many people; but if the state of nature were partial, decisions about what laws to enforce among family members would require additional political choices that would affect authority and roles within families.

Market Model

A second way the state might seem to be neutral among family members is based on the opposite strategy of enforcement. The state could treat each member of a family as a juridical equal and treat their family status as irrelevant. Marriage and parentage would become private relationships, not recognized by the state. Courts would treat as irrelevant the fact that litigants were married to one another or that one was the parent of the other, and enforce lawsuits as between any unrelated people or strangers. This approach essentially ignores the family relationship and treats family members just as strangers are treated. Such a policy would not fit contemporary views of nonintervention in the family, especially as regards children. For example, under the Market Model, parents who disciplined their children by sending them to their rooms might be guilty of kidnapping and the children could have a valid cause of action for false imprisonment. Parents would have neither an obligation to support children nor a right to keep them from living away from home. Children and parents would be free to cut their own deals. Contracts entered into between children and their parents, or between any other family members, would be just as enforceable as contracts between any unrelated individuals.

The concept of nonintervention based on the Market Model is not only unacceptable to most people, but it is also no more coherent than laissez faire. All the arguments put forth by the legal realists to show the incoherence of laissez faire apply to nonintervention under the Market Model. The neutrality of the Market Model would be formal neutrality only, even as between adults. The particular tort, contract, and criminal laws the state chose to create and enforce would affect the relative power of individuals and thus the bargains they could negotiate with their spouses, children, or other relatives. For example, strong battery laws are likely to help wives and children; weakened self-defense doctrines limit their ability to protect themselves, and would seem to help husbands.

To illustrate further, consider the laws that forbid prostitution and nullify contracts when sexual services constitute all or part of the consideration on one side of the agreement. In our present society, the effect of nullifying such contracts usually enriches the male at the expense of the female. The public policy against prostitution might have something to do with refusing to reduce women to sex objects, but it might have as much or more to do with preserving for men the economic resources that reinforce their prestige and power. The result of policies that enrich men and impoverish women is that even if the law were to refuse to permit "family" defenses to contract, tort, or criminal actions, wives would still often bring to the marriage a position lower in the social and economic hierarchy, and thus a weaker bargaining position vis-à-vis their husbands. [....]

WHY IT MATTERS

The protective intervention argument, that the state should intervene in the family when necessary, has gained so much acceptance—just as the protective intervention argument against laissez faire has gained widespread acceptance—that one might wonder why we need the incoherence argument, that intervention and nonintervention are meaningless concepts. First, it is not the case that the exception has swallowed the rule. Under the protective intervention argument, the state is treated as having a policing function—to detect and correct those rare circumstances that disturb and disrupt the family, without questioning any of the basic individualistic foundations of society. The assertion that the state can and should avoid "intervention" in the family plays an important but generally unrecognized ideological role. Further, focusing on "nonintervention" tends to mush and confuse the ethical and political choices we make. It directs our attention to a false issue and obscures genuine issues of ethics and policy. Finally, both laissez faire and nonintervention in the family have sprung up in modern versions—law-and-economics in place of laissez faire and the individual right to privacy in place of nonintervention in the family. These new forms, one labeled conservative, the other liberal, are flawed in the same way the originals—laissez faire and nonintervention—are flawed. The standard liberal criticism of law-and-economics and the standard conservative criticism of the right to privacy are both versions of the protective intervention argument. In each instance, I believe the incoherence argument presents a more important critique.

10

Just Marriage

Mary Lyndon Shanley

American conservatives pride themselves on moral clarity. And that clarity is nowhere greater than on the topic of marriage and family. The essentials of marriage are, they say, well-defined: it unites a man and a woman; it provides the foundation for a family that may include biological or adopted children; it assigns different roles to men and women; and it is a union for life, indissoluble except for the most grievous offenses. These essentials are, according to conservatives, not a product of the vagaries of social convention or contingent cultural choices but are instead given by nature, scripture, or tradition. Moreover, preserving them is intrinsically good for individuals and has great public benefits: marriage is the foundation of society, and a strong foundation will protect against society's ills, from crime to poverty.

For the past decade conservatives have worked energetically to implement this vision—more precisely, to restore it in the face of the demographic, economic, and cultural changes of the past forty years. They have defended two-parent marriage by requiring (in the 1996 Welfare Reform Act) that single parents who receive welfare must work outside the home for wages, while allowing one parent in a two-parent family that receives welfare to stay home to take care of children. They supported President George W. Bush's "marriage initiative," which allocates federal funds to programs aimed at persuading unwed parents to marry, by rewarding, for example, a single mother who marries her child's father. And they have opposed efforts to legalize same-sex marriage in individual states and praised the federal Defense of Marriage Act (DOMA), which exempts states from recognizing same-sex marriages entered

179

into in other states. The Catholic bishops of Massachusetts, for example, have recently been pressing the state legislature to pass a constitutional amendment against same-sex marriage: such marriages will, they say, have "devastating consequences." And Ken Connor, president of the conservative Family Research Council, has promised to make a "big, big issue in 2004" out of the idea that "marriage is a sacred covenant, limited to a man and a woman."

Critics argue that these efforts to shore up the traditional family represent an assault on thirty years of sensible reforms of marriage and divorce law that have helped to free women and men from stultifying or abusive relationships; that they threaten to reimpose oppressive gender roles; that they stigmatize and disadvantage unwed mothers and their children; and that they condemn gay men and lesbians to second-class citizenship. In short, the conservative program is characterized as the enemy of equality and a threat to personal liberty.

But these critics have been less clear about their own constructive moral and political vision. One response to the conservative project has been to concentrate on efforts to legalize gay and lesbian marriage by reforming state marriage laws. This strategy is attractive and shows some promise in a few states, but even if it succeeds it leaves other elements of the conservative project untouched. It does nothing to address the concerns of those who regard marriage itself as oppressive, to remedy the poverty that deters some people from marrying, or to support single parents and their children.

A second, more comprehensive proposal—put forward by, among others, Lenore Weitzman in *The Marriage Contract* and Martha Fineman in *The Neutered Mother*—is to abolish state-defined marriage altogether and replace it with individual contracts drawn up by each couple wishing to marry. A regime of individual contract would allow spouses to decide for themselves how to arrange their lives, and it would enable people of the same sex, or more than two persons, to marry. On this view, which I will call contractualism, the best way to treat citizens as free and equal adults is to stop treating marriage as a special public status, and permit the parties themselves to define its terms and conditions.

Contractualism has considerable force, but it suffers from two deficiencies. First, the contract model treats persons as rational and bounded individuals while paying insufficient attention to the mutual need and dependence that arise in marriage and other close relationships. It thus rests on an incomplete view of the person and fails to take account of the ideal of marriage as a relationship that transcends the individual lives of the partners. That ideal has deep cultural resonance, and contractualism unnecessarily concedes this ground to conservatives. Second, while emphasizing the need for liberty in the choice of partners, contractualism fails to give sufficient weight to positive state action to enhance equality and equal opportunity along with liberty and freedom of association. It thus is founded on too narrow a conception of justice.

A third line of response, then, would preserve the idea that a married couple is something more than its separate members, and that spouses can make claims in the name of their relationship that are not identical to claims that each could make as individuals. But it would also open up marriage so that both women and men, regardless of race, class, or sexual orientation, can, as equals, assume the responsibilities and reap the rewards of family life. I will call this the equal status view. Its defining aspiration is to preserve the idea that marriage is a special bond and public status while rejecting—as incompatible with liberty and equality—important elements of the traditional view of the purpose and proper ordering of marriage.

Can marriage be reformed to serve as a public status that promotes equality and liberty? Is the happy combination of justice and committed intimacy and love suggested by the equal status view a real possibility?

FROM FIXED STATUS TO NO-FAULT

The traditional view of marriage in the United States has roots in Christian religious views and church law. The English common law, which provided the basis for the marriage laws of most US states, reflected the tenets of marriage promulgated by the Anglican (and before it the Catholic) Church. When jurisdiction over marriage and children was transferred from church to common-law courts, for the most part public law simply incorporated aspects of church doctrine.

The Traditional View

In the Church's view marriage was first and foremost a covenant, like God's covenant with the Jews and Christ's covenant with the church (the community of the faithful). Christian marriage was thus an unbreakable bond (for Catholics, a sacrament). Marriage was to be lifelong and marital faithfulness was to include monogamy.

Marriage was also regarded as a hierarchical relationship in which husband and wife played complementary roles. The man was given authority as head of household. Blackstone, the eighteenth-century legal authority, explained that since Genesis declared husband and wife to be "one flesh" in the eyes of God, they were to be "one person" in the eyes of the law, and that person was represented by the husband. This suspension of the wife's legal personality was known as the doctrine of spousal unity or "coverture." Under coverture a married woman could not sue or be sued unless her husband was party to the suit, could not sign contracts unless her husband joined her, and could not make a valid will unless he consented to its provisions. As a correlate to these powers and his role as head of the family, a husband was obligated to support his wife and children. And since he would be held responsible for her actions, a husband had a right to correct his wife physically and to determine how and where their children would be raised. As late as 1945 a New Jersey court wrote:

> The plaintiff [husband] is the master of his household. He is the managing head, with control and power to preserve the family relation, to protect its members and to guide their conduct. He has the obligation and responsibility of supporting, maintaining and protecting the family and the correlative right to exclude intruders and unwanted visitors from the home despite the whims of the wife.

Marriage was to be a structure in which the roles of the spouses were distinct and complementary: the wage earner and the housewife, the protector and the protected, the independent and the dependent.

The husband was expected to govern his household with neither interference nor help from the state. By and large, police turned a blind eye to violence between spouses. In most jurisdictions wives could not prosecute their husbands for marital rape because the law assumed that by marrying, spouses gave blanket consent to sexual relations (they were, after all, "one body" and "one person" in law). And judges enforced obligations of support only if spouses separated, not in an ongoing marriage.

When people married, then, they consented to enter a relationship whose terms were set by the state. Of course, consent was necessary to enter the married state, but the agreement to marry brought with it rights and duties that were not set by the partners but were treated as intrinsic to the status of being married.

The First Wave of Reform

The unequal provisions of marriage law became the object of reform efforts in the mid-nineteenth century. Reformers were critical, for example, of the fact that many states granted divorce only for a wife's adultery and not a husband's. Moreover, adultery was in many states the *only* grounds for divorce, and some men and women began to insist that other wrongs, particularly physical cruelty and domestic violence, were significant offenses against the marriage that justified dissolving the marital bond. To forbid divorce in such instances, they said, was to make the home a "prison" for unhappy and wronged spouses, depriving them of essential personal liberty.

Feminist reformers also challenged coverture by invoking equality. They organized campaigns in a series of states to pass laws which would allow wives to hold property, sue and be sued, and enter contracts in their own names. By the end of the nineteenth century, many states had passed married women's property statutes, freeing married women from many of the legal effects of coverture.

While this first wave of marriage-law reform increased both the freedom to leave unsatisfactory marriages and equality between husbands and wives, dissatisfaction with marriage law remained. The grounds for divorce remained restrictive: thus, several states granted divorce only for adultery. And law still treated married men and women differently: for example, many states imposed alimony only on husbands, a stipulation that assumed, and perhaps helped to perpetuate, women's exclusion from the paid labor force. The age at which females could marry without their parents' consent was often younger than that for males, suggesting that boys needed to stay in school or learn a trade before marrying and that girls did not. Custody laws varied widely, but often contained a preference for mother's custody, again assuming that the mother was and would in the future be the better caregiver.

The Second Wave of Reform

In the mid-twentieth century a variety of factors (which I can only briefly allude to here) converged to spark a second wave of marriage-law reform. Demographic changes after 1900 were dramatic. Life expectancy for women was fifty-one years in 1900 and seventy-four in 1960; increased life expectancy meant that most parents had years together in an "empty nest" after their children had left home; at mid-century women began childbearing at a later age and bore fewer children than in 1900. In addition, economic changes in the decades following World War II led women, including married women and women with children, into the paid labor force in unprecedented numbers. This drew women out of the home for part of the day and gave them greater economic independence. The introduction of the birth control pill in the 1960s gave women more control over pregnancy, and the ability to plan the timing of their children encouraged women to work outside the home and to think of "careers" rather than temporary jobs.

These and related changes provoked a dramatic transformation of divorce law between 1965 and 1974. Herbert Jacob has called the adoption of no-fault divorce the "silent revolution": revolution because it involved a series of "radical changes in legal expectations about family life"; silent because the changes resulted from "routine" policy processes that never became the focus of media and public attention.

In the mid-1960s, lawyers in California began the push for no-fault divorce in large part to get rid of the subterfuge in many divorce proceedings that took place when couples tailored their stories to make them fit the legal requirements for divorce. Although California courts were lenient in granting divorce, in order to obtain a divorce a husband or wife had to prove that the other had committed an offense such as adultery, cruelty, willful neglect, habitual intemperance, or desertion. In most cases the wife was the plaintiff, and she usually charged her husband with "cruelty," which could range from disparaging remarks to physical violence. The charges were often fabricated and the testimony rehearsed, the couple having decided to end the marriage. The dishonesty, even perjury, that pervaded some divorce proceedings prompted activists to press the legislature to adopt a no-fault divorce law, which enabled a spouse to obtain a divorce without proving wrongdoing by the other.

No-fault divorce emerged prior to modern feminism, and its proponents did not aim to promote greater equality for women or greater choice among alternative family forms. Nor did they intend or anticipate the demographic watershed in US families that resulted from no-fault divorce. In the wake of no-fault legislation the divorce rate rose dramatically, from 2.2 per thousand population in 1960 to 4.8 per thousand population in 1975. And by the last quarter of the twentieth century only one-fourth of US households fit the supposed "norm" of a wage-earning husband and homemaker wife living with children.

Alongside its dramatic demographic consequences, no-fault divorce prompted a sea change in conventional understandings of marriage. The idea that marriage partners themselves could simply decide to end their marriage was revolutionary; it affected thinking about the very nature of marriage and its permanence. The observation by nineteenth-century legal historian Henry Maine that the movement of the law in the nineteenth century was "a movement from status to contract" was finally coming to be true of marriage.

Although no-fault divorce preceded the resurgence of feminism, the idea that individuals should be able to extricate themselves from unhappy marriages resonated with feminist ideas about women's liberty and equality—and later with the movement by gays and lesbians to end legal discrimination against homosexuals and the ban on same-sex marriage. The conjunction of no-fault divorce, renewed attention to equality, and gay liberation, as Nancy Cott observed, sparked proposals to "reinvent marriage" by "extend[ing] its founding principle of consent between the couple to all the terms of the relationship, allowing the contractual side of the hybrid institution to bloom." If personal choice suffices to end a marriage, why, the contractualist asks, shouldn't personal choice define the terms of marriage right from the outset?

A THIRD WAVE OF REFORM?

Marriage and Liberty

Liberty, the first foundational value of a liberal polity, is central to the question of who is allowed to marry. When the law stipulates who may and may not marry, it restricts the freedom of those excluded from marriage. Some exclusions are relatively uncontroversial, such as prohibiting marriage below a certain age, with a close relative, or while in prison (although each of these has been attacked as an unjustifiable limitation on individual freedom). Other restrictions are more contentious. Law precluded slaves from marrying. And only in 1967, in the case of *Loving v. Virginia*, did the Supreme Court decide that anti-miscegenation laws were unconstitutional.

Advocates of contract marriage favor legal recognition of same-sex marriage, a position consistent with their dedication to individual liberty. When marriage is a public status, they say, law inevitably draws a line separating those who may marry and those who may not. The repeated refusal by states to formalize unions of same-sex couples represents, according to the contractualists, a failure to take pluralism, privacy, and personal choice seriously. States, of course, may enforce agreements between marriage partners, just as states enforce other contracts; and they may prohibit marriages below a certain age, as they impose age restrictions on other contracts. But states may not legitimately decide who may marry whom or how spouses should order the personal and material aspects of their relationship.

I might be tempted to become a contractarian if contract marriage were the only way to achieve legal recognition for same-sex marriage, but—as current political initiatives at the state level underscore—it is not. Marriage for same-sex couples can be achieved by either legislation or court decisions that change the content of marriage law; it does not require us to replace a regime of marriage law with a regime of private contract. The fact that many municipalities have adopted "domestic partnerships" and that Vermont has recognized "civil unions" may be a harbinger of legislative victories to come. And courts may someday decide that there is a constitutionally protected right to marry that encompasses same-sex couples. The ground was laid in *Loving v. Virginia* when the Supreme Court declared "The freedom to marry has long been recognized as one of the vital personal rights essential to the orderly pursuit of happiness by free men. Marriage is one of the basic civil rights of man, fundamental to our very existence and survival." If marriage is a fundamental liberty protected by the 14th Amendment's due-process clause, then any restriction on marriage must be tailored to advance a compelling state interest. And while some religious views may condemn homosexual unions, no state interest rises to a sufficiently compelling level to justify prohibiting same-sex marriage.

The debate here is not for and against same-sex marriage, but between contractualists who would provide legal recognition of same-sex marriage by abolishing marriage law and those who would instead alter marriage law itself. Is there any reason to prefer the latter? I think there is.

The individualism and emphasis on rational bargaining that are at the heart of contracts rest on misleading models of the person and of the marriage relationship. Marriage partners are not only autonomous decision-makers; they are fundamentally social beings who will inevitably experience need, change, and dependency in the course of their lives. The prenuptial agreements that set forth how economic assets each partner brings to the marriage are to be held and distributed recognize the individuality of the partners, although they strike some people as unromantic. But the question of who should have a claim to property obtained by either spouse during the course of the marriage is more problematic, because when people marry they become part of an entity that is not always reducible to its individual components. Some states hold all such property to be held in common (community property), reflecting the notion that marriage creates a single entity and a shared fate (and hence shared resources) for marriage partners. Other states give title to the person who earned or otherwise obtained the property, but allow title to be overridden in the interests of a fair distribution at the time of divorce, reflecting a belief that marriage creates claims growing out of a shared life. The relational entity is also reflected in common language when spouses say they are doing something "for the sake of the marriage," such as choosing a place to live that would be neither partner's first choice if single. It is reflected in legal practice when one spouse is prohibited from testifying against the other in certain proceedings because the law wants to express the notion that the marriage relationship itself should be protected.

Married life is not only deeply relational, but it is also unpredictable. Not all of what spouses may properly expect of one another can be stipulated in advance. Contracts are useful devices for facilitating communication about each partner's expectations and aspirations. But contracts create obligations by volition and agreement; they do not account well for the obligations that may arise from unforeseen circumstances, including illness or disability of an aging parent, a spouse, or a child.

Finally, contract suggests that each marriage is a particular agreement between individuals, not a relationship in which the public has a legitimate interest. But the public does have an interest in the terms of marriage. It has, as the equal status view argues, an interest in promoting equality of husband and wife, both as spouses and as citizens, and in securing what Martha Nussbaum calls the social bases of liberty and self-respect for all family members. And it has an interest in sustaining marital and other family relationships in the face of poverty or illness.

One way to think about the differences in these two approaches is to consider whether polygamy should be legalized in the United States. As *Boston Globe* columnist Jeff Jacoby asks, "If the state has no right to deny a marriage license to would-be spouses of the same sex, on what reasonable grounds could it deny a marriage to would-be spouses ... who happen to number three or four instead of two?" Would a continuation of the ban on plural marriage simply shift the boundary between who's in and who's out?

For contractualists, the case for a right to plural marriage is straightforward: it expresses individuals' rights to form affective and sexual relationships free from state interference. Martha Fineman said in 2001 that "if no form of sexual affiliation is state preferred, subsidized, and protected, none could or should be prohibited. Same-sex partners and others forming a variety of other sexual arrangements would simply be viewed as equivalent forms of privately preferred sexual connection." The law would have to be gender-neutral, allowing marriages with plural husbands as well as plural wives. But as long as protections against coercion, fraud, and other abuses that invalidate any contract were enforced, people could choose multiple marriage partners.

Proponents of the equal status conception fall on both sides of the question. Laurence Tribe, supporting legal recognition of polygamy, asks rhetorically in *American Constitutional Law* whether the goal of preserving monogamous marriage is "sufficiently compelling, and the refusal to exempt Mormons sufficiently crucial to the goal's attainment, to warrant the resulting burden on religious conscience." Peggy Cooper Davis condemns in *Neglected Stories* the "cultural myopia" that led the Supreme Court to outlaw Mormon polygamy in *Reynolds v. United States* in 1879, and argues that a principled objection to polygamy in a multicultural society would require more than "a political majority's wish to define and freeze the moral character of the polity." But the flaws in the *Reynolds* decision do not mean polygamy should be legalized. Many people are convinced that polygamy is profoundly patriarchal. The "larger cultural context of female subordination" is too deeply rooted and strong even for gender-neutral principles that allow both women and men to have more than one spouse to overcome its effects. In this view, plural marriage reinforces female subordination and is unacceptable on grounds of equality.

The answer to the question, "If we legalize same-sex marriage, won't we have to legalize plural marriage?" is not, then, an obvious "yes." Equality as well as liberty is implicated in marriage law and policy. In assuming the equal agency of the parties to the contract, the contract model leaves aside the question of whether choices themselves may lead to subordination. In order to decide whether plural marriage should be legalized, one must address the question of whether polygamy can be reformed along egalitarian lines. Equality must be a central attribute of any marital regime based on considerations of justice.

Marriage and Equality

Most people today endorse "equality" as a general cultural value, but there is deep disagreement about what kind of *spousal* equality we want and how best to achieve it. Advocates of gay and lesbian marriage who are concerned principally with restrictive rules about who may marry whom typically do not engage this issue. But a vision of the proper relationship between spouses is central to the conservative project; a compelling alternative to it will require its own core vision.

Under nineteenth-century marriage law the fact that a wife's legal personality was subsumed in that of her husband, that she was not able to vote, and that she was excluded from many occupations was regarded by many not as inequality but as complementary difference. Today some traditionalists contend that although men and women, husbands and wives should enjoy equal rights both in marriage and as citizens, they have different roles to play in family and civil society. For example, Chad Brand explains the Southern Baptist Convention's position that "while the Bible teaches equality, it does not affirm egalitarianism or interchangeability in all things." He contends that "male-female equality and male headship may seem paradoxical, but they are both taught in Scripture, much like a thread of two strands." In a secular vein William Kristol asserts that women and men must be taught "to grasp the following three points: the necessity of marriage, the importance of good morals, and the necessity of inequality within marriage." Because the nation needs strong and even aggressive men to flourish, the price women pay for marriage and morals is submission to the husband as leader within the family.

Angered by the endorsement of male dominance in these views, advocates of contract marriage such as Martha Fineman argue that "abolishing marriage as a legal category is a step necessary for gender equality." Marriage by contract replaces the gender stereotyping and protectionism of traditional marriage law with the recognition of the individuality and equal agency of the partners. Marriage partners should be treated as rational actors capable of knowing and articulating their interests. Contract reflects autonomy and self-direction in general, and marriage partners are individuals who, according to the American Law Institute's *Principles of the Law of Family Dissolution,* need to "accommodate their particular needs and circumstances by contractually altering or confirming the legal rights and obligations that would otherwise arise."

Supporters of contract marriage are right to reject male dominance and state protectionism. But as Carole Pateman argued in *The Sexual Contract,* while contract may be the enemy of status, it alone is not adequate to defeat the legacy of patriarchy. The contract model is an insufficient foundation for spousal equality. Ensuring conditions of fair contracts is not in itself enough to establish this kind of equality in marriage and in civic life. Instead, marriage law and public policy must work to ensure that neither partner is precluded from participating in social and political life or rendered unable to provide care to family members. Vigorous state action is needed to promote spousal equality, and one important justification for such action is provided by vision of marriage as a relationship between equals that enriches both their individual and joint lives. While marriage and divorce laws themselves are now usually drafted in gender-neutral terms, cultural norms and employment practices perpetuate a division of labor at work and at home that results in a system of gender and racial hierarchy. So even if reforms are animated by concerns about joining domestic equality with special respect for marital bonds, those reforms will need to focus on the labor market as much as the domestic arena.

Most jobs, whether professional or nonprofessional, still assume the model of what Joan Williams in *Unbending Gender* calls the "ideal worker": a full-time, paid employee married to an at-home caregiver. Employment practices in the United States developed around the sexual division of labor. Jobs were designated "male" or "female," and men's jobs tended to pay higher wages than women's. Different pay scales applied to men and women doing the same work (men being presumed to be the family provider, women to be working for "pin money"). Health, unemployment, and other benefits were tied to full-time work. The workday and workweek were based on the assumption that someone else was cleaning, cooking, and caring for family members. The ideal worker model had enormous influence on both the economic resources and caregiving skills of men and women.

Although discrimination against women in the workplace has diminished, the ideal worker model continues to affect both decisions to marry and the dynamics within marriage. As Susan Okin argues in *Justice, Gender, and the Family*, the difference in wage earning capacity between men and women gives men more resources with which to deal with the world, and this in turn affects dynamics within the family. The disparity still remains despite a narrowing wage differential between men and women of all races: while women in 1979 earned 62.5 cents for every dollar men earned, in 1998 they earned 76 cents. Because uninterrupted time in the work force increases one's potential earning power, wives who stay out of the paid labor force for a number of years fall behind. This diminishes their decision-making authority within marriage and their options to leave an unsatisfactory union.

The arrangement of the workplace also affects decisions about caregiving, for children as well as elderly or sick relatives. Because benefits such as health insurance may depend on full-time work, and because the pay scale is often higher for full-time work, one partner may have to work full-time. Because many jobs are sex-segregated and wages for men's jobs are higher than those for women's, it will make economic sense in some families for the husband to work full-time and his wife to do the caregiving. The division between "workers" and "caregivers" not only harms women in the workplace but makes it less likely that men will develop interpersonal and caregiving skills.

In the Supreme Court's recent decision upholding the right of a man denied family leave to take care of his sick wife to sue the State of Nevada under the Family and Medical Leave Act, Justice Rehnquist noted the effects on both home and workplace of the assumption that women caregivers free men to be ideal workers.

> Because employers continued to regard the family as the women's domain, they often denied men similar accommodations or discouraged them from taking leave. These mutually reinforcing stereotypes created a self-fulfilling cycle of discrimination that forced women to continue to assume the role of primary caregiver, and fostered employers' stereotypical views about women's commitment to work and their value as employees. [*Nevada Department of Human Resources v. Hibbs*, No. 01-1368, decided May 27, 2003.]

Congress acted reasonably, Justice Rehnquist ruled, in mandating a family leave that would help to break these stereotypes about male and female social roles. The tight linkage between work and family is influenced not only by gender but also by race and class.

Racial prejudice meant that historically fewer Black than white families had an "ideal worker" and stay-at-home caregiver. The economic need created by racial discrimination meant that the labor force participation of married Black women was always higher than that of white women. Black men were relegated disproportionately to agricultural and other low-paid labor, Black women to domestic and other service jobs. Since the last decade of the twentieth century the high unemployment rate among Black males has had an additional impact on family life, as marriage rates have fallen: William Julius Wilson, Orlando Patterson, and others have argued that some people won't marry when they have no reasonable hope of being able to support a family.

As to social class, the increasing number of never-married mothers living in poverty led authors of the Welfare Reform Act of 1996 (the Personal Responsibility and Work Opportunity Act) to insert a provision requiring mothers who receive welfare to identify the biological fathers of their children. The state could then go after the father for child support, and if he did not provide enough money to lift mother and child out of poverty, the mother was required to work outside the home. Sponsors hoped that if the woman identified the father the state might induce them to marry. Even if they did not marry, the man and not the government would support the child. Many women eligible for welfare, however, did not want to identify the fathers of their children, some because they preferred to parent with someone else or alone, some because they feared abuse from the father, and some because they knew the father had no money (and often no job).

Marriage is not an effective anti-poverty program, nor is it appropriate to use it as such. Unemployment rates are high because the number of jobs that pay a living wage are far below the number of unemployed seeking work. The wages available to many men who can find work are inadequate to support a family, and adding a wife's wages is of little help unless affordable childcare is available. Addressing women's poverty by attaching them to men who can support them reproduces inequality and vulnerability within marriage. Inducing women to marry men may expose them and their children to domestic violence while failing to provide them with either the personal or community resources to extricate themselves from intolerable living conditions.

The understanding of marriage as a contract does not by itself generate the reforms necessary to alter family and workplace structures, welfare, and social services in ways necessary to give both men and women the opportunity to engage in both public and caregiving work. The next phase of the struggle to achieve sexual and spousal equality must entail a public commitment to liberty and equality and tackle not only marriage law but economic circumstances as well.

A number of reforms would move society toward greater justice in marriage. One such reform would be to ensure that people can find jobs that pay a living wage. There must be equal pay for equal work, whether performed by full- or part-time employees. Benefits must be extended to all workers, not just those who meet the ideal worker model (and basic health benefits should not be tied to employment status). Work must also be restructured in such a way that it accommodates caregiving, through a shorter workweek and more flexible scheduling, for example. If caregivers are not to be marginalized, quality, affordable childcare must be part of any comprehensive family policy, as must the kind of child allowance common in European countries. Paid parental leave for both men and women would create an incentive for men to participate in child care, particularly if a father could not transfer his leave time to someone else but had to use it or forego the benefit. In the event of divorce the wages of both a primary wage earner and a primary caregiver should be treated as joint property, reflecting the commonality of marriage, particularly if there are children or other dependents.

These measures certainly do not exhaust the possibilities. They make the point that in order to meet the principle of spousal equality men and women alike must be able to perform the tasks necessary to both the public and the private realm, to shoulder the responsibilities of workers outside the home as well as family caregivers.

PUBLIC STATUS OR INDIVIDUAL CONTRACT?

The contractual image has much to be said for it. It captures what Milton Regan Jr., in *Alone Together* calls the "external stance" toward marriage, which focuses on the ways in which marriage serves the interests of distinct individuals. Contract represents well the role that choice and negotiation play in any marriage. Drafting a marriage contract is a useful exercise for a couple because it encourages potential partners to asses their individual needs and sources of personal satisfaction, make their expectations explicit, and identify areas of both agreement and conflict. Legal notions of spousal unity and the sentimentalization of a woman's role as "the angel in the house" have often served to undercut married women's agency and autonomy. The external stance provides an important antidote.

Contract does less well in capturing what Regan calls the "internal stance" toward marriage, which regards it from within the relationship and focuses on shared experience rather than lives lived in parallel association. The internal stance reflects the fact that when people marry they become part of an entity that is not reducible to or identical with its individual components. Historically this concept of a marital entity distinct from either spouse was oppressive to women. The doctrine that husband and wife were "one" and formed a new "person" in the eyes of the law deprived married women of their independent right to hold property and enter into contracts in their own name until the latter half of the nineteenth century. Prior to the advent of no-fault divorce in the late 1960s a court had to find that one of the spouses had committed an offense "against the marriage" before granting a divorce. "Incompatibility" was not a valid ground for divorce even when both partners wanted to end their marriage. Even in our own day, police may ignore complaints of domestic violence because they do not want to "intrude" on the private realm of the married couple.

Despite this dismal history, the notion that marriage creates an entity that is not reducible to the individual spouses captures a truth about significant human relationships and could be used to reshape social and economic institutions in desirable ways. This understanding of the marriage relationship as something distinct from the individuals could be used in the future not to subordinate women but to press for marriage partners' rights to social and economic supports that sustain family relationships and enable spouses to provide care to one another. Such a right to provide care to and receive care from a spouse is not the same as an individual's right to health care or social services. Nor does public protection and support for associational and affective ties need to be limited to marriage partners and parents and children. Rather, recognition of the inevitability of dependency and the importance of caregiving should lead people to ask what other relationships deserve public support.

Marriage suggests, as contract does not, the role of committed relationships in shaping the self. The promise to love someone else, in a marriage or in a friendship or in a community, binds a person to act in ways that will fulfill that obligation. Contract also does not express the notion of unconditional commitment, both to the other person and to the relationship. Contract in lieu of marriage rests upon a notion of quid pro quo, in which each party offers something and agrees on the terms of any exchange as a rational bargainer. But the marriage commitment is unpredictable and open-ended, and the obligations it gives rise to cannot be fully stated in advance. What love attuned to the well-being of another may require is by its nature unpredictable.

With so much of our public discourse reducing individuals primarily to consumers in the market, it is especially important to insist on the social and relational sides of our lives. The contractual model for marriage that presents marriage, as Hendrik Hartog says in *Man and Wife in America*, as "nothing more than a private choice and as a collection of private practices" is insufficient to the tasks of reconfiguring marriage. Marriage entails respect for individuals and for their relationships. It is a particularly striking instance of a practice founded on both individuality and "a shared purpose that transcends the self" (Regan). If such a commitment is a valuable aspiration and one that our political community wants to facilitate, then we need to examine and remove impediments to such relationships. Those impediments are legion, especially among the poor. Removing them thus confronts us with a formidable agenda—reforms of the workplace, of welfare, and of caregiving. But with notions of the public good and collective responsibility under constant assault, withdrawing the state from the pursuit of justice in marriage and family moves in the wrong direction. We need to insist instead that marriage and family law can and must be made to conform to the principles of justice that affirm the equality and equal liberty of all citizens.

11

The Liberal Case for Disestablishing Marriage

Tamara Metz

INTRODUCTION

What role should the liberal state have in recognizing and regulating marriage as such? Until recently this question received surprisingly little attention among liberal political theorists. Yet with its numerous public-private border crossings marriage challenges and unsettles one of liberalism's most cherished methods for protecting liberty, equality, and fairness. Hence, the question of how, if at all, the state—the most public of forces—should engage with this most insubordinate of institutions is elemental. Tensions in contemporary debates suggest that these challenges remain unaddressed and thus, invite attempts to formulate a coherent and compelling model of the relationship between marriage and the liberal state. This article offers a partial response to this invitation.

Marriage—though not the question I pose—has long been a concern of liberal thinkers. From John Locke to Susan Moller Okin, the conjugal institution has received steady, if under appreciated, attention in the liberal canon. Typically this attention focused on the dual (contract/status) character of marriage, or more recently, on its role in (re)producing gender inequality. Especially those thinkers concerned with gender have exposed the ideological character, and often obfuscating and oppressive effects of the "public/private divide." While both concerns and the critical insights they bear out are essential to any adequate account of marriage and the state, they do not account for all that must be covered. If we wish to grasp the sources of confusion and silences in contemporary debates, and formulate a robust liberal model of marriage and the state, we must examine the functions—intended and effective—of public recognition of marriage.

In light of such an examination, the relevance to the marriage-state relationship of familiar liberal approaches to negotiating the religion-state relationship becomes apparent. Drawing on these approaches and liberal feminist thought, I sketch a model of marriage and the state that aims to expand the area of protected freedom without sacrificing equality, fairness, or marriage. I argue that the optimal balance of these liberal commitments would obtain were marriage to be disestablished. No longer would the state confer marital status, or use "marriage" as a category for dispersing benefits. Legitimate public welfare goals traditionally treated through marriage—guarding privacy, protecting the vulnerable, supporting intimate caregiving, and securing property—would be addressed through an intimate caregiving union (ICGU) status. [....]

ESTABLISHMENT OF MARRIAGE

To argue that marriage should be disestablished is to imply that marriage is established. Although in this article I refer primarily to the United States, this description aptly applies to other liberal democracies. The American arrangement, for instance, has deep roots in British political history—where church and state courts jointly governed marriage since the earliest stirrings of the liberal state in the late seventeenth century until well into the nineteenth century. While neither synonymous with nor a direct effect of the establishment of religion, the establishment of marriage is historically correlated with and conceptually akin to the former. I use the term to refer to a historically specific arrangement where the state actively controls, privileges, and utilizes a particular account of marriage to regulate the intimate and caregiving lives of its citizens.

To say that marriage is established is to imply that citizens hold deeply divergent views of what marriage is and how intimate life ought to be arranged. Debates concerning same-sex marriage, high divorce rates, and divergent views on infidelity, polygamy, and the proper roles of husband and wife, evince profound disagreement about what marriage is. Flourishing diversity of family forms highlights the lack of consensus—in theory and practice—regarding intimate caregiving life. In this context, to define and promote "marriage" is to privilege one version of the institution over all others and, crucially, over all other kinds of intimate caregiving arrangements. In the United States, as in most other polities, the current variety of choice is the declaredly monogamous, heterosexual, ideally childbearing, and life-long union.

The state establishes its preferred version of marriage by providing exclusive material, legal, and expressive benefits to those who (may) opt for marital status, and by punishing those who violate the norms embodied in the status. Benefits are, by now, well-rehearsed. Punishments for non-conformity may seem less obvious. But current and historical examples abound: criminalization and prosecution of polygamous and interracial marriage, non-recognition of marriage between slaves and individuals of the same sex. The establishment of marriage is also facilitated by the state's jealously defended, final control of the public definition and conferral of "marriage"—against religious, cultural, and individual authority. A striking example of how vigorously the state guards this control is the recent prosecution of Mormon polygamist Tom Green. Although he and his many wives claimed to be married under religious but not legal authority, Green received a five-year prison term for his hubris. So vital is final control of the label that even non-legal use of the marital appellation, it appears, is unacceptable (*Utah v. Green* 2001).

The language of establishment and religion-state relations draws attention to how, through its control of marital status, the state plays a pivotal role in an institution, a unique, unavoidable—if often underplayed or ignored— purpose of which, I shall argue, is to inculcate a comprehensive account of intimate life and its place within the community into its citizens. The force of this aspect of the analogy becomes clearer as we address prominent tensions and awkward silences in contemporary debates. [....]

THE EXTRA VALUE OF "MARRIAGE" AND THE AMBIVALENCE IT ENGENDERS

The case for disestablishing marriage begins with tensions, confusions, and silences lurking in the shadows of contemporary debates. Consider two recent court cases, *Baker v. State of Vermont* (1999) and *Goodridge v. Dept. of Public Health* (2003). In both, the courts ruled that same-sex couples could not be justly excluded from the civil benefits of marital status. The Vermont case produced civil union status, while the Massachusetts court held that marital status had to be expanded to include same-sex couples. Lost in the hubbub caused by the bold steps taken by these courts is a peculiar ambivalence concerning the value of what one prominent participant called "the 'm' word."

At first glance, Baker portrays the goods at stake in the battle over legal recognition of same-sex marriage as the myriad concrete legal and material benefits and burdens attached to marital status. On this logic the court could suggest that marital status and civil union status are essentially the same—the sum of the delineable benefits attached to the status. Put another way, this position assumes that "marriage" is simply what I call an instrumental status, that is, one that conveys concrete, delineable goods (material or legal) and, at most, a generic, coincidental kind of public sanction that would attach to any benefits-bearing legal status. At least when "marriage" is defined and conferred by the state, the appellation carries no unique expressive value. Or so the court assumed. For only by assuming that marriage is an instrumental status could the court equate marital and civil union status.

This account of state-conferred marital status has a long history in liberal political thought. From John Locke to John Stuart Mill and contemporary scholars, liberal thinkers have tended to focus on the material side of marriage and the instrumental purpose of marital status—at least when considering the state's role therein. The focus makes sense because it allows marriage to fit easily into a liberal tradition that depicts the state as properly limited to matters of material concern, of action and behavior, not belief and meaning.

But, to return to Baker, if marital status and civil union status are the same, why create civil union status at all? Why not bestow marital status on all? Or, conversely, why not civil union for all? If the value of legally defined and conferred marital status is the sum of a delineable set of benefits and burdens, then why not avoid the perils of negotiating competing definitions of "marriage" and simply use "civil union" to convey these goods?

Here the subterranean incoherence in the marriage debates becomes evident. The court's explicit reasoning cannot explain the reservation of the marital label. The immediate answer seems obvious: it was a prudent political move. The court and legislature knew that a majority of Vermonters would find legal recognition of same-sex marriage unacceptable. And so, to soften the blow, they called the same-benefits-bestowing status by another name. But the fact that Vermonters might care about the name, and the court's resulting equivocation reflects a deeper, unspoken logic. The reservation suggests that "marriage" adds something extra to the instrumental status—something that the court seems to want to both deny and protect.

What is the extra value of marital status that caused the court's reluctance to embrace it fully? The Baker court gave only hints of the source of its ambivalence. The court's emphasis on the instrumental purposes of state control of marital status suggests that its reluctance had something to do with seeing state control of this extra value as incompatible with traditional liberal views of the proper role of the state.

The Massachusetts court took a different tack in dealing with the political and principled challenges posed by same-sex marriage. In *Goodridge v. Dept. of Public Health*, the court ruled that the state's exclusion of same-sex couples from the legal status of marriage—not just the concrete benefits attached to it—was unconstitutional.

To many, the Goodridge decision corrected the contradictions of the earlier Baker decision by acknowledging that "marriage" is more than an instrumental status: "Marriage ... bestows enormous private and social advantages on those who choose to marry. Civil marriage is at once a deeply personal commitment to another human being and a highly public celebration of the ideals of mutuality, companionship, intimacy, fidelity, and family." Marital status is a unique kind of expressive good, the value of which exceeds the sum of the delineable benefits and burdens that attach to it. Thus, to withhold it from same-sex couples would be to treat them unequally. In contradistinction to the Baker court, the Goodridge court openly embraced marital status as both an instrumental and, without fully explaining or defending it, as a constitutive status.

One might think that in acknowledging that "marriage" carries expressive cachet the Goodridge court answered the question raised by Baker: What is the extra value attached to marital status and why should the state be wary of it? Unfortunately, the court did little more than assert the importance of this extra value. The Massachusetts court did not explain or defend fully the content of the ideals of marriage, or how these ideals affect the desired outcome. The court failed to explain how state control of the status is essential to its extra value or why this special status is essential for the state to achieve its goals. Nor did the court defend the state's capacity to effectively produce and trade in this extra-value status, or the legitimacy of its doing so. In other words, despite the fact that dissenting Justice Sosman explicitly raised the possibility, the court never explained why the state should not replace marital status with a universal civil union status. But the position that the state properly and necessarily defines and confers marital status is one that must be defended. Stowed away in the inarticulate confusion of contemporary debates are questions about marriage, the functions of public definition and conferral of marital status, and the role of the state therein that remain unanswered at the potential peril of basic commitments to freedom, equality, and fairness.

The tensions and awkward silences in these two cases reflect a long history of the unacknowledged and unresolved challenges posed by marriage to liberal theory and practice. The challenge is this: In liberal polities marriage has long been a vital social institution firmly grounded in both sides of the public/political–private/non-political divide; marriage is both a religious and a civic institution, it involves material and expressive goods, influences behavior and belief, and is quintessentially familial and political, personal, and communal. How, if at all, can the liberal state support and rely on marriage without violating commitments to freedom, equality, and fairness?

To answer this question we must address questions raised but often ignored in contemporary debates. First, we must elaborate the extra value attached to marital status. What makes marital status different from civil union status? What are its products and how does it produce them? What does this extra-value status assume of those who receive it and those who bestow it?

Second, in light of answers to these questions, we must consider whether the liberal state should deal in the currency of this extra value. Should the state be in the business of defining and conferring any constitutive status and marital status in particular? What are the legitimate aims of the liberal state with regard to intimate caregiving life? Must the state control marital status in order for marriage to flourish or for the state to secure its legitimate public policy goals?

To address the first set of questions, I begin with G. W. F. Hegel. For the second set, I draw on liberal traditions governing religion-state relations and attempt to sketch a model of marriage and the state that is true to the values of liberty, equality, and fairness, and to the very public nature and importance of marriage.

THE EXTRA VALUE OF MARITAL STATUS: ITS CONSTITUTIVE POTENTIAL

What is the extra value attached to marriage? Answering this question requires thinking about the meaning side of marriage—that is, the social, psychological, and moral meaning that the institution and the status do, or are intended to, represent, inculcate and reproduce in individuals and communities. Liberal thinkers, canonical and contemporary, have tended not to consider the meaning side of marriage. Thus, I turn outside of the liberal tradition to Hegel. Hegel placed the social-psychological influence of social and political institutions at the center of his political philosophy. Thus, unlike many liberal thinkers, he placed the meaning side of marriage at the heart of his analysis of the institution and its place in political life. His descriptions of marriage and the functions of public recognition of the conjugal union thus help elaborate the logic implicit in the contemporary view of marriage as a constitutive institution.

To avoid confusion: I use Hegel's account of marriage for very limited purposes, more for suggestive insights about the unique social-psychological dynamics at play in the public control and exchange of marital status than for an argument about what the relationship between marriage and the state is or ought to be. Hegel's full account of marriage contains elements that liberals rightly reject, including his views about women and, crucially for our purposes, his idea that the state must control marital status in order for its extra value to be realized. We can and should reject both of these elements of Hegel's account and still gain useful lessons from his description of the functions of public definition and conferral of marital status. In fact, my point is precisely this: his account helps us identify and better understand illiberal moments in contemporary marriage law of polities like the United States.

The marriage contract, Hegel argues, is different from other kinds of contracts. Its unique purpose is to facilitate the transcendence of its contractual starting points. Marriage starts as a legalistic agreement between two distinct individuals. Its ultimate purpose, however, is realized when these two individuals no longer see themselves in that light, as two separate parties to a contract, but rather as partners in something bigger than themselves—individually and as a couple. The initial legalism of contract is transcended when the individuals to the marriage contract understand themselves as a unit, deeply intertwined with each other and with the community that confers marital status.

The public—and for Hegel, the legal—definition, conferral, and acceptance of marital status play integral parts in affecting this transformation. He argues that when the state confers marital status, it is not—as the instrumental view suggests—merely tagging individuals as appropriate recipients of legal recognition, and material support. Rather, it is conveying, and is understood to be conveying, its weighty moral approval and a complex story about the meaning of marriage. The bestowal and acceptance is a communally understood performance intended to alter how all involved see themselves.

Hegel insists on state control of marital status for reasons of both cause and effect. Receiving marital status from the state causes citizens to experience and understand the state as the source of and guide to their true freedom. At the same time, because citizens experience the state in this manner, the public conferral and acceptance of marital status effectively alters their self-conception vis-à-vis their conjugal partner and the state. Leaving aside the complexities, or some would say incoherence, of Hegel's apparently tautological reasoning, the useful point for our purposes is this: to transform self-understandings marital status must be bestowed by what he calls an ethical authority, that is, a representative of the conferring community whose commands are experienced by individuals in the community as freedom-guiding, not freedom-limiting.

Traditionally, liberals have treated the commands of the state as limiting action (not belief) for the narrow purposes of insuring social order, protecting citizens from harm, and guaranteeing political fairness. Generally, the state confers legal status for instrumental convenience, not to alter self-understanding in any deep and enduring way. Hence, we call this instrumental status. The familiar idea behind the limited state is that freedom consists, in large part, in individuals being free from interference to live according to their own design. In contrast, on Hegel's account, the state's commands are, or ought to be, experienced as freedom-guiding in the sense that the citizen understands, and accepts that the commands guide her to some freedom or good beyond that which she, herself, may currently perceive. For an authority's commands to be experienced as freedom-guiding, then, the commanded individual must believe that the authority possesses special insight into her true good and that the authority can be trusted to guide her in that direction. The power of ethical authority rests on the belief, shared by commander and commanded, in the ethical nature of their relationship. In the case of marital status, effective ethical authority assumes shared understandings about the nature of the relationships (between the parties to marriage and between the couple and

conferring community) it labels, about the purposes of the status, and, crucially, about the appropriateness of that authority's commands in matters of
the most intimate nature. Recognition intended to alter self-understanding in
this way, we may call constitutive recognition and the related status, constitutive status. [....]

While Hegel's description of the state's commands as freedom-guiding,
and the relationship between citizen and state it assumes, contrast with the
liberal picture of the state, his more general claims about the functions of
public recognition of marriage are familiar. Something like this is what many
understand to be happening when a couple stands in front of their community—whether a collection of hippies in a northern California redwood
grove, or a traditional congregation in a Catholic church—and accepts the
marital status bestowed by that community. The community's conferral and
the couple's acceptance of marital status are understood as intentionally,
mutually constitutive acts.

I propose that this—the expansively transformative potential of marital
status—is what distinguishes "marriage" from "civil union." The extra value
attached to the marital title is the community's constitutive recognition, the
weighty moral approval and the complex normative account of the relationship it names and that is intended to reconstitute the most intimate aspects
of self-understanding. The transformative power of mutual recognition and
obligation between couple and community is the special value widely but often
inarticulately attributed to marriage that feeds the ferocity of contemporary
debates.

We can now see why it is especially appropriate to speak of marriage
as established. Just as the "establishment of religion" refers to the state's
involvement in defining, inculcating, and reproducing a particular religious
worldview and institution, so the "establishment of marriage" highlights
the state's integral role in reproducing and relying on belief in a particular,
comprehensive account and institutional form of intimate life and its tie to
the community.

The comparison to religion suggests causes of the prevalent silences and
ambivalences with regard to state control of marital status in liberal theory
and practice. Hegel describes the promise of freedom as bound up in the state
functioning as an ethical authority. In contrast, liberal freedom is assured when
the state functions as a limited authority, protecting citizens from each other,
protecting the vulnerable from harm, and supporting only those institutions,
norms, and actions essential to a functioning liberal democracy. It is no wonder
then that liberals have both embraced and rejected state control of marital
status: at least since the rise of liberal political theory in the late seventeenth
century, marriage has served as a, if not the, primary institutional home for
many of any society's most important social relationships and distributive
mechanisms. In addition, it advertises unparalleled potential to integrate public

and private, individual and community. Yet this potential appears to depend on qualities that the liberal state does not and ought not reliably possess. So: If marriage requires constitutive recognition from an ethical authority, yet the liberal democratic state cannot (and should not try to) effectively provide such recognition, what is to be done? Must we choose between a healthy marital institution and liberal commitments and institutional arrangements? My answer is no.

THE CASE FOR DISESTABLISHING MARRIAGE

The suggestion implicit in the comparison to religion—that there may be good reason for the state to withdraw from its pivotal role in controlling marital status—is compelling. Marriage should be disestablished. We can and should distinguish between instrumental and constitutive statuses. We can and should distinguish between the marriage and the actions, intimate associations, and caregiving often, though not always, housed within its ideational folds. The state can achieve its legitimate public welfare goals—in this case, of protecting intimate association and caregiving—without defining and conferring marital status. In a diverse, liberal democratic polity, freedom, equality, fairness, and marriage itself would be better served were marriage disestablished and an ICGU created.

Freedom and Marriage

Disestablishing marriage would be a boon for both liberty and marriage. On the most basic level, releasing "marriage" from the hands of government would protect a unique kind of expression. Unlike under the current regime where citizens can be prosecuted for unsanctioned use of the marital title—as was polygamist Tom Green—under the proposed regime, citizens who wished to call themselves married could do so without fear of state punishment (*Utah v. Green* 2001). As with baptismal status, nongovernmental authorities would confer the label. While it would carry no legal weight, marriage would still carry its constitutive potential. Call this the freedom of marital expression.

This may seem a trivial freedom, or worse, a trivializing freedom. Leaving the conjugal appellation to the whims of individual choice, one might argue, would effectively undercut its constitutive and transformative power for all by undermining its necessarily communal foundation. While understandable in the context where "public" and "state" are often conflated, this concern is misguided. If I am right about the extra value of marital status, then state control is not essential to its realization. In fact, it is reasonable to conjecture that the unique expressive value of the status and therefore marriage would benefit were the state to relinquish control over the institution. Like its religious kin, ethical authority depends on being chosen in one sense—i.e., not forced—but also not chosen, in the sense of simply being experienced as ethical authority by its adherents. Thus, the constitutive potential of marital status is more likely to be realized or felt when the conferring authority is chosen/not chosen in this sense. Such an authority might, for some people, be a religious leader. For others an ethical authority might be the head of a cultural group, or the esteemed representative of one's family. The key to effective ethical authority in marriage is that the conferrer and recipients share the understanding that the conferrer possesses the authority to bestow and wield the resulting responsibility that their shared vision of marriage entails. Non-state entities—associations of civil society—represent just such potential authorities. So, by releasing "marriage" from state control into the arms of these entities, the non-establishment of marriage places control of a constitutive status into the hands of those best suited for wielding it effectively. In addition, under the proposed regime, acquiring marital status would be the ticket to one thing—the constitutive recognition of a community of shared understandings—and not to a vast array of legal and material benefits. Changing the benefits would change the motivations for seeking the status. As many same-sex couples do already, couples would acquire marital status when they wanted meaningful recognition from a community that held ethical sway in their lives. Moreover, shifting control of marital status to voluntary groups in civil society would increase the likelihood that marital status be assumed in the context of a community of shared understandings about marriage. This improved fit between the couple's understanding of marriage and that of their conferring community could also bolster the force of the special value of marital status. By changing incentives for acquiring marital status, increasing the fit between conferring community and recipients, and invigorating cultural authorities and their diverse—and, admittedly, not always liberal, a point to which I return shortly—accounts of marriage, the proposed regime would benefit marriage by invigorating the constitutive force of the status.

Disestablishing marriage would guard freedom in another way: it would protect particularly vulnerable individuals from unnecessary state coercion, exclusion, and undue punishment. Just as the non-establishment of religion ensures that a citizen's right to vote cannot depend on her religious affiliation, so too the disestablishment of marriage would guarantee that government-provided benefits for intimate caregiving would not hinge on an individual's public acceptance of a particular vision of marriage. Martha Fineman persuasively shows that when the state uses marital status as the primary avenue through which to support caregiving, it significantly disadvantages many actual caregivers. Social welfare policies aimed at discouraging unwed, single-motherhood are powerful examples of this dynamic. Not only do such policies perpetuate the view that single motherhood is bad in itself and the cause of a great many social evils, but they actually make it more difficult to be a successful single mother. By disentangling marriage from state support of intimate caregiving, the state would no longer unduly burden caregivers who chose not to clothe their relationships in the thick, normative dressing of marriage.

Freedom of intimate association would also benefit under the proposed regime. In the American constitutional tradition, for instance, marriage has long served to justify protection of this freedom (*Griswold v. Connecticut* 1965; *Loving v. Virginia* 1967; *Zablocki v. Redhail* 1978; *Bowers v. Hardwick* 1986). And yet, as Drucilla Cornell persuasively argues, the marital origins of this protection obscure the wider ethical and political importance of a protected imaginary domain. Doing away with the marital category would be one crucial step in dislodging marriage from its seat as the reigning proxy for relationships that need and deserve such protection. The move would help highlight the fact that all human beings, married or not, heterosexual, homosexual, single, paired, sexual, or celibate, need a space within which to imagine and enact their "sexuate" lives.

Care, Equality, and the Case for ICGU

Disestablishing marriage might well bolster the meaning side of the institution, and protect important kinds of expression and association, but what about equality and fairness—especially with regard to the material side of marriage, and the legitimate public welfare concerns that the state currently addresses through marriage? Does liberal commitment to liberty outweigh those to equality and fairness?

Equality, fairness, and protecting the vulnerable are no less important than liberty. Further, any account of marriage and the state that ignores the historical connections among marriage, intimate caregiving, and inequality (gender, sexual, and familial) would be inadequate. Fortunately, disestablishing marriage and creating an ICGU status would do better by these commitments than do legal regimes common in contemporary liberal democracies. Leaving the definition and conferral of marital status to civil society is no different from leaving the control of baptismal status to civil society. In neither case do we assume that the state thereby withdraws from its role in protecting the vulnerable and promoting equality. What we do assume is that the best way to balance liberty, equality, and fairness in a diverse society is for the state to be concerned primarily with regulating action, not expression or thought, and then only to the extent necessary to protect other citizens from harm, or to guarantee a reasonably fair distribution of the benefits and burdens of social cooperation. We can and should distinguish between the meaning side of marriage—the normative accounts expressed by "marriage" that infuse the institution with particular meaning—and the material side of marriage—the associated goods and relationships: divisible goods (money, property), practices (labor distribution), and all forms of intimate caregiving.

Fairness (or justice), equality, and prudence recommend state involvement with elements of the material side of marriage, and intimate caregiving relationships more generally. Justice, because care is essential, always already given, and risky. Equality, because intimate caregiving has long been the site and source of significant but remediable social and political inequalities. Prudence, because in our society care is most often and most effectively given and received in intimate caregiving relationships. [....]

In short, care is essential for the survival and flourishing of both individuals and society. But giving care, especially intimate care, in a market-based economy is risky. To ensure that intimate care is given—at all, and well—and that its benefits and burdens are distributed fairly, the state rightly protects intimate caregiving.

When the distraction of marriage is removed, it becomes clear that the real challenge with state involvement in intimate affiliations is how to balance liberty—and especially privacy of intimate association—against equality and just caregiving arrangements. How do we protect freedom of thought, expression, and action (in intimate association) and, at the same time, ensure that the burdens and benefits of caregiving are realized and distributed fairly? I propose that an intimate caregiving union status (ICGU) best balances these demands. It does so by limiting the object and intent of state action to the material and instrumental. The distinctions between material and meaning sides of marriage, and instrumental and constitutive status may be imperfect. But they are recognizable. These distinctions make civil union acceptable to many who are unwilling to conscience same-sex marriage. They underpin some in the gay community's tepid acceptance of civil union. The difference may be matters of intent and degree, but for reasons I hope I have made clear these matters do and should matter.

In many ways, an ICGU status would look a lot like marital status today. It would afford legal recognition from which would flow various legal presumptions (i.e., lines of rights and responsibility), protection (i.e., from certain types of intrusion), and material benefits (i.e., tax benefits, etc.). As with marital status now, an ICGU status would be defined, conferred, and, if necessary, dissolved by the state. Unlike marriage, however, ICGU would be expressly tailored to protecting intimate care in its various forms. So, for example, the status would reflect assumptions of longevity and resource sharing. Also, to protect the norms of unmonitored reciprocity and to protect caregivers, at dissolution property would be divided to achieve substantive post-dissolution equality. Crucially, ICGU status would be designed with instrumental not constitutive purposes in mind. Any special expressive significance attached to ICGU status would be incidental (as opposed to the intentionally mind-altering significance of a constitutive status).

Disestablishing marriage and creating an ICGU status would better serve equality, fairness, and care than do legal regimes currently in place in most liberal democracies. First, this change would shift the focus of public discussion from interminable disagreement about the definition of marriage to questions about the importance, nature, and distribution of intimate care. Exposing the real costs and benefits of caregiving would increase the chances that they would be distributed fairly and that actual caregivers would be supported adequately. Defining caregiving would undoubtedly evoke controversy. But controversy is inevitable and is far better than obfuscating silence. In addition, a civil status expressly tailored to protecting intimate caregiving would be more appropriately crafted and accurate in its target. Therefore, it would be more effective than "marriage" as a tool for realizing the legitimate public welfare goals of supporting intimate caregiving broadly defined (and therefore the material side of marriage as well). Similarly, the proposed changes would make it easier for the state to simultaneously meet its legitimate public welfare goals and realize the aspiration to treat citizens equally. Replacing the imprecise and distracting prism of marriage as the primary means for supporting intimate caregiving with a narrowly focused instrumental status would increase the chances that all actual caregivers would be served equally by the law. Such a status would be less likely to exclude and punish actual caregivers and therefore, actual caregivers would be equally served.

The proposed changes would benefit gender equality. By bringing the reality of caregiving to the fore of public discussion, disestablishing marriage would shine light on the derivative vulnerabilities and gender inequalities often created by current intimate caregiving arrangements. No longer hidden behind the veil of marriage, questions of how the unpaid elements of intimate caregiving are distributed, at what cost and benefits, and to whom, would move inexorably to the center of public discourse, and thus, increase the chances that the costs and benefits would be distributed fairly.

THREE OBJECTIONS

My proposal is likely to elicit three important objections. The first objection concerns equality: If marriage is left to associations of civil society, do we not run the risk of pushing further from public scrutiny the inequality and oppression often shrouded behind the conjugal veil? For instance, would not disestablishing marriage effectively allow polygamy and therefore promote gender inequality?

This worry invites three responses. First, yes: were marriage disestablished, some groups would openly sanction polygamous marriage and undoubtedly gender inequality would flourish in many of these unions. Even more: if these groups both fit and chose to assume the socially determined but functionally defined prerequisites of an ICGU status, they would gain support and protection from the state. Crucially, however, they would receive support by virtue of their willingness to enter into the civil status, with its protection and responsibilities for caregiving activities, not by virtue of being married. In this sense, my proposal promotes gender inequality no more than do current regimes that permit but do not—ostensibly—promote traditional (gendered) marriage. Second, gender equality would benefit under the proposed regime because the increased recognition of and support for caregiving would ensure that even women who opted for polygamous or, less radically, traditional gendered marriages would be less vulnerable as a result of gendered division of power and labor within their families. Still, the critic might say, by increasing the power of potentially illiberal communities the proposal promises to increase their sway over the way people think and therefore, behave, and even on your own account, this is no small power. To this, I offer my third response: we must balance liberty and equality. Even with this very real danger, I believe that the proposed model does a better job balancing these two commitments. It increases liberty by limiting the objects and intent of state action (along lines that have deep roots in liberal theory and practice) without relinquishing influence over the most significant sources of inequality.

The second objection accepts that marriage is a constitutive status, that it conveys a comprehensive normative account of the relationships it labels, and that its function is to alter behavior and belief. Self-identified liberal advocates of this position think, however, that the state should be in the business of defining, conferring, and privileging this status because, they believe, it is a uniquely effective mechanism for supporting families. They admit that such an approach puts the state in the role of robust ethical authority, but are untroubled by this fact. After all, they would say, even an ICGU status casts the state in the role of ethical authority. These scholars tend to be untroubled by the exclusions caused by using marriage to convey social support for intimate caregiving. Against what they see as an "anything goes" policy, they advocate one that promotes caregiving in a particular form.

My proposal is neither an "anything goes" policy, nor is it grounded on libertarian intuitions. Both marriage and ICGU status reflect value judgments. In defining and conferring either status the state is acting in a way that reflects particular political commitments. This is true, and it is good. As I argue, there are compelling reasons for the state to recognize, protect, and support intimate caregiving. The case against state control of marriage is not that it reflects a substantive commitment, but rather that it entangles the state in an institution, the unique and perhaps primary purpose of which is to alter self-understanding in ways that go beyond what is necessary to the legitimate public welfare concerns of the state. State actions that reflect political commitments are not the problem; casting the state in the role of robust ethical authority is. Instrumental and constitutive statuses differ on precisely this count. I agree that "marriage" matters: it carries a unique value, beyond the material and legal benefits that attach to it, even beyond the generic expressive goods that come with any legally privileged position. To ignore this extra value is naïve and detrimental for marriage, equality, liberty, and fairness. But marriage is not the only or even the best means by which stable caregiving relationships can be understood and protected. It is, for the potential benefits to those who are moved by marriage, an institution that should be afforded public support and protection. From civil society it can receive its constitutive recognition. From the state marriage, and all other caregiving relationships can and should receive instrumental support. If state-controlled marital status were the only way for the state to recognize and support intimate caregiving, this objection would be more compelling. However, I have shown that this is not the case. On the contrary, we have good reason to believe that disestablishing marriage and creating an ICGU status would bolster both marriage and intimate caregiving.

The third objection claims the opposite of the second: "marriage" can function as an instrumental status and therefore the state is justified in using it to promote legitimate public welfare ends. As far as the state is concerned, this position implies, "marriage" is simply shorthand for "those who commit to caring for each other and for their offspring." Whether individuals attach more normative significance to the title is irrelevant as far as the state is concerned. The conferring power neither assumes ethical authority, nor aims to reconstitute the self-understandings of those labeled. Given its historical effectiveness and current popularity, this objection holds, the state should continue to support and use marriage, albeit in ways that bolster gender equality and incorporate same-sex couples.

In essence, this is the position with which we started in Baker and Goodridge. But, as I argue, the awkward silences of these cases both highlight and obscure the fact that "marriage" is loaded with a unique kind of meaning. Even if the explicit purposes of state control of marital status are instrumental, the history of marriage in Western societies means that the status is imbued, unavoidably, with a constitutive purpose. Politicians say, "civil union, yes; same-sex marriage, no," because "marriage" carries unique social meaning. Why use a label so obviously laden with diverse, incommensurable, and deeply normative meanings if it is meant to serve only as a convenient proxy for a set of instrumental rights, benefits, and obligations? If the state's reasons for controlling marital status are instrumental, then a label that more directly identifies these commands and expectations is appropriate. To use the appellation "marriage" is to imply more than a straightforward set of legal and material benefits. An ICGU status has the advantages of status without the problems of constitutive status and without leaving adult intimate caregiving affiliations to the drawbacks of contract.

Suggested Further Readings for Part IV

David Blankenhorn, *The Future of Marriage* (New York: Encounter Books, 2007).

Elizabeth Brake, *Minimizing Marriage* (Oxford: Oxford University Press, 2012).

Claudia Card, "Against Marriage and Motherhood," *Hypatia* 11, no. 3 (Summer 1996): 1–23.

John Corvino and Maggie Gallagher, *Debating Same-Sex Marriage* (Oxford: Oxford University Press, 2012).

Lisa Duggan, "Queering the State," *Social Text* 39 (Summer 1994): 1–14.

Maxine Eichner, *The Supportive State: Families, Government, and America's Political Ideals* (Oxford: Oxford University Press, 2010).

Elizabeth F. Emens, "Monogamy's Law: Compulsory Monogamy and Polyamorous Existence," *New York University Review of Law and Social Change* 29 (2004): 277–376.

Martha Fineman, *The Neutered Mother, the Sexual Family and Other Twentieth Century Tragedies* (New York: Routledge, 1995).

Martha Fineman, *The Autonomy Myth: A Theory of Dependency* (New York: The Free Press, 2004).

Robert George and Jean Bethke Elshtain, eds., *The Meaning of Marriage* (Dallas, TX: Spence, 2006).

Tiffany R. Jones and Larry Peterman, "Whither the Family and Family Privacy," *Texas Review of Law and Politics* 4 (1999): 193–236.

Stephen Macedo and Iris Marion Young, eds., *Child, Family, and the State: NOMOS XLIV*, (New York: New York University Press, 2003).

Tamara Metz, *Untying the Knot: Marriage, the State, and the Case for Their Divorce* (Princeton, NJ: Princeton University Press, 2010).

Jonathan Rauch, *Gay Marriage: Why It Is Good for Gays, Good for Straights, and Good for America* (New York: Henry Holt and Company, 2004).

Alice Ristroph and Melissa Murray, "Disestablishing the Family," *Yale Law Journal* 119 (2010): 1236–1279.

Susan Shell, "The Liberal Case Against Gay Marriage," *The Public Interest* 156 (Summer 2004): 3–16.

Karen Struening, *New Family Values* (Lanham, MD: Rowman and Littlefield, 2002).

Andrew Sullivan, ed., *Same-Sex Marriage: Pro and Con* (New York: Vintage, 1997).

Michael Warner, *The Trouble with Normal: Sex, Politics, and the Ethics of Queer Life* (Cambridge, MA: Harvard University Press, 1999).

Barbara Bennett Woodhouse, "The Dark Side of Family Privacy," *George Washington Law Review* 67 (1999): 1247–1262.

V

Multiculturalism, the Family, and Dilemmas of Justice

Introduction to Part V

The chapters in Part V pick up on a number of themes from the previous three sections, including gender equality, children's rights, family privacy, and marriage laws, but recast them in the context of discussions about multiculturalism and family practices. In many ways, the issues here are distinctly modern: Mill is the first of the classical thinkers to consider challenges of deep cultural difference to liberal justice. In *On Liberty,* for instance, he addresses Mormon polygamy and Islamic dietary laws. Yet Mill's unadorned privileging of his own culture is now seen by many as patently unjust. The diversification of modern societies in recent decades has spurred contemporary Western political theorists to search for ways to balance respect for cultural differences with their commitment to common norms of justice.

Alison Dundes Renteln's piece recounts a wide variety of child rearing practices associated with immigrants and minority cultures in England and the United States in order to ask: Where should the state draw the line? Does the state behave in culturally imperialistic ways when it prohibits individuals from raising their children according to their cultural traditions or religious views? Not necessarily, Renteln answers. Although the state should give parents wide scope to raise their children according to their cultural and religious beliefs, it has legitimate grounds, on her account, for proscribing parenting practices that cause irreparable physical injury or are potentially life-threatening to children.

In "Polygamy in America," Sarah Song highlights the hypocrisy that sometimes lies behind majority criticisms of minority cultural practices, arguing that these criticisms can serve to shield the majority from oppressive elements within their own culture. The anti-polygamy movement in nineteenth-century America, for example, diverted attention from the patriarchal marriage practices of the majority culture. Even today, Song argues that the ban on polygamy tends to cause more harm than good to women and children in polygamous cultures. Taking these considerations into account, Song argues that the competing demands of gender and cultural justice would best be met with "qualified recognition" of polygamous marriage as well as a number of other minority cultural practices.

12

Cultural Diversity and Child Protection

Alison Dundes Renteln

It is generally agreed that parents should be punished if they maliciously inflict serious harm on their children. It is far less obvious what to do with parents who may inadvertently cause their child harm through actions they sincerely believe are in the child's best interest. The outcomes of such cases invariably turn on the questions of the degree of harm and the reasonableness of the parent's belief that the action would be beneficial for the child. Deciding these kinds of questions is rarely easy. It becomes particularly problematic when the parents involved belong to a cultural or religious minority group, because different peoples have such vastly different conceptions of what constitutes acceptable child-rearing practices. Nevertheless, courts are sometimes confronted with cases such as these, requiring them to balance the safety and welfare of the child against the cultural autonomy of the parents. [....]

Two sorts of cases can be distinguished, which the official legal system would broadly classify as "abuse" and "neglect." In abuse cases the parent actively engages in a certain form of behavior that is considered by the state to be deleterious to the health of the child; by contrast, in neglect cases the state asserts that the parents fail to act in such a way as to maintain or restore the health of the child. These categories are, of course, ethnocentric. For instance, parents may actively apply folk remedies or faith healing to cure an ailing child, but because the child is not taken to a Western medical doctor, this is interpreted as neglect by the state.

The first category to be discussed involves parents who act according to tradition where the act in question is viewed as a crime: ritual scarification, female circumcision, discipline, folk medicine, and touching. The second category is a set of cases in which parents refuse to authorize medical treatment. They may prefer alternative remedies such as folk medicine or faith healing, or they may be opposed to any intervention because they believe the child was intended to have the condition in question. An important distinction will be drawn between life-threatening and non-life-threatening conditions, as the legal standards are much more firmly established for the former than the latter. Of particular interest will be the attempt to identify legitimate criteria for legal intervention.

The common thread that unites all these cases is the interplay between culture and culpability. In response to the charges brought against them, the parents in these cases typically invoke some sort of cultural defense, asserting that their actions are consistent with, and in some cases required by, their cultural traditions. Cultural defenses are used in civil proceedings as well to determine custody of the child.

These divergent approaches to justice are reflected in the disputes concerning proper child-rearing practices. The United Nations has taken a strong, absolutist position condemning traditional practices. Others, for example, Jill Korbin, take a position diametrically opposed to that of the United Nations. Provided individuals treat their children in accordance with their own rules, Korbin's view would not support intervention. In this chapter I argue that an intermediate standard offers the best solution to this challenging problem. It is my hope that through the analysis of the categories of conduct discussed in this chapter I will be able to provide a justification for a standard that proscribes traditional practices only in certain extreme cases.

WHEN PARENTAL ACTION IS CONSTRUED AS CRIMINAL CONDUCT: ABUSE CASES

Scarification

The much publicized unreported English case of *R. v. Adesanya* (1974) concerning the interpretation of ritual scarification illustrates well how courts typically contend with culture conflict. Mrs. Adesanya, a Yoruba woman from Nigeria, claimed to be following custom when, during the New Year celebrations, she made small incisions with a razor blade on the faces of her two sons, aged nine and fourteen. Apparently, she decided to place the traditional marks on their faces in order to ensure that her boys perceived themselves as Yoruba. The boys were said to be more than willing participants. The foster parents with whom the boys had been living reported the markings to the police.

Adesanya was charged at the Old Bailey, the Central Criminal Court in London, with assault occasioning actual bodily harm under section 47 of the Offences against the Person Act 1861. She pleaded not guilty to the charge of assault and offered a cultural defense. From her cultural viewpoint, failure to make the facial scars would be condemned: "Without such markings, her boys would be unable to participate as adults in their culture. A failure to assure one's children of such scarification would thus be viewed as neglectful or abusive within the cultural context of her tribe." Judge King-Hamilton QC held, however, that "the existence of the Nigerian custom was no defence to the charge brought." The judge contended that scarification differed from the piercing of girls' ears and the circumcision of young boys, noting the great danger posed by the razor on the face(!). Since the cutting of the skin was a wound under the law, the judge instructed the jury that it had no choice but to convict her. Because the judge understood that Mrs. Adesanya did not realize she was breaking the law and because it was the first case of its kind, the judge granted her an absolute discharge. But he offered a warning at the same time:

> You and others who come to this country must realize that our laws must be obeyed.... It cannot be stressed too strongly that any further offenses of this kind in pursuance of tribal traditions in Nigeria or other parts of Africa ... can only remit in prosecution. Because this is a test case ... I am prepared to deal with you with the utmost leniency. But let no one else assume that they will be treated with mercy. Others have now been warned.

[....]

Female Circumcision

A quite different type of surgery required by some cultures is known variously as female circumcision, female genital surgery, or female genital mutilation (FGM). The custom involves removal of some or all of a woman's external genitalia. The practice has existed for thousands of years and approximately 85 to 114 million women in the world have been circumcised. The practice is prevalent in Africa and the Middle East, but has also been documented in Islamic Indonesia, South America, and Australia. It exists in more than forty countries, and the number is growing because of migration. European nations have had to come to grips with this custom, which was previously unknown within their national boundaries. While some countries have adopted new laws targeting the practice, others apply existing general laws.

Anthropologists have explained the cultural justifications for the practice. Though religion (Islam) does not require the surgery, many cultural reasons are given for it. Among the reasons must often cited are (1) it guarantees the virginity of girls before marriage and chastity afterward; (2) it is a rite of passage, and without it a girl will be unable to marry; if unmarried, she will be ostracized; (3) if the clitoris touches the baby's forehead during the delivery, it will harm or kill the baby; (4) the clitoris would otherwise grow to the size of a penis. The crucial point is that the cultural logic dictates that the surgery be performed. Without it the uncircumcised girl will be a social outcast.

Feminists view women's support of the practice as a consequence of their having been victims of patriarchal systems and hence cite their attitude as an example of "false consciousness." But although many contend that this custom is the ultimate form of female oppression, women in many cultures favor its continuation. Educated women seem to be opposed to it, but some evidence indicates that even they succumb to social pressures to have the surgery performed.

It is important to point out, however, the growing number of critics of the practice within the countries where it is prevalent. Many governments have banned it, for instance, Sudan in 1945 and Kenya in 1982. There have also been consciousness-raising programs coordinated with the help of non-governmental organizations and the United Nations. Even where the custom persists, it may be performed among the same people in certain areas and not in others. Though it remains widespread, there is growing opposition to it.

The international strategy has been to condemn female circumcision as unhealthy. Indeed, it may be a classic example of a "traditional practice prejudicial to the health of [female] children." The manner in which the surgery has traditionally been performed has led to many severe health complications. One difficulty with the health critique, however, is that with the dissemination of Western medical techniques, the operations can be carried out under thoroughly antiseptic conditions. This is certainly the case when Africans migrate and have their daughters circumcised by well-established surgeons in Europe.

In some countries, the parents or women who perform the surgery have been prosecuted under general sexual mutilation laws and then sentenced to lengthy prison terms. More prosecutions have occurred in France than in any other country. The cultural defense has been raised as a discrete argument in these cases. Although defense attorneys claim that "ignorant Africans" were unaware that excision was prohibited in France, courts reject this based on the principle that ignorance of the law is no excuse. One French attorney argued against allowing the custom on equal protection grounds: "We accept for the little African what we would violently refuse for our own children.... In France customary laws should in no case pretend to substitute the enforcement of national law."

As of 1999, twenty-six cases had been prosecuted, resulting in twenty-five convictions. Relatives prosecuted in France originally received suspended sentences; this followed the pattern of discouraging the practice without imposing punishment. Although punishment in the only two cases brought to the criminal court as of May 1990 were suspended sentences of three years imprisonment each, since then, defendants have been sentenced to actual jail time. [....]

Discipline

The issue of corporal punishment of children is a highly divisive one. Some sort of punishment seems to exist in all cultures; the difficult question is what constitutes "excessive force." This is because there is considerable cultural variation in interpreting this notion. So, parents sometimes discipline their children and then find, much to their surprise, that their techniques are "unacceptable" in their new country. Most often, courts reject the cultural defense and insist that immigrants adhere to the standards of the dominant culture.

In the British case of *R. v. Derriviere* (1969) the judge had to grapple with the problem of how to balance the requirements of law with justice. A West Indian father was charged with assault that led to actual bodily harm. This was the result of a family altercation: when his son misbehaved and refused to apologize to his mother, his father punched him several times, leaving him with bruises, swellings, and lacerations. The issue was whether other views of child discipline would be allowed to be practiced in England.

The judge accepted as true the claim that standards of parental correction differ in the West Indies but concluded that this was an unacceptable "savage attack":

> There can be no doubt that once in this country, this country's laws must apply; and there can be no doubt that, according to the law of this country, the chastisement given to this boy was excessive and the assault complained of was proved.
>
> Nevertheless, had this been a first offense, and had there been some real reason for thinking that the appellant either did not understand what the standards in this country were or was having difficulty adjusting himself, the Court would no doubt have taken that into account and given it such consideration as it must. The really outstanding fact in this case is that this was not the first offense.

[....]

In the United States judges take differing views of the relevant of culture in adjudicating child abuse cases. Sometimes a court purports to take it into account, as in *Dumpson v. Daniel M.* (1974), a case that took place in family court in New York City. A Nigerian father allegedly used excessive corporal punishment, and the issue was whether the court should affirm a lower court decision to remove the children from their parents' home. During a meeting with an assistant principal to discuss his son's misbehavior at school, the father hit his seven-year-old son, Ekenediliz, repeatedly. He explained his conduct saying

> he struck his son because according to his culture pattern this type of punishment was necessary and appropriate. In Nigeria ... if a child misbehaves in school and causes shame to the family, the parent has the duty to punish immediately and in any manner he sees fit.

The court acknowledged that there are diverse child-rearing practices but concluded that it had to decide the neglect issue according to the applicable legal standards of the dominant culture: "While recognizing individual and cultural differences, this court has the obligation to apply the law equally to all men." But the court, in reality, disregarded cultural factors: "The sole issue for determination here is whether the respondents' conduct constitutes excessive corporal punishment as would warrant a finding of neglect under the statute. We think it does." The challenge of interpreting "the best interests of the child" standard in this context seemed unproblematic to the court:

> Any reasonable man knows that it is not in the best interests of a child for its parents to punish in the manner we have seen here. While we are sympathetic and understanding of the respondents' motives, we must conclude that motive is irrelevant when we are confronted with the type of punishment this seven-year-old boy has received.

Thus, the court, denying the relevance of cultural motivation, decided to endorse the order authorizing temporary removal of the son.

Dumpson is instructive because it illustrates the standard judicial approach in cultural defense cases. There is a clear presumption that the reasonable man thinks like a member of the dominant culture. In addition, the court explicitly disregards motive, the cultural justification for the action under scrutiny. It also demonstrates how cultural defenses arise in legal proceedings other than criminal prosecutions.

This case suggests that we ought to be concerned with the impact judges' decisions will have on the ethnic community affected by the adjudication. Here the court states that its finding of neglect "is not meant to cast any negative overtones on the respondent's ability to function as a parent in any other respect." Nevertheless, the ruling could well humiliate the family. The father commented that "he was ashamed just to have to be in the courtroom." It is hard to imagine how the finding of neglect would not be interpreted as a judiciary casting aspersions on Nigerian child-rearing. Even if the decision was justifiable, it is sheer nonsense to assert that the outcome has no broader implications.

Cases involving Southeast Asian methods of discipline have reached American courts. Traditional practices such as beating a child with a bamboo rod are regarded as child abuse by American authorities. In some cases the claim that the physical abuse is part of the culture may be false. Moreover, even if the harsh discipline was once allowed, the tradition may have been discarded. In other instances it is possible that the discipline is traditional, but when it results in potential irreparable harm, it must be prohibited, nevertheless.

Even if the public policy of the state is to intervene when parents use what is considered "excessive" force, it is crucial that the intervention be handled with care. In Oakland, California, social workers removed four children, including a five-week-old baby, from a Laotian home after a teacher reported seeing bruises on a child. The social service authorities suspected that the father, Jio Saephan, had "inappropriately" disciplined his son. Kouichoy Saechao, a spokesperson for the Lao Iu Mien Culture Association, explained that his group accepts some forms of physical punishment. The Department of Social Services, however, was opposed to any discipline that leaves marks and favors intervention. Apparently the social worker removed the children while two police officers stood guard. The baby died while in foster care, apparently of sudden infant death syndrome, and one can only imagine what the Laotian community must think of the US government. It is likely that removing the children from the home was an overreaction on the part of the social workers who may have feared that they would be sued if they failed to take the children out of the house.

Even if one favors intervention to halt corporal punishment among ethnic minority communities, there are unintended consequences worth considering. For example, by conveying to children the message that parents cannot use traditional discipline, the parents are emasculated and the children are empowered. If children engage in deviant behavior, parental authority has been shattered. Furthermore, failure to intervene as zealously in nonminority families will be viewed as a sign that a double standard is operating. [....]

Touching

Another cross-cultural misunderstanding involves differing interpretations of touching children. There are several publicized cases in which relatives accused of sexual abuse claim that their behavior is innocent. These "fondling" incidents have been documented in various ethnic communities, including Albanian, Afghani, Cambodian, Eskimo, Filipino, Pakistani, and Taiwanese cultures. The legal question in these cases is whether or not the adults are touching the children for the purpose of sexual gratification. Ordinarily, it is only if adults have this motivation that the touching is illegal. In these cases the key notion is that the behavior is a form of expressing affection and is not intended to be erotic.

In a Texas case, Sadri (Sam) and Sabahete (Kathy) Krasniqi, Muslim immigrants from Albania, lost their two children in 1989 when Mr. Krasniqi was accused of sexually molesting his four-year-old daughter in a public school gymnasium during a martial arts event. After the Texas Child Protective Service initially took the children out of the parents' home, the Krasniqis appealed. When Mrs. Krasniqi took the children to see their father, in violation of the court order, the court terminated their parental rights; the Texas Supreme Court affirmed the termination. According to the program aired on *20/20,* the parents claimed the touching was entirely innocent and a part of Albanian culture. An anthropologist at the University of Massachusetts, Amherst, Barbara Halpern, explained the cultural aspects of the behavior.

Although Dr. Halpern's expert testimony was decisive in winning an acquittal in the criminal case against Mr. Krasniqi, this had no bearing on the family court decision terminating the Krasniqis' parental rights. The two children were legally adopted by their foster parents and forced to convert from Islam to Christianity. This case demonstrates an almost unbelievable abuse of state power. Termination of parental rights should be reserved for the most serious cases only.

In some jurisdictions a defendant from another culture can successfully use de minimis statutes. Statutes of this kind, often modeled after the Model Penal Code, are designed to avoid unjust outcomes. They represent legislative authorization for judges to monitor prosecutorial discretion. In *State v. Kargar* (1996), an Afghani refugee, Mohammad Kargar, was convicted of two counts of gross sexual assault for kissing his eighteen-month-old son's penis. The court sentenced him to two concurrent terms of eighteen months in prison, then suspended the terms and placed him on probation for three years on the condition that he learn English. On appeal he argued that the trial court erroneously denied his motion to dismiss under the state de minimis statute. The Maine Supreme Court agreed and vacated the lower court's judgments.

At the de minimis hearing testimony was presented from many Afghani people familiar with the practice of kissing a young son. They explained that "kissing a son's penis is common in Afghanistan, that it is done to show love for the child, and that it is the same whether the penis is kissed or entirely put into the mouth because there are no sexual feelings involved." Kargar's attorney submitted written statements from Professor Ludwig Adamec, University of Arizona's Center for Near Eastern Studies, and from Saifur Halimi, a religious leader in New York. Kargar himself testified at the hearing that by kissing the penis, which is not the cleanest part of the body because of urination, a father demonstrates how much he loves his child. [. . . .]

It is wrong to imprison a person who has engaged in culturally motivated behavior and who is unaware of the prohibition of the conduct. If the touching is considered socially unacceptable, rather than incarcerating the individual, it is preferable to inform him that the behavior is not allowed in the new country. Even if forcing assimilation is the only option, it is certainly more humane to rely on education rather than imprisonment whenever possible.

WHEN PARENTS REFUSE TO AUTHORIZE WESTERN MEDICAL TREATMENT: NEGLECT CASES

In some neglect cases parents do not provide Western-style medical treatment because their religion or culture forbids it. While in some instances they opt for "alternative" or traditional techniques that are compatible with their worldview, in others they prefer not to have any treatment whatsoever. The failure to ensure that children receive medical care can lead either to dependency proceedings to remove a child from a home on a temporary or permanent basis or to criminal prosecution of parents; under all state child abuse and neglect laws, parental failure to provide "adequate" medical care is a criminal offense.

Traditionally, courts would not intrude in family decision-making regarding the health care of children unless the child had a life-endangering condition. In the past few decades they have gradually moved toward an approach that has been described as ad hoc. Intervention in non-life-threatening cases has become easier to justify and can be authorized to ensure "quality of life." The crux of the issue, of course, is deciding just what constitutes a life of quality. The presence of divergent views on this issue among the peoples of the world virtually guarantees that conflict will occur.

Finally, I turn to a consideration of Christian Science faith-healing cases. Although the parents in these cases are not immigrants and refugees, they are members of a group whose worldview differs substantially from that of the majority. Furthermore, many of the culture conflict cases considered in this chapter are in essence religious conflicts, so it is instructive to consider how these conflicts are dealt with when the defendants are in every other respect part of the American "mainstream." As will be seen, the way in which faith-healing cases are handled reveals serious biases in the legal system.

Non-Life-Threatening Conditions

The child neglect statutes permit the state to intervene and order medical treatment when children are seriously ill. If a child has a life-threatening condition, there is generally a consensus that intervention is justifiable. While in the past courts would not authorize forced medical treatment for non-life-threatening illness, increasingly they are doing so. American judges have compelled children to submit to medical treatment, even though their health problems were not life-endangering.

A fascinating case that has received relatively little attention is that of Kou Xiong. In a Fresno, California, case a court ordered a six-year-old Hmong boy by the name of Kou to have surgery to correct a club foot, despite the vehement protestation of his parents. The Fresno County Social Services Department wanted Kou to have surgery because physicians said without it he would eventually lose the ability to walk and become "wheelchair-bound." The petition stated that he came within the provisions of Welfare and Institutions Code section 300(b) because his parents had failed to obtain surgery to correct his "congenital deformities"—a dislocated right hip and clubfeet. The physicians in the case testified that there was no guarantee that the surgery would ultimately be successful. Moreover, several operations would be required over a period of years. Even though Kou's own attorney argued his interests should supersede those of his parents, he stated that it was "not clear at all what course of conduct [would be] in the minor's best interest."

Evidence was presented to the court to show that the Hmong believed the surgery would interfere with the natural order; misfortunes might well befall other members of the family or community. The family believed he was born with clubfeet as punishment for wrongs committed by an ancestor. In fact, the family was convinced that this had already happened—after surgery in a Thai refugee camp his mother became violently ill, and the Xiongs' next two sons were born with cleft palates. The Hmong Council also informed authorities that in another case where surgery was performed against the advice of the shaman, the child's father died. The parents' objections to surgery were based on sincerely held religious and cultural beliefs. It was not apparent what compelling state interest outweighed these constitutional rights, as Kou had a disability and not a life-threatening condition.

There was some question as to whether the surgery was immediately necessary to enable Kou the ability to walk. It seems that it was already considered late to perform the surgery and that the longer he waited to have it, the more radical the medical approach would have to be. But even if it was medically advisable to have the surgery sooner rather than later, it is not at all obvious that the court should authorize surgery over the parents' religious and cultural objections. Kou himself said both that he did not want surgery and that he did not want to be in a wheelchair. He was concerned that were he to have surgery, he might be ostracized afterward. The psychologist attested to this fear on his part in his description of how Kou played with dolls during the evaluation.

The family's attorney attempted a series of appeals all the way to US Supreme Court justice Sandra Day O'Connor, but lost at every level. Interestingly, however, despite the legal outcomes, as of 1992 no doctor was willing to perform the surgery without the parents' cooperation. After all the litigation, the original judge decided to vacate his earlier ruling ordering the surgery. What changed his mind was a psychiatric report which concluded that Kou would be at "grave psychological risk" if the operation were performed over parental objections. Kou said he was afraid of being separated from his parents if the surgery took place. He was also fearful that something bad would happen to his siblings (and that he would be responsible). Basically, he would be rejected by the community—he would be a social outcast. So, in spite of the protracted litigation, which appeared to disregard the cultural objections for the most part, the Hmong family, in the end, succeeded in avoiding the surgery.

What is striking about this case is that the court ordered the surgery even though the boy's condition was not life threatening. With only a couple of exceptions, courts generally have not intervened in family decision making concerning children in cases that were not life threatening. One can only speculate as to why the court felt the urgent need to depart from the standard doctrinal approach.

Here again it is worth pointing out the tremendous effect the court order had on the Hmong community, where the case was the source of much consternation. The Hmong Council, representing the eighteen Hmong clans, wrote a letter to the Department of Social Services imploring its director not to force the surgery on the boy. It seems likely that the Hmong learned that they could not expect justice, from their point of view, from American courts. American courts, in their eyes, ceased to be credible institutions.

It is also important to realize how the disabled community might view the court's treatment of the issue. Though it was certainly not a conscious suggestion, the lawyer for Kou implied that life in a wheelchair was unacceptable: "The parents' right to raise their child in the way they see fit must give way to the child's right to have an opportunity to live a productive and pleasant, or at least bearable life." An explicit presumption was that it is sufficiently important for children to walk that even surgery with uncertain results can be ordered over family objections.

Life-Threatening Conditions

Although it may be problematic to justify intervention in non-life-threatening cases, courts are more than willing to intercede on behalf of a child whose life is in immediate danger. In the process, courts sometimes ride roughshod over the parents' cultural beliefs, resulting in greater suffering by the family.

In 1984 a Hmong family in Columbus, Ohio, refused to authorize surgery for their four-month-old boy, Franklin Kue, who had been diagnosed as having cancer in both eyes (malignant retinoblastoma). As Hmong, the parents had extremely serious reservations about the surgery. The Hmong fear surgery for several reasons, one of which is that people will remain forever in the afterlife as they are at the time of death. Thao, a Hmong medical student, explains: "When the person dies, he will not be recognized by his ancestors in the 'spirit' world, he will not be reborn as another human being in the next life, and his soul will bring sickness to the living family members." Another reason for their apprehension is "the belief that cutting open the body allows good spirits to leave and bad spirits to enter." There is also fear that they will be used as experimental subjects. Because they were distraught about the surgery, the parents in this case supposedly even contemplated a murder-suicide.

American officials intervened because doctors said the child had a 90 percent chance of survival if they removed his eyes before the cancer spread. So, when the hospital's emergency order granting custody of the child to the county failed to produce the desired result, the public officials involved in the case returned to court. This time Judge Clayton Rose Jr. ordered immediate hospitalization of the infant for the purpose of surgery. He was reported as saying, "The only exception in the law is if the child is treated by prayer from a well-recognized religion. That is not the case in this instance." Mr. Kue, who attended the hearing, became visibly angry after the judge issued the order and argued vehemently through an interpreter with the doctor who had requested the surgery. A police officer then escorted the baby to the Children's Hospital.

The lack of cross-cultural understanding prompted the family to spirit the infant away from the hospital and transport him to Detroit to see a shaman. Apparently, they fled Columbus to avoid arrest and the enforcement of the court order requiring surgery. Meanwhile, they became the objects of a multistate search by the police and FBI. After receiving counseling in Detroit through the intervention of a refugee resettlement organization (aided by Tou-Fu Vang, a bilingual Hmong refugee resettlement expert), the parents consented to surgery. The prosecutor dropped the felony charges of endangering a child, but threatened to refile them if the child was not returned for treatment by a certain date. A social worker who aided the family said that "having the pressure of prosecution off their backs" helped them decide to have the operation performed. It is thought that a major factor in their decision was their recognition that the infant was already blind.

The surgery proved successful in averting further cancer, but Hmong confidence in American justice may have been permanently undermined. The father explained his actions: "They came to the door and took our baby away. That never happened in our country." Mr. Kue also said he felt rushed and frightened by the authorities.

The judge in this case might have played a crucial role in facilitating cross-cultural understanding but missed the opportunity to handle this culturally delicate situation with care. While Americans may view a breach of the law (here the failure to comply with the court order) as a serious offense, the Hmong believe that no institution can usurp parental authority. If this transpires, it shames the parents. Had the officials been more aware of Hmong attitudes and practices, they might have handled this case more sensitively.

Fatalities: Faith-Healing Cases

Having considered cases involving judicial intervention to authorize medical treatment for children with non-life-threatening and life-threatening conditions, I now turn to cases in which parents choose to treat their children according to spiritual means and are subsequently prosecuted for manslaughter when their children die. There are several reasons why it is appropriate to consider faith-healing cases here. First, the Christian Science parents, in refusing to consent to "conventional" medical treatment, are acting on the basis of religious motivations that are part of their worldview, just as, for example, the Xiongs were. Second, because of this, the religious arguments put forward as a defense in these cases are strikingly similar to the cultural arguments put forward in the cases involving immigrants.

The faith-healing cases arise because, according to the Christian Science worldview, disease is simply an illusion created by God, often as a result of sin. The tenets of their religion require that "cosmopolitan" medicine not be consulted. In fact, Christian Scientists are told that by seeking medical help, they will undermine the efficacy of faith healing. Thus, faith healing and modern medicine are, at least according to official dogma, mutually exclusive. Consequently, they believe they cannot seek medical help for their children when they are ill.

Despite similarities between faith-healing cases and other cultural defense cases, however, there is one significant difference: religious exemptions in all but a few states protect Christian Scientists from prosecution; ethnic minority groups have not benefited from any similar sort of legislative exemption relating to their culture. The existence of these exemptions accounts for the differential treatment by courts of faith-healing cases and other culture conflict cases. In particular, a large number of faith-healing cases revolve around the issue of which takes precedence, the exemption or the manslaughter law.

When parents whose children died for lack of medical treatment have been prosecuted for manslaughter in the United States, the cases have turned on the question of due process. For instance, in Minnesota, Kathleen and William McKown were indicted for second-degree manslaughter when they relied on Christian Science spiritual healing for their eleven-year-old son, Ian, who died of diabetic ketoacidosis. The defendants won a dismissal in the lower court, basing their argument on the due process fair notice requirement. That is, because the relationship between the neglect law exemption and the homicide law was ambiguous, they had not received notice as to the requirements of the law. The parents were, therefore, unable to make their conduct conform to legal standards:

> Respondents contend the child neglect statute misled them in that it unequivocally stated they could, in good faith, select and depend upon spiritual means or prayer without further advising them that, should their chosen treatment method fail, they might face criminal charges beyond those provided in the child neglect statute itself. In short, respondents argue that the child neglect statute does not go far enough to provide reasonable notice of the potentially serious consequences of actually relying on the alternative treatment methods the statute itself clearly permits.

The state appealed, but lost. Both the Minnesota Court of Appeals and the Minnesota Supreme Court accepted the fair notice claim and affirmed the lower court's decision to dismiss:

> The exception is broadly worded, stating that a parent may in good faith "select and depend upon" spiritual treatment and prayer, without indicating a point at which doing so will expose the parent to criminal liability. The language of the exception therefore does not satisfy the fair notice requirement inherent to the concept of due process.

Commentators note that religious defenses are rejected specifically in cases where parents withhold medical treatment from dependent children: "Courts have long recognized that religion affords no defense to a statutory obligation to provide medical care for dependent children." Thus, from constitutional decisions one infers that there is little sympathy for a free exercise defense in criminal prosecutions, especially those involving children. Consequently, faith healing has only been possible because of the existence of statutory exemptions.

Statutory exemptions have been challenged on constitutional grounds. One argument has been that they violate the Establishment clause because they effectively promote Christian Science. Another claim is that the exemptions deny equal protection to parents because parents of some religions are favored over others. For example, although there exist religious exemptions for faith healing, which often leads to death, there are no "religious" exemptions for coining or cupping, which never leads to death. It seems as though only members of "organized" religions benefit from exemptions, which suggests favoritism inherent in the law. More serious is the contention that exemptions deny equal protection of the laws to children, because the state fails to protect the health of children without regard to their religious affiliation.

Of all the objections to exemptions (religious or otherwise), the strongest one is the equal protection argument vis-à-vis the children. The real issue in the faith healing cases is whether the state should permit parents to risk the lives of their children in the name of religion. From the children's point of view, the legal requirement that necessary medical treatment be provided them should not depend on the group to which one's parents belong. In order to institute exemptions, children's rights may be sacrificed, including their right to religion. After all, without medical treatment to save their lives, they cannot choose to follow any religion.

In most of the cases the children are too young to be competent to decide what is in their own best interest. If, however, an older child wanted to forego medical treatment and have faith healing instead, such a case might present a different issue. It might be that a mature minor's right to refuse treatment would have to be treated no differently from other cases in which there is no religious objection. For the younger children it is questionable whether parents should retain the right to choose faith healing to the exclusion of medical treatment when the children have life-threatening conditions. Certainly the exemptions deny the children their rights to medical care.

It is a sad irony that the only formal cultural defense that has been established to date is the statutory religious defense used in faith-healing cases. Surprisingly, not only are parents whose children die for lack of medical treatment charged with manslaughter instead of murder, but their convictions have, for the most part, been overturned. While I support the consideration of the parents' motive—that is, to heal their children—the appropriate punishment should be that assigned to manslaughter rather than simply probation. To allow their religious worldview to reduce their culpability any further would be unjust. Until the faith-healing exemptions are repealed, it seems probable that the courts will continue to quash the convictions of parents based on the due process argument.

The statutory exemptions seem to be based on a recognition that parents intend to heal their children rather than to harm them. But this method of accommodating the beneficent motive of parents may suffer from constitutional defects and may also jeopardize the health of children. For these reasons religious exemptions must be subject to the closest scrutiny by the judiciary.

INTERVENTION

In the faith-healing cases just discussed the children died, and the question was what to do with the parents. Much of the discussion about these matters centers on the exemptions and the question of whether religiously motivated conduct constitutes a defense. But what about the case in which a child has not yet died? It is important to note that the faith-healing exemptions do not preclude child welfare authorities from reporting cases of children who are in need of medical treatment. If someone detects a problem in time, it is possible that courts could authorize child protective services departments to order medical treatment. There is no question that preventative intervention is preferable to prosecution after the fact, as the child's life might be saved. It is to the question of intervention that we now turn.

Under what circumstances, if any, should the state be empowered to intervene to protect children from cultural or religious practices that are regarded as deleterious to their health? Scholars take varying positions—supporting practically no intervention to intervention any time the health of the child might be perceived to be at risk.

The important work of Jill Korbin best exemplifies the view that intervention is never justified as long as the parents are complying with the rules of their community. Her position on traditional practices is that intervention by a national legal system should only occur if several criteria are met. Ellen Gray and John Cosgrove summarize the elements of her framework succinctly:

> If the following conditions are satisfied in Korbin's scheme, the behavior should not be considered abusive: (1) the behavior in question actually reflects a sanctioned practice of that culture; (2) it falls within the limits of (behavior and) deviation acceptable in that culture; (3) the intent of the responsible caretaker is consistent with the cultural "rules" governing the practice; (4) it is the perception of the child that this is an appropriate practice in the situation; (5) the practice is important in the development of the child as a member of the culture.

This theoretical position does not allow for criticism of a practice provided that there is apparent consensus supporting its continuation. Even if the internal standard conflicts with the external standard, she assumes, without justification, that the internal one takes precedence.

Although Korbin is to be commended for her culturally sensitive analysis, she conflates two distinct scenarios. One situation exists when outsiders invade another society and then try to outlaw many aspects of the indigenous way of life, as for example, in colonialism. The other situation is where a group migrates and wants to preserve its traditions despite the fact that they violate the law of the new country. While Korbin may be right with respect to the first situation—that it is unwise to criticize customs in foreign jurisdictions (at least in the absence of domestic dissent—the second situation poses a different question, and it is not self-evident that all traditions must be permitted in this context.

If we assume that some degree of intervention is justifiable, then the question becomes one of finding the appropriate standard. Those who fear that the state will abuse its power argue that minimal governmental intrusion in the family is the most defensible public policy. Judith Areen, after noting that "there is little consensus about when a court should find that a particular child is neglected or abused" offers the following principles:

1. Standards for court intervention in a family should focus on the emotional and physical needs of the children rather than on parental fault.
2. Decisions on whether and how to intervene in a family should serve to enhance the social and emotional bonds of that family.
3. Courts should require a permanent placement for any child who has been removed from his family and who cannot be returned safely within a period of time that is reasonable in view of the age and needs of the child.

The principles are intended to limit intervention by promoting family autonomy and by using the least intrusive methods of addressing intrafamilial conflict.

Other approaches to intervention are based on concepts such as irreversible or irreparable harm, serious bodily harm, and so forth. The difficulty with these standards, of course, is determining the scope of their application. In some cases, as with scarification and female circumcision, an irreversible or irreparable harm standard would require that immigrants discontinue these practices. However, discipline and folk medicine do not ordinarily cause irreversible or irreparable harm. Thus, children's rights advocates might find such a standard inadequate because it is too narrow to prevent practices they view as detrimental. Serious bodily harm might be preferable because it is more inclusive, and yet it may outlaw practices that are not harmful.

The United Nations decided to adopt an extremely broad standard in the Convention on the Rights of the Child: any practices that are "prejudicial" to the health of the child are to be abolished. This gives the greatest latitude to those who seek to eradicate cultural practices that harm children in some way, whether the harm is permanent or not. Such a standard may appeal to those who want to protect children from repressive customs, but it also runs the risk of authorizing excessive public intrusion into private family affairs. [....]

As a general argument I take the view that the legal system should sanction intervention when the parental action will lead to irreparable physical injury. Although there will be debate about what conduct is encompassed by the standard, it would authorize intrusion into the family to prevent scarification, female circumcision, and some types of corporal punishment, but not necessarily for the practice of folk medicine.

In neglect cases courts should authorize surgery over parental religious or cultural objections if there is a potentially life-threatening situation. In the absence of a threat to life, there is time to try to persuade a family of the benefit of medical intervention. There is no need to intimidate families with the law unless the child is in jeopardy. [....]

BALANCING CULTURAL RIGHTS AGAINST CHILDREN'S RIGHTS

The challenge is to decide how a national legal system should handle culture conflict cases involving children. Although the state must be culturally sensitive, it must, at the same time, serve to uphold fundamental human rights standards. There is a particular need to enforce the law when children's rights are implicated because children are vulnerable and unable to act as their own advocates.

In order to strike the proper balance between children's rights and cultural autonomy, I have argued for intervention to prevent irreparable harm. It is my view that the legal system should try to preserve choice for children. Thus, courts should intervene when a child's life is at stake because otherwise the child cannot decide whether or not to remain a member of the cultural group or to opt for a different cultural identity. Likewise, in cases where parents plan to make irreversible physical changes, the state should act to prevent it.

Where the issue is medical neglect because parents object to medical treatment on religious or cultural grounds, I favor a return to the life-threatening/non-life-threatening standard. I would, however, amend the rule to authorize state intervention when children have potentially life-threatening conditions. The current trend toward use of a "quality of life" standard permits excessive intrusions into family life. The notion of irreparable harm may be pertinent here as well since in some cases the question is whether delaying surgery until the child reaches the age of majority may mean that it can never be successfully performed. In general, intervention is unwarranted if the decision to withhold medical treatment will not be permanently devastating for the child. Otherwise, family and cultural autonomy will be unjustifiably undermined.

If the state discovers the abuse or neglect after it has already occurred, however, the question is how cultural arguments should figure into decisions concerning the guilt and punishment of the parent defendant. An understanding of a defendant's culture is crucial to determining whether or not criminal motivation underlies his or her actions. Indeed, it seems hard to imagine how courts can avoid cultural factors in determining the guilt or innocence of parents.

13

Polygamy in America

Sarah Song

[....]

The movement against Mormon polygamy provides an early example of a minority group's demand for accommodation—in this case, a demand for immunity from prosecution, an exemption—and the dominant culture's overwhelmingly negative response. As one legal historian put it, the federal government pursued the campaign against polygamy with "a zeal and concentration" that was "unequalled in the annals of federal law enforcement." Opponents of polygamy called for federal intervention to dismantle what was widely considered a deeply patriarchal practice. Some might look approvingly at the outcome of this case, pointing to it as a model for how liberal democratic states might deal with illiberal and nondemocratic groups. What they would miss, however, is not only how such intervention failed to improve the status of Mormon women but also how condemnation of polygamy helped divert attention from the majority culture's own patriarchal norms. The focus on polygamy helped shield Christian monogamy and the traditional gender roles associated with it from criticism. It also served as a useful tool in the government's assault on what was probably its bigger concern, the political power of the Mormon Church.

In this chapter, I examine the politics of the American antipolygamy movement to explore the intercultural dynamic of diversion. Antipolygamy activists gave two main arguments against polygamy: that it violated Christian public morals and that it subordinated women. Turning to examine the contemporary practice of polygamy, I consider whether the concern for equal protection of women supports a case for qualified recognition of polygamy with an emphasis on ensuring a realistic right of exit, as well as discuss other contemporary cases in which the diversionary effect is at work.

THE RISE AND FALL OF MORMON POLYGAMY

In 1830, Joseph Smith, a New York farmer, founded the Church of Jesus Christ of Latter-Day Saints. The Book of Mormon, as translated by Smith, described the Hebrew origins of Native Americans and established America as God's chosen land. In 1843 in Nauvoo, Illinois, Smith had a revelation mandating "plural marriage," but the revelation was not made public until 1852 after the Mormons had settled in Utah. While Mormon leaders began practicing plural marriage in Illinois, it was on the western frontier that the practice grew, offering a systematic alternative to Christian monogamy. Responding to what they perceived to be the increasing secularization of marriage in the dominant culture, Mormon leaders solemnized marriages without state involvement. Public outrage against the practice grew. The Republican Party condemned the "twin relics of barbarism—polygamy and slavery" in its party platform of 1856 and asserted the sovereign power of Congress over the territories.

Efforts by American citizens and government officials to dismantle Mormon polygamy spanned from 1862 to 1890. In 1862, Congress criminalized bigamy in the territories. The law proved unenforceable since Utah did not register marriages and Mormon juries would not convict polygamists. In 1874, Congress followed up with the Poland Act, which transferred jurisdiction of criminal and civil cases from probate courts in the Utah Territory, whose judges were often Mormon bishops, to federal territorial courts and gave federal judges considerable power over selection of jurors. In 1879, the US Supreme Court upheld a bigamy conviction in *Reynolds v. US*, but the decision did not eliminate the practice since prosecutors could not easily prove plural marriage. Congress followed up in 1882 by renaming the offense described as "bigamy" to "polygamy" and made it easier to procure polygamy convictions by criminalizing "unlawful cohabitation." It also denied polygamists the right to vote and hold public office and required a man to swear he was not a polygamist and a woman to swear that she was not married to one. Some Mormons who were denied the vote in the 1882 election because they refused to take the oath sued the registrar of ballots. Two years later, the US Supreme Court held that it was appropriate for Congress to make marital status "a condition of the elective franchise," adding that a sovereign power could legitimately "declare that no one but a married person shall be entitled to vote."

In 1887, Congress stepped up the assault by repealing the incorporation of the Mormon Church and directing the US Attorney General to expropriate its property holdings over $50,000. The act also disenfranchised Mormon women, who had had the vote for seventeen years before that point. The

Mormons resisted and continued to practice polygamy, but in 1889, the Supreme Court upheld Congress's power to dissolve and expropriate the church's property against the church's claim that it was a protected religious body. Finally, in 1890, Mormon President Wilson Woodruff issued a manifesto accepting the federal prohibition of polygamy and encouraged members to refrain from contracting any further polygamous marriages.

THE ANTIPOLYGAMY MOVEMENT AND THE DIVERSIONARY EFFECT

Why did American citizens, legislators, and judges in the nineteenth century deem polygamy to be intolerable? The leading arguments against polygamy were that it offended Protestant public morals and that it was deeply patriarchal. While patriarchal power was not unique to the polygamous form of marriage, citizens and government officials targeted it because it was seen to embody an extreme of patriarchy inconsistent with democracy. If we examine the broader social and political context in which antipolygamy activism arose, however, we see that while motivated by a concern to improve the status of Mormon women, the antipolygamy movement was also fueled by a concern to protect traditional monogamous marriage and dismantle the political power of the Mormon Church. The focus on polygamy served these latter goals well by shielding monogamy from feminist criticism and gathering support for the federal attack on the political power of the Mormon Church.

The context in which antipolygamy arose was a period of increasing anxiety over sexual values, family structure, and the proper role of women. Social changes in the majority culture—the spread of prostitution, the rising incidence of divorce, and lax morality of growing cities stirred anxieties about the preservation of Christian-model monogamy. By the time the issue of polygamy arose on the national political stage, nineteenth-century women's rights activists had already been unsettling prevailing gender norms. By the 1840s, family reformers, fearful of utopian experiments and the demands of women's rights activists, diagnosed a "crisis of the family" and expressed "moral panic" around the issue of marriage reform. The antipolygamy movement's persistent focus on the theme of sexual perversion allowed members of the majority culture to displace its anxieties about these social changes onto subversive minorities. In addition to subversive sexual practices, Mormonism's association with lenient divorce laws and female enfranchisement fueled fears that all three were part of a plot to undermine the traditional American family and Christian civilization itself.

Polygamy challenged the Christian concept of marital unity and the related common law concept of coverture. In the eyes of the law, the husband and wife were one legal person represented by the husband with the legal existence of the wife "covered" by his authority. According to the preeminent expert on common law, William Blackstone, a woman's legal identity was subsumed by her husband's upon marriage. What helped soften the image of the patriarchal nature of monogamy, in contrast to polygamy, was the rising ideology of romantic conjugal love, premised on consent and focused on one person. The metaphor of "one flesh" was recast as the spiritual union of the couple based on mutual love and consent, offering a gentler version of coverture.

The patriarchal nature of polygamy was the focus of the *Reynolds* case. The Court held that the establishment and free exercise clauses did not protect local difference in domestic relations. Writing for the majority, Chief Justice Morrison Waite recognized polygamy as a religious doctrine, but he argued that the First Amendment protection of religious freedom extended to belief, not action. In justifying government restrictions on religious action, he did not address Mormon arguments that highlighted questions of jurisdiction and the powers of Congress over the territories, focusing instead on questions of sexual behavior and the connection between marriage structure and political structure. Chief Justice Waite expressed concern for the "pure-minded women" who were the "innocent victims of this delusion," and argued for upholding Congress's proscription on polygamy on the grounds that it "leads to the patriarchal principle which, when applied to large communities, fetters the people in stationary despotism, while that principle cannot long exist in connection with monogamy." Such condemnation of patriarchy seems disingenuous insofar as nineteenth-century opponents of polygamy neither challenged patriarchal power within monogamy nor advocated the equality of women outside marriage. Yet, the Court was genuinely concerned with the patriarchal nature of polygamy: Mormon life was seen to embody patriarchy of a nature and degree unmatched by monogamy. Such extreme patriarchy was seen to be inconsistent with democracy. Considered against notions of romantic conjugal love that (at least in theory) promised marital unions based on consent and mutual love, polygamy was truly a form of bondage.

The Court cast the conflict as between a secular state and religion and affirmed the state's civil interest in preserving monogamy. The case for the civil interest in marriage was based on the widely accepted view that marriage structure was intimately connected with political order:

> Marriage, while from its very nature a sacred obligation, is nevertheless, in most civilized nations, a civil contract, and usually regulated by law. Upon it society may be said to be built, and out of its fruits spring social relations and social obligations and duties, with which government is necessarily required to deal. In fact, according as monogamous or polygamous marriages are allowed, do we find the principles on which the government of the people, to a greater or less extent, rests.

To buttress his claim about the state's civil interest in protecting monogamy, Chief Justice Waite drew on dominant ideas in the political thinking of his day—in particular, the claim that monogamy fostered democracy, whereas polygamy led ineluctably to despotism. [....]

Yet, even as it recast a religious conflict between Christians and Mormons as a conflict between a secular state and religious individuals, the Reynolds court endorsed the marriage form of America's dominant religious tradition. The Court's conception of marriage and its view of the connection between marriage and public order were undeniably Protestant. Chief Justice Waite drew on the theory and history of state court rulings on religion, which deemed the Christian structure and meaning of marriage as integral to the flourishing of democracy. As the chief justice himself observed, the offense of polygamy was considered an offense against Christianity. Civil courts assumed the authority formerly wielded by ecclesiastical courts, but this did not mean that religious understandings of marriage were then supplanted with secular or more ecumenical understandings. Rather, the Court integrated the protection of Christian marriage into the First Amendment. In subsequent cases involving the Mormons, the Court's religious favoritism was more explicit: polygamy was "a return to barbarism contrary to the spirit of Christianity and of the civilization which Christianity has produced in the Western world." To call polygamy "a tenet of religion is to offend the common sense of mankind."

The perceived threat of Mormon polygamy to Christian monogamy and civilization was heightened by Mormonism's association with easy divorce and women's suffrage. On the divorce question, in 1852 the Utah territorial legislature enacted a divorce statute that simply required the petitioner to demonstrate that he or she was "a resident or wishes to become one." In addition to this lenient residency requirement, Utah's divorce law also included an omnibus clause allowing a divorce "when it shall be made to appear to the satisfaction and conviction of the court, that the parties cannot live in peace and union together, and that their welfare requires a separation." These provisions made Utah the most permissive of any jurisdiction in America on divorce. Some scholars contend that divorce was more prevalent among nineteenth-century Mormons in Utah than in any other jurisdiction in the United States, especially when divorces in polygamous marriages (granted by ecclesiastical courts after plural marriage was made illegal in 1862) are included in the total. Historians Lawrence Foster and Louis Kern have argued that Mormon women had the primary initiative in determining when to end a relationship, while the husband could not so easily divorce if his wife was opposed. Kern finds that 73 percent of all divorce actions in Utah territory were taken by women and argues that divorce may have served as a means to redress the dissatisfactions of plural wives, suggesting that polygamy actually worked out as serial polyandry. Residents of other jurisdictions also took advantage of the lenient divorce laws. Divorce rates rose in the 1870s after the transcontinental railroad was completed; Utah's lenient residency standard allowed Eastern lawyers to flood local courts with divorce petitions.

Antipolygamy activists found common cause with advocates of stringent divorce laws: both polygamy and divorce treated marriage as a capricious thing and threatened to destroy it. Antidivorce activists called divorce "the polygamic principle" or "polygamy on the installment plan." The mobility of the population after the Civil War undercut the ability of state governments to control the law of marriage and divorce, and there was increasing anxiety over rising divorce rates and abandonment. Antidivorce and antipolygamy reformers joined forces in calling for a "United States marriage law," which would establish uniform marriage and divorce laws. In 1886, Republican Senator George Edmunds, Congress's leading antipolygamy spokesman, attempted to get a bill through Congress that would authorize the government to collect divorce statistics as a first step toward restricting divorce.

In addition to lenient divorce laws, the Mormon experiment with women's suffrage heightened their image as cultural subversives. In 1870, the Mormon-controlled Utah territorial legislature had unanimously approved the enfranchisement of women, including all female citizens over twenty-one and all the wives, widows, or daughters of native or naturalized men. These women of Utah were among the first women to vote in America, and they had the vote for seventeen years before they were disenfranchised by the Edmunds-Tucker Act. Mormon leaders seem to have endorsed women's suffrage largely out of the desire to ensure their own political domination in Utah by "voting their wives," which doubled their constituency in the face of rapid settlement of "gentiles." In the 1870s, suffragists outside Utah also defended the enfranchisement of Mormon women on the grounds that revoking women's suffrage would aid polygamy. The expectation here was that once women in Utah had a political voice they would use it to unshackle themselves from polygamy. Indeed, in 1869, a congressman from Indiana had actually introduced a women's suffrage bill to the Committee on Territories with the hope that female enfranchisement would lead to the abolition of polygamy.

Instead, Mormon women voted the way their husbands did and mobilized in defense of polygamy, and this played into the hands of those who opposed Mormon women's suffrage on the grounds that they were too degraded to exercise an independent political voice. As one observer put it, "Mormon women hold mass-meetings in Salt Lake City that are engineered by the church and assert that they are perfectly satisfied with their condition. Before the abolition of slavery the world was assured that negroes were happy in their chains, and individual slaves may have said as much." Even liberal Republicans sympathetic to women's suffrage outside Utah distanced themselves from the issue. The *New York Times,* which had supported federal legislation to enfranchise the women of Utah, argued after the Female Suffrage Bill passed the Utah legislature that "the downfall of polygamy is too important to be imperiled by experiments in woman suffrage." A few prosuffrage Republicans and women's rights activists argued against revoking female enfranchisement in Utah; they asked why former polygamists should keep the right to vote while their wives lost it. A few Southern Democrats, all of whom opposed women's suffrage as a matter of federal policy, argued that suffrage was better left to the states and territories. But there was overwhelming support in favor of revocation. Moderate Republicans led the campaign, which met with little resistance in Congress. Republican Senator George Edmunds, the sponsor of the bill that disenfranchised the women of Utah, expressed a widely shared sentiment that likened Mormon women to slaves, stating that revocation would "relieve the Mormon women of Utah from the slavehood of being obliged to exercise a political function which is to keep her in a state of degradation." The disenfranchisement bill had the support of middle-class evangelical women, who were concerned to protect Christian-model monogamy. In 1884, Angie Newman, founder of the Woman's Home Missionary Society and a leading antipolygamy spokeswoman, drafted a petition calling for Congress to abolish women's suffrage in Utah and obtained 250,000 signatures from among the nation's organized Christian women's groups in support of the bill.

Polygamy, easy divorce, and women's suffrage were all linked in the minds of antipolygamy activists. To condemn these practices by the Mormon minority was to stand with Christian monogamy. But women's rights activists, including Elizabeth Cady Stanton and Susan B. Anthony, recognized that polygamy and these other "subversive" Mormon measures served as a handy foil that deflected criticism of monogamy and downplayed the limited but not inconsequential improvements in women's status brought about by Mormon-led reforms on divorce and suffrage. While the enfranchisement of women in Utah may not have been intended to advance women's rights, it had the consequence of encouraging women's political participation, especially as Congress's assault against polygamy gained momentum. Shortly after they were enfranchised, Mormon women began publishing the *Woman's Exponent*, which ran articles criticizing the inequitable treatment of women in all domains of life and defended polygamy in the name of women's rights. They also established contact with leading women's rights activists, and by 1872, Mormon women held office in the National Woman Suffrage Association (NWSA), the suffrage organization led by Stanton and Anthony. Emmeline B. Wells, the editor of the *Woman's Exponent,* printed news of suffrage activities, and Mormon women helped gather signatures for the NWSA in support of the woman suffrage amendment.

Stanton and Anthony were invited by Mormon suffragists to speak in Salt Lake City in 1871. In her lecture from the pulpit of the Mormon Tabernacle, Stanton attacked patriarchal power and the subordination of women by organized religion and argued that there was just as good reason for polyandry as there was for polygyny. Accompanied by NWSA members, two prominent Mormon women, Emmeline B. Wells and Zina Young Williams, delivered a memorial to the House Judiciary Committee on behalf of all Mormon women, defending their practice of polygamy and asking Congress to repeal the Morrill Act of 1862. They maintained that Mormon women were contented wives and mothers and the effect of enforcing antipolygamy legislation would make fifty thousand women outcasts and their children illegitimate. The alliance between the NWSA and Mormon women was possible in part because NWSA members questioned women's status within all forms of marriage and within all religious communities. Unlike many public officials and citizens of their day, they did not see the form of marriage as the key to women's emancipation, emphasizing that women were subordinated within all forms of marriage.

It is within this larger context of mainstream gender practices that Stanton and Anthony viewed the controversy over Mormon polygamy. Stanton herself distinguished among three kinds of "polygamy": Mormon polygamy, bigamy based on fraud, and polygamy involving one wife and many mistresses "everywhere practiced in the United States." Rather than condemn Mormon polygamy and defend Christian monogamy, Stanton criticized all contracts of marriage as oppressive for women: "In entering this contract, the man gives up nothing that he before possessed—he is a man still; while the legal existence of the woman is suspended during marriage, and henceforth she is known but in and through the husband." She sought to improve women's status within marriage by arguing for greater equality within marriage and greater freedom to divorce. Similarly, Anthony urged suffragists to avoid "shouts of puritanic horror" against polygamy and offer a "simple, loving, sisterly clasp of hands" in order to help abolish "the whole system of woman's subjection to man in both polygamy and monogamy." As she would stress many years later, what was important was women's independence, regardless of marriage form: "What we have tried to do is to show ... that the principle of the subjection of woman to man is the point of attack; and that woman's work in monogamy and polygamy is one and the same—that of planting her feet on the ground of self-support." The NWSA were careful to separate support for Mormon women from support for the Mormon religion and polygamy, but they did not focus their efforts on attacking Mormon polygamy, as many middle-class evangelical women did, in part because they saw all forms of marriage as subordinating women and because Mormons had enfranchised women and provided women with greater freedom to divorce. When the federal government moved to disenfranchise the women of Utah with the Edmunds-Tucker bill, NWSA activists argued against the use of "federal power to disenfranchise the women of Utah, who have had a more just and liberal spirit shown them by Mormon men than Gentile women in the States have yet perceived in their rulers."

Antipolygamists who sought to defend Christian monogamy in the face of attacks by women's rights activists found a convenient diversion in Mormon polygamy. As legal historian Sarah Barringer Gordon puts it, "The popular appeal of antipolygamy gave legislators a convenient out—here was a form of marriage that *truly* replicated 'slavery' for white women. By enacting laws to prohibit the 'enslavement of women in Utah,' congressmen could deflect attention from domestic relations in their own states and direct it towards a rebellious territory. In this sense, Utah became a handy foil." Antipolygamists attacked what they believed to be a deeply patriarchal practice, but the focus on polygamy served the cause of those who defended Christian-model monogamy and the patriarchal roles associated with it. Both Anthony and Stanton's remarks on Mormonism and their emphasis on women's subordination within all forms of marriage suggest that they saw past the diversionary rhetoric.

The focus on polygamy was not only a handy foil against critiques of monogamy, but also a diversion from the federal government's attack on what was probably its bigger concern: the political power of the Mormon Church. In contrast to other nineteenth-century American communal experiments, such as the Shakers and Oneida Perfectionists, the Mormon Church had grown too politically powerful to be ignored. As President Hayes recorded in his diary in 1880, "Laws must be enacted which will take from the Mormon Church its temporal power. Mormonism as a sectarian idea is nothing, but as a system of government it is our duty to deal with it as an enemy of our institutions, and its supporters and leaders as criminals." Reverend Josiah Strong put it more colorfully: Mormonism was "an *imperium in imperio* ruled by a man who is prophet, priest, king and pope, all in one ... he out-popes the Roman by holding familiar conversations with the Almighty, and getting, to order, new revelations direct from heaven." The real danger of Mormonism was "ecclesiastical despotism"; polygamy is "not a root, but a graft." The Mormons were not merely a small separatist community seeking a free exercise exemption from civil marriage laws; they challenged the political authority of the American state by claiming a right to self-government in the Utah Territory. In 1849, Mormons established an autonomous state of Deseret and envisioned a western empire in the Great Salt Lake basin of Utah that was to encompass all of Nevada and Utah and parts of California, Oregon, Arizona, New Mexico, Colorado, and Wyoming. Mormons petitioned for statehood for the Utah Territory in 1850, and when the federal government rejected it, Brigham Young, the first governor of the territory, continued to rule it as a theocracy. They had to accept federally appointed judges, but the Mormon-dominated legislature appointed probate judges in each county with jurisdiction over divorce, alimony, guardianship, and property cases. Children of polygamous wives were recognized and permitted to inherit property, and the courts upheld a variety of living and support arrangements for polygamous families.

Supreme Court Justice Bradley summed up the political threat of Mormonism by pointing to "the past history of the sect, to their defiance of the government authorities, to their attempt to establish an independent community, to their efforts to drive from the territory all who were not connected with them in communion and sympathy." Mormonism was more than a deviant religious group; it was also an "immense power in the Territory of Utah" which was "constantly attempting to oppose, thwart, and subvert the legislation of Congress and the will of the government of the United States."

Polygamy proved an effective weapon for those whose real concern was Mormon political power. As Senator Frederick T. Dubois of Idaho explained,

Those of us who understand the situation were not nearly so much opposed to polygamy as we were to the political domination of the Church. We realized, however, that we could not make those who did not come actually in contact with it understand what this political domination meant. We made use of polygamy in consequence as our great weapon of offence and to gain recruits to our standard. There was a universal detestation of polygamy, and inasmuch as the Mormons openly defended it, we were given a very effective weapon with which to attack.

Scholars of Mormon history disagree about whether polygamy or Mormon political power was the real issue behind federal intervention. What is clear is that the use of polygamy as the federal point of attack proved politically effective, not only for dismantling Mormon power but also for deflecting attention from monogamy and the patriarchal norms associated with it.

MORMON POLYGAMY TODAY

Which arguments from the nineteenth-century debate on polygamy, if any, are relevant for the contemporary practice of polygamy among fundamentalist Mormons in America or any minority group engaging in the practice in liberal democratic societies?

With regard to Mormon polygamy today, government officials have largely taken a laissez-faire approach, a departure from their approach in the earlier part of the twentieth century. In 1935, the Utah legislature declared cohabitation with "more than one person of the opposite sex" a criminal felony. Although the code is vaguely worded, this law was invoked in several polygamy cases in the 1930s and 1940s. Using the 1935 legislation on cohabitation, Utah and Arizona authorities took several actions against fundamentalists, including a raid on the Short Creek fundamentalist Mormon community in 1935 and a raid on various locales on charges of kidnapping, cohabitation, criminal conspiracy, and "white slavery" in 1944. The charges of kidnapping and conspiracy were not upheld, but on appeal, the US Supreme Court affirmed convictions based on the Mann or White Slave Traffic Act, which forbids the transportation of women across state lines for immoral purposes. The Court focused on the question of whether Mormon polygamy was a practice of debauchery and immorality within the reach of federal law. Drawing upon arguments from nineteenth-century decisions against Mormon polygamy discussed above, Justice William O. Douglas, writing for the majority, affirmed that it was. In his dissent, Justice Frank Murphy introduced an unprecedented pluralistic perspective into the nation's highest court. He called polygamy "one of the basic forms of marriage" and argued that it did not constitute sexual enslavement, nor was it "in the same genus" as prostitution or debauchery. Citing anthropological findings that monogamy, polygamy, polyandry, and group marriage were four different forms of marriage practiced by different cultures, Justice Murphy argued that Mormon polygamy was "a form of marriage built upon a set of social and moral principles" and ought to be recognized as such.

State and federal authorities have not followed Murphy's lead and gone as far as recognizing polygamy as a legitimate form of marriage; polygamy is still illegal. In practice, however, government officials have increasingly taken a "don't ask, don't tell" approach toward Mormon polygamy. The last major raid against Mormon polygamy took place in 1953 against the Short Creek community in Arizona. There was much public criticism in reaction to photographs of children being torn from their parents and taken to foster homes. Since then, government officials have taken a more tolerant stance. In 1991, the Utah Supreme Court ruled that polygamous families were eligible to adopt. A leader of the Fundamentalist Church of Jesus Christ of Latter-Day Saints hailed the Canadian court decision that overturned the ban on polygamy on grounds of religious freedom as a sign that the United States would soon legalize polygamy. This prediction was supported by then Republican Governor Michael O. Leavitt's public statement that polygamy might enjoy protection as a religious freedom. After protests from women who had left polygamous marriages, the governor quickly amended his stance, saying that "plural marriage is wrong, it should stay against the law, and there is no place for it in modern society."

In such a laissez-faire legal climate, the number of individuals living in polygamous families in various communities in Utah and Arizona has increased steadily, and the total number of individuals living in polygamous families is estimated to be between 20,000 and 40,000. In explaining why these communities are growing and few people exit, anthropologists Irwin Altman and Joseph Ginat suggest that the main reason appears to be religious devotion. Mormon fundamentalists are committed to the founding doctrines regarding plural marriage. In speculating about whether there are sexual motives, Altman and Ginat contend that for men "any sexual motives must surely pall after a while, as the day-to-day pressures of plural family life cumulate—the financial burdens, the needs of large families, family tensions and conflicts." They add that the widespread occurrences in America of serial marriages and divorces, cohabitation of unmarried couples, and affairs and mistresses appear much simpler and more "romantic."

For Mormon women today, as in the nineteenth century, there are strong economic motivations to enter and remain within polygamous relationships. While many women convert to fundamentalism on the grounds that they've discovered the true and underlying basis of Mormonism, many are also divorcées or widows in need of economic support. These women gain "the security of a community and family, the support and assistance of other women, someone to care for their children, and a highly structured set of roles with respect to their husband and children." Women who enter polygamous marriages tend to be women seeking economic security; for them, conversion to the group is usually followed by striking upward social and economic mobility. Janet Bennion notes that the Mormon fundamentalist group provides "lower-class female recruits" the chance to "ascend to a position of higher marriage (hypergamy)" and a higher level of economic satisfaction than male recruits to Mormon fundamentalism. Compared to women from the mainstream LDS Church, Bennion finds that Mormon fundamentalist women participate more in social and religious work and also pursue paid work outside the home at higher rates. She argues that polygyny "develops independent women who bear much of the financial responsibility for their families." But her study also finds that men in these communities seek to counteract egalitarian values from the wider with harsher rules and restrictions for women.

If we listen to what Mormon women themselves are saying about polygamy, we find a contested practice. On one side is Tapestry of Polygamy, a group of former polygamous wives, who support the legal ban on polygamy and favor its strong enforcement. They argue that de facto accommodation of polygamy reinforces women's subordination within fundamentalist Mormon communities. On the other side are women living in polygamous relationships, such as members of Women's Religious Liberties Union, who favor decriminalization of polygamy in the name of religious freedom. They also argue that polygamous arrangements are good for women because they allow them to pursue both career and family by sharing childcare and household responsibilities. A website they maintain denounces forced marriage and incest, and echoing the sentiments of Stanton and Anthony, states that "abuse is not inherent in polygamy and can exist in any society." Non-Mormons have also made secular arguments in favor of polygamy. In contrasting monogamy and polygamy, one advocate maintains that frequent divorce and remarriage, separation of children from parents, multiplication of step-relationships, and total breakdown of paternal responsibility suggest that the institution of serial monogamy is in serious trouble and may be no better than polygamy per se.

A CASE FOR QUALIFIED RECOGNITION

What then is the appropriate response to the contemporary practice of polygamy? The charge that polygamous relationships are oppressive is contingent, and needs to be investigated by looking at individual relationships and their context, just as monogamous relationships should be. On a rights-respecting accommodationist approach, the importance of polygamy for Mormon fundamentalists must be weighed against protecting the basic rights of Mormon women and children. On the one hand, liberal democracies should respect people's religious liberty and the liberty to pursue the kinds of intimate relationships that accord with their convictions and desires. Mormon fundamentalists maintain that polygamy is of great importance to their beliefs and way of life. If Mormon women maintain that they have freely chosen to remain in polygamous marriage in accordance with their religious convictions, the state should respect their choices but on the condition that they are free to exit. Determining whether women have realistic rights of exit is no easy matter; it requires consideration of the sorts of conditions necessary for genuine consent and exit, as well as contextual inquiry to see whether such conditions obtain in any given case.

Exit has recently received considerable attention as a solution to the problem of internal minorities. Some liberal political theorists defend toleration of illiberal religious and cultural groups, endorsing a principle of state nonintervention, when these groups meet certain minimal conditions necessary for exit: The central claim here is that religious and cultural groups should be let alone so long as membership in these groups is voluntary. Not voluntary in the sense that a religious belief and cultural attachments are experienced as choices, but rather that individual members can, if they wish, exit groups. The appeal of exit as a solution to the problem of internal minorities has not only to do with its providing vulnerable members with a way to escape internal oppression but also with the transformative potential that the threat of exit can have. As Albert O. Hirschman famously argued, the threat of exit can enhance one's voice in decision making. In the context of minority groups, the idea is that if many members can credibly threaten to exit the group on account of their disagreement with particular aspects of group life, the group's leaders would be compelled to reform those aspects. In the Mormon polygamy case, if the threat of exit by women opposed to polygamous marriage was serious enough, it could compel group leaders to reform their marriage practices or to abolish polygamy altogether.

While exit is a real option for members of many religious and cultural minority groups in contemporary America, whether it really is in any particular case depends on the costs of exit and the nature of the group in question. Describing people's convictions and attachments as voluntary seems appropriate against, as Nancy Rosenblum puts it, "a background of fluid pluralism, where other religious homes are open to splitters and the formation of new associations is a real possibility." So long as members are free to exit, religious and cultural associations need not be congruent with public norms and institutions "all the way down." But how far down state intervention will have to go in order to ensure realistic rights of exit for vulnerable internal minorities is an open question. First, there is the issue of how isolated or open the group is to the wider society. Groups that are relatively isolated and which socialize their members into the inevitability of sex hierarchy, as may well be the case with Mormon fundamentalist communities, are especially worrisome. There is also the issue of the costs of exit, not just the material costs of leaving but also intrinsic and social costs. Leaving means losing not just the cultural or religious affiliations themselves and the intrinsic value they hold for members (intrinsic costs) but also the social relationships afforded by membership (associative costs). In addition, there may be extrinsic costs of educational and employment opportunities or other material benefits associated with membership. There is not much the state or the wider society can do about intrinsic or associative costs, but it can assist those trying to leave their communities with the extrinsic costs of exit.

Okin's criticism of the strategy of exit highlights a different kind of obstacle having to do with the *capacity* for exit, conditions of knowledge and psychology, which require a different sort of response than providing material resources. In many minority groups, there may be strong countervailing pressures that undermine the capacity for exit for women and girls in particular. Okin highlights three such pressures: girls are much more likely to be short-changed than boys in education; they are more likely to be socialized in ways that undermine their self-esteem and that encourage them to defer to existing hierarchies; and they are likely to be forced into early marriages from which they lack the power to exit. Under such conditions, women and girls within religious groups can hardly be said to enjoy a realistic right of exit.

These concerns suggest the need to think carefully about the sorts of conditions under which women can genuinely make free choices to stay or leave and what the state can do to foster those conditions. Minimal standards necessary to ensure the worth of a right of exit include members' freedom from abuse and coercion; access to decent health care, nutrition, and education; and the existence of genuine alternatives among which to make choices, including real access to a mainstream society to exit to. To address the concerns about capacity raised by Okin, education must play a key role. Children should be taught about their basic constitutional and civic rights so they know that liberty of conscience exists in their society and that apostasy is not a legal crime.

Some argue that even these minimal standards are too robust, and that the existence of a surrounding market society is all that is required for exit to be a meaningful option. But such an approach overlooks the serious obstacles to exit that the state can help ameliorate and assumes that any state action to address these obstacles would be worse in terms of violating basic individual freedoms (especially freedom of association) than leaving vulnerable members to cope on their own. This minimalist position is right to stress that states have oppressed minority groups. [....]

What do these considerations about exit suggest for the contemporary case of Mormon polygamy? A legal regime of qualified recognition of polygamy can, I think, more effectively ensure Mormon women's rights to exit their communities than outright proscription. The current ban on polygamy leaves polygamous wives and their children even more vulnerable to domination by driving polygamous communities into hiding. In May 2001, Tom Green, a husband of five and father of twenty-nine, was convicted on four counts of bigamy, the first prosecution of polygamy since 1953. Green's conviction has caused anxiety among some members of polygamous communities. They fear that prosecution of polygamy will discourage the group's most vulnerable members from reporting abuse of women and children. As Anne Wilde, who has been in a polygamous marriage for thirty-two years, put it, "This has pushed people a little further underground." She adds that the *Green* case had done a major disservice to the estimated 30,000 polygamists who live in Utah and neighboring states by presenting a false image of their chosen way of life. She contends that Green is an anomaly among polygamists for having wives and children in far greater numbers than average polygamist husbands. A more common family includes two to three wives and eight to ten children. Even worse, she says, the separate charge of child rape against Green for having one wife who was thirteen at the time of their marriage may leave the impression that all polygamist husbands marry underage girls and abuse children when in fact most do not. Sidney Anderson, director of Women's Religious Liberties Union, also argues that fear of prosecution for polygamy almost assures that when child abuse does happen it is more likely to go unreported: "The state is forcing them into an abusive situation, and some men are using it to convince women that they have to live in isolation for the unit to be safe. So women who need help can't get it out of fear." Ms. Anderson argues that the best way to help vulnerable members within polygamous communities is to decriminalize bigamy altogether, which would make it easier for members of plural families to seek help when they need it.

A strategy of qualified recognition of polygamy was pursued in reforming the customary marriage laws in South Africa, and this case is instructive for the case of Mormon polygamy. Drawing on provisions in the South African constitution, reformers sought simultaneously to respect customary law and protect women's rights. On the one hand, the constitution recognizes the rights of cultural and religious groups, including various systems of customary African law. On the other hand, it specifies equal individual rights and prohibits racial and sexual discrimination, among other forms of discrimination. In the discussions leading up to reform, many different groups were consulted, including the traditional leaders' Congress, women's groups, legal reform groups, and scholars of constitutional and customary law. The actual lived practices of customary marriage were at the center of discussion. The chiefs were persuaded that reforming the customary marriage laws was less likely to erode their authority than retaining traditional customary marriage laws.

What emerged from the deliberations was the Recognition of Customary Marriages Act of 1998. It recognizes all past customary unions as "marriages" while also reforming customary marriage itself. The law declares women and men formal equals within marriage and grants the state a role in regulating customary marriage. The law requires all marriages to be registered with a government agency, and it requires that divorce and child custody proceedings be conducted by a family court judge, as opposed to a tribal court. Customary groups are permitted to retain *lobolo* (bride price) as a condition of valid marriage, and polygyny was preserved in a modified form. In order to take a second wife, a man must make a written contract with his existing wife fairly dividing the property accrued at that point and persuade a family court that the contract is fair for all involved.

Qualified recognition of polygamy, as in the case of the modified customary marriage law in South Africa, can offer Mormon women the protection of the law while also respecting their religious commitments. If the law were to recognize polygamy, it could secure legal rights for polygamous wives and ex-wives by regulating the conditions of entry into and exit from such relations. As in the South African case, the state might require a man seeking an additional wife to obtain the consent of his existing wife and to draw up a contract that fairly divides the property they had accrued at that point. If she approved, the couple would then have to obtain the approval of a family court judge. A state that recognizes polygamy could also secure rights for ex-wives and the rights of inheritance for children of polygamous relationships by regulating the terms of property division after divorce. Currently, a polygamous husband may abandon any wife beyond his first without providing any assistance to her and her children. Securing Mormon wives' exit rights could help strengthen their voice within polygamous relationships.

Utah authorities have moved toward a de facto regime of qualified recognition. They have shifted away from prosecuting polygamy per se toward cracking down on abuses that occur within polygamous marriages. The Utah attorney general publicly advised prosecutors to avoid prosecuting cases of consensual adult bigamy. Instead, Utah authorities have reached a consensus to crack down on child abuse, statutory rape, and incest. In 1998, the Utah Legislature raised the age for statutory rape to seventeen from sixteen. In 1999, the Legislature raised the minimum marriage age from fourteen to sixteen. The attorney general said he planned to ask the state legislature for money to hire additional investigators for matters relating to "closed societies" so that more traditional crimes do not go unpunished. He favors reducing the charge of bigamy from a felony to a misdemeanor in order to encourage people to provide information about serious crimes in polygamous families. These reforms may stem more from the practical difficulties of prosecuting polygamy: as in the nineteenth century, polygamous men generally obtain marriage licenses only for their first wives and subsequent marriages are performed secretly. But in addition to these prudential concerns, there are principled arguments in favor of decriminalization. The public morals argument pressed by nineteenth-century antipolygamy activists, that polygamy was offensive to Christian public morals, does not offer a compelling reason, but the other argument, the concern for equal protection, does. We have good reasons to think that qualified recognition of polygamy can better protect the basic rights of Mormon women and children in polygamous households than a ban on polygamy. [....]

Suggested Further Readings for Part V

P. Alston, ed., *The Best Interests of the Child: Reconciling Culture and Human Rights* (Oxford: Clarendon Press, 1994).

Bryan Barry, *Culture and Equality* (Cambridge: Harvard University Press, 2001).

Monique Deveaux, *Gender and Justice in Multicultural Liberal States* (Oxford: Oxford University Press, 2006).

William Galston, "Families, Associations, and Political Pluralism," *Fordham Law Review* 75, no. 2 (2006).

Jill Korbin, "What Is Acceptable and Unacceptable Child-Rearing—A Cross-Cultural Consideration," in *Child Abuse: A Community Concern,* ed. Kim Oates (New York: Brunner/Mazel, 1982), 256–265.

Chandran Kukathas, *The Liberal Archipelago* (Oxford: Oxford University Press, 2003).

Susan Okin, *Is Multiculturalism Bad for Women?* (Princeton, NJ: Princeton University Press, 1999).

Rob Reich, "Minors within Minorities: A Problem for Liberal Multiculturalists," in *Minorities within Minorities: Equality, Rights, and Diversity,* ed. Jeff Spinner Halev and Avigail Eisenberg (Cambridge: Cambridge University Press, 2005): 209–226.

Ayelet Shachaar, *Multicultural Jurisdictions: Cultural Differences and Women's Rights* (Cambridge: Cambridge University Press, 2001).

Iris Marion Young, *Justice and the Politics of Difference* (Princeton, NJ: Princeton University Press, 1990).

VI

Globalization and the Family

Introduction to Part VI

Globalization is usually associated with the intertwining of national economies, the expansion of multinational corporations, vast improvements in global communication and transportation technologies, and more fluid movements of people across borders. All of these developments have important implications for families. Commuter families, for example, where at least one member lives and works for large periods of each year in another state or country, are becoming more common. Permanent family divisions across national borders, particularly as individuals from poor countries seek better paying jobs in wealthier countries, are also becoming widespread.

This final part explores some of the repercussions of globalization for family justice. In "Global Care Chains and Emotional Surplus Value," Arlie Russell Hochschild discusses one of the most significant but unnoticed aspects of globalization: the increased migration of women from developing countries to industrialized countries to serve as care workers. As more and more women in industrialized countries enter the paid labor force, and public policy fails to respond, the demand for nannies and child care workers increases. Much of this demand is now met by women from poor and developing countries who leave their own children behind to earn wages caring for the children of others. Many of these women, in turn, pay other women back in their home countries to care for their own children. Although Hochschild acknowledges the need to know more about the effects of these global care chains on families before reaching a final judgment about them, she offers a number of reasons for thinking that they are unjust. Moving beyond the claims of other theorists, her argument thus suggests that family life and family policies have important implications not only for the justice of domestic societies but also for justice across nations.

In the final chapter in this section, "Deportation and the Parent-Child Relationship," David Thronson explores the rights of children and parents at the intersection of family law and immigration law. Focusing on US immigration law, Thronson describes the complicated issues that arise with regard to "mixed status" families, that is, families in which all family members do not share the same immigration status or citizenship. Although US law generally allows parents to legally immigrate with their children or petition to bring their children into the country, it does not allow children who are born in this country (and hence are citizens) the right to family integrity. As a result, citizen children may see their parents deported or may face de facto deportation themselves under current law. Thronson questions the justice of these arrangements and argues for legal reforms based upon the fundamental rights of children and parents to preserve the parent-child relationship.

14

Global Care Chains and Emotional Surplus Value

Arlie Russell Hochschild

Vicky Diaz (a pseudonym) is a thirty-four-year-old mother of five. A college-educated former schoolteacher and travel agent in the Philippines, she migrated to the United States to work as a housekeeper and as nanny to the two-year-old son of a wealthy family in Beverly Hills, Los Angeles. She explained to the researcher Rhacel Parrenas:

> Even until now my children are trying to convince me to go home. The children were not angry when I left because they were still very young when I left them. My husband could not get angry either because he knew that was the only way I could seriously help him raise our children, so that our children could be sent to school. I send them money every month.

In her forthcoming book *The Global Servants*, Rhacel Parrenas tells this disquieting story of the "globalization of mothering." "Vicky" is her name for the respondent whom she quotes here. Vicky's story as well as other case material in this chapter is drawn from Parrenas's University of California dissertation.

The Beverly Hills family pays Vicky $400 a week and Vicky, in turn, pays her own family's live-in domestic worker back in the Philippines $40 a week. But living in this "global care chain" is not easy on Vicky and her family. As she told Parrenas:

Even though it's paid well, you are sinking in the amount of your work. Even while you are ironing the clothes, they can still call you to the kitchen to wash the plates. It was also very depressing. The only thing you can do is give all your love to the child [the two-year-old American child]. In my absence from my children, the most I could do with my situation is give all my love to that child.

Paradoxically, Vicky got her job by telling her prospective employer that she had experience raising children. As she recounted: "I found out about the job in a newspaper ad and I called them and they asked me to come in for an interview. I was accepted after that. They just asked me if I knew how to take care of a child and I told them that I did because I had five children of my own. But come to think of it, I was not the one watching after them because I had a maid to do that."

Global capitalism affects whatever it touches, and it touches virtually everything, including what I call global care chains—a series of personal links between people across the globe based on the paid or unpaid work of caring. Usually women make up these chains, though it's possible that some chains are made up of both women and men, or, in rare cases, made up of just men. Such care chains may be local, national, or global. Global chains—like Vicky Diaz's—usually start in a poor country and end in a rich one. But some such chains start in poor countries, and move from rural to urban areas within that same poor country. Or they start in one poor country and extend to another slightly less poor country and then link one place to another within the latter country. Chains also vary in the number of links: some have one, others two or three—and each link varies in its connective strength. One common form of such a chain is: (1) an elder daughter from a poor family who cares for her siblings while (2) her mother works as a nanny caring for the children of a migrating nanny who, in turn, (3) cares for the child of a family in a rich country. Some care chains are based on the object of care (say, a child, or an elderly person for whom a carer feels responsible), others on the subjects of care (the carers themselves, as they too receive care). Each kind of chain expresses an invisible human ecology of care, one kind of care depending on another and so on. The head of the International Organisation for Migration estimates that, in 1994, 120 million people migrated—legally and illegally—from one country to another: 2 percent of the world's population. According to Stephen Castles and Mark Miller, over the next twenty years this migration will continue to globalize and accelerate. An increasing proportion of those migrants, they say, will also be women. Already in 1996 over half of those who legally emigrated to the USA were women, and their median age was twenty-nine. It is hard to say how many of these women form links in a care chain. But most of Parrenas's young female care workers were young female legal immigrants too.

In this chapter, I would like to ask: How are we to understand the impact of globalization on care? What do we know about it and how do we think and feel about it? If more global care chains form, will their motivation and effect be marked by kindness or unkindness? Given the harshness of poverty itself, these are by no means simple questions. But we haven't fully addressed them, I believe, because for most of us the world is globalizing faster than our minds or hearts are. We live global but feel local.

However long the chain is, wherever it begins and ends, many of us focusing at one link or another in the chain see the carer's love of a child as private, individual, circumscribed by context. As the employer above might think to herself, "Mothers know how to love children." Love always appears unique, and the love of a carer for the child in her care—like that of Vicky for the child she cares for—seems unique and individual. It has no other context than itself. From time to time, Vicky herself may feel keenly the link between her love for the children she is paid to care for and love of her own children whom she pays another to nurture. But her American employers are far more likely to see this love as natural, individual, contextless, private. "Vicky is a loving person," they might say, and "Vicky loves Tommy."

There are many good studies of globalization that can help us overcome our localism. But they focus on people in the aggregate and don't shed a strong light on individual human relationships. Some scholars, however—especially those exploring globalization and gender—have very much helped us see links between global trends and individual lives. Building on the pioneering work of Sylvia Chant, Pierrette Hondagneu-Sotelo, Beneria Lourdes, Maria Mies, Saskia Sassan, Sau-ling Wong, and, especially, Rhacel Parrenas, I propose to set down some thoughts on the globalization of care. In doing so I am drawing on various areas of research that scarcely connect. Most writing on globalization focuses on money, markets and labor flows, while giving scant attention to women, children and the care of one for the other. At the same time, research on women in the USA and Europe focuses on a detached, chainless, two-person picture of "work-family balance" without considering the child-care worker and the emotional ecology of which these workers are a part. Meanwhile research on women and development traces crucial links from the International Monetary Fund or the World Bank, through the strings tying Third World loans, to the scarcity of food for women and children. But this research, important as it is, does not trace the global links between the children of service-providers and those of service-recipients. The new work on care workers thus addresses a blind spot in our knowledge and to it I add a thought about the global pattern on displaced feeling. The task, as I see it, is to draw threads from each area of research, with an eye to both the macro- and micro-side of the story.

The straight globalization literature tends to focus on three issues—marketization, mobility, and distribution of resources. Each of these sheds light on Vicky Diaz's dilemma. Money provides a powerful incentive to work, and the yawning global wage gap provides a powerful incentive to move, as Vicky Diaz's story shows, from a place where one is paid relatively little even for professional work to a place where one is paid more. Before they migrated from the Philippines to the USA and Italy, the Filipina domestic workers in Parrenas's study had averaged $176 a month—often as teachers, nurses, and administrative and clerical workers. But by doing less skilled (though not easier) work as nannies and maids and care service workers, they can earn $200 a month in Singapore, $410 a month in Hong Kong, $700 a month in Italy, and $1,400 a month in Los Angeles.

People like Vicky Diaz want not just better pay but also more security. Having access to a variety of jobs, and even a variety of national economies, can become an insurance against the very instabilities globalization creates. Migration is a ticket to a better life but also an insurance policy against currency devaluations and business failures at home. As the migration expert Douglas Massey notes, the more globalization, the more insecurity, and the more people try to insure against insecurity by migrating. In short, the more globalization, the more globalization.

And it should be said that while these care providers move to get better pay, they do not become money-making machines. One Filipina caretaker interviewed by Charlene Tung cared for an elderly Alzheimer's patient and had this to say: "We [her friend and she] took care of him for so many years we cannot leave him at this time because we care for him very much. We don't stay for the pay. We could get more elsewhere. He's a very nice man."

In response to the marketization of care, then, many women migrate. But in what sense do they leave home? Studies suggest that migrants such as Vicky Diaz remain attached to the homes and people they leave. Vicky Diaz remained poised to return home, though she did not get back there for five years at a stretch. Indeed, most of the migrant workers Parrenas interviewed talked of going back but, in the end, it was their wages that went home while they themselves stayed on in the USA and Italy. Many of the migrants Parrenas interviewed seemed to develop a "hypothetical self"—the idea of the person they would be if only they were back home. They spoke of the birthdays, the school events they would attend, the comfort they would give if only they were there. Although families are separated, sometimes for decades at a time, they are not in the Western sense "broken." They become what Parrenas calls "transnational families" for whom obligations do not end but bend.

Analysts of globalization also focus on the maldistribution of resources between the First and Third Worlds. Globalization has clearly lifted populations of some countries out of poverty—Malaysia, Korea, and parts of China, for example—while it has also depressed economic conditions in others. According to a recent report published by the United Nations Development Programme, sixty countries are worse off in 1999 than they were in 1980 and inequities in wealth are likely to grow in the future (*New York Times*, July 13, 1999). But we need to ask exactly what resources are being unequally distributed. The obvious answer is "money," but is care or love also being inequitably redistributed around the globe? Marx's idea of "surplus value" may help us form a picture of what's happening. For Marx, surplus value is simply the difference between the value a laborer adds to the thing he makes (say, a car, a pair of blue jeans) and the money he receives for his work. Factory owners and shareholders profit from the value a worker adds to a product; they do not share that skimmed-off "surplus" value with the worker. In the material realm, we can say that one person gets money that another deserves.

Marx was talking about exploitation of workers in the public realm and he left human relations in the private realm out of the picture. But if we look at connections between events in the public realm (the love Vicky Diaz feels for the small boy in Beverly Hills she is paid to care for) and events in the private realm (her love for her five children back in the Philippines) the picture is far more complex than that which Marx discussed. For one thing, caring work touches on one's emotions. It is emotional labor, and often far more than that. For another thing, we are talking about the relation of children to their caregivers, which is partly visible, partly invisible. For, globalization separates the worlds of the actors in this care chain. In contrast to a nineteenth-century industrialist and worker, the employer may have no clue about the world the nanny has left behind and the child there may know little about its mother's First World surrogate child. In contrast to the nineteenth-century industrialist and worker, also, given their options each party in a care chain would seem to be a voluntary participant, except, we might presume, for the children left behind. But the one thing both examples share in common is that the people lower down the class/race/nation chain do not share the "profits."

How are we to understand a "transfer" of feeling between those cared for? Feeling is not a "resource" that can be crassly taken from one person and given to another. But nor is it entirely unlike a resource either. According to Freud, displacement involves a redirecting of feeling: one doesn't give up a feeling but finds a new object onto which to project that feeling. For Freud, displacement was neither right nor wrong, but simply a process to which our feelings are subject. The most important displacement for Freud was of sexual feelings: the original object is the mother (for a boy) or the father (for a girl) and the later displacement is toward a sexually appropriate adult partner. While Freud applied the idea of displacement mainly to relations within the nuclear family, we can apply it to relations extending far outside it. In the words of Sau-ling Wong, nannies and au pairs often divert toward their young charges feelings that were originally directed toward their own young. As Wong puts it, "Time and energy available for mothers are diverted from those who, by kinship or communal ties, are their more rightful recipients."

Can attention, solicitude, and love be "displaced" from, say, Vicky Diaz's son Alfredo, back in the Philippines, onto, say, Tommy, the son of her employers in Los Angeles? And is the direction of displacement upward in privilege and power? How is the emotional need of Vicky Diaz's five children back in the Philippines "related to" that of the two-year-old child in Beverly Hills for whom Vicky is the nanny? Can we think of "distribution" and emotional caring in the same breath? Are First World countries such as the United States importing maternal love as they have imported copper, zinc, gold, and other ores from Third World countries in the past?

Within our own families we easily think of "distribution" and "care" in the same breath. A parent might love all the children equally or might favor one over another. But globalization forces us to broaden our perspective on this question of "distribution." We are not accustomed to thinking in such widely ranging terms but, again, the Marxist idea of "fetishization" and "de-fetishization" is extremely useful here. To fetishize a thing—like an SUV—is to see the thing simply as that and to disregard who harvested the rubber (and at what rate of pay) that went into the tires. Just as we can mentally isolate a thing from the human scene in which it was made, so too we can do this with a service—like that between Vicky Diaz and the two-year-old child for whom she cares. Seen as a thing in itself, Vicky's love for the Beverly Hills toddler is unique, individual, private. But elements in this emotion might be borrowed, so to speak, from somewhere and someone else. Is time spent with the First World child in some sense "taken from" a child further down the care chain? Is the Beverly Hills child getting "surplus" love?

The idea is unwelcome, both to Vicky Diaz who very much wants a First World job and to her well-meaning employers who very much need someone to give loving care to their child. Each person along the chain feels he or she is doing the right thing for good reasons.

How do nannies feel about their decision to come abroad to work? In Pierrette Hondagneu-Sotelo and Ernestine Avila's "I'm Here, but I'm There: The Meanings of Latina Transnational Motherhood," the authors described how Latina nannies in Los Angeles saw their work (hard), and their employers (rich and egotistical). But about their own motherhood they seemed to feel two ways: on one hand, being a "good mother" was earning money for the family, and they were used to a culture of shared mothering with kith and kin at home; at the same time, they felt that being a good mother required them to be with their children and not away from them. Being in a care chain, the authors conclude, is "a brave odyssey ... with deep costs."

The person these Latina nannies most preferred as care for their children was their own mother. But she was not always available. In Parrenas's sample, one domestic worker relies on a paid domestic worker to care for her children in the Philippines as she takes care of the household work of a professional woman in Italy; another hires a domestic worker for the care of her elderly mother while she works in Los Angeles as a teacher (but previously as an elder-care worker); and another woman cleans houses of dual wage-earning families in Rome while she depends on her sisters-in-law for the care of her elderly mother.

Such chains often connect three sets of care-takers—one cares for the migrant's children back home, a second cares for the children of the woman who cares for the migrant's children, and a third, the migrating mother herself, cares for the children of professionals in the First World. Poorer women raise children for wealthier women while still poorer—or older or more rural— women raise their children.

Some migrant care workers care not just for one person all day long, but for many children, or many elderly and sick people. Given many clients, it might seem that an "original" love would be harder to "displace." As Deborah Stone has observed, care in public settings is now subject to pressures to reduce costs, and to follow bureaucratized rules. For example, medical workers have to monitor and limit their time with clients and document specific medical problems for a patient while ignoring other perhaps pressing problems if these aren't listed as a reason for needing home care. As Stone notes, "the main strategy of keeping costs down in home health care is to limit care to medical needs and medically related tasks, and to eliminate any case that is merely social" (1999: p. 63).

But despite the prohibitions of a deadening bureaucracy, feelings of concern and love passed from carer to cared-for. Stone observed that one care worker dropped off milk to an elderly man on her way to work, though she wasn't paid to do so. Others kept in touch by telephone, visited and otherwise cared for clients above and beyond the call of duty. Since it wasn't in the rule book, they felt guilty and furtive for doing so. Given the growing power of the market-place and bureaucracy, carers are pressured to deliver care in a standardized time-limited way. It is often women of color who are on the front lines of institutional care and who thus fight the system to stay human.

Paid care fits a racial pattern. In the American South, before and after the Civil War, African American mammies cared for the children of their white masters while older siblings or kin took care of their own, as in a story told by Toni Morrison in her novel *The Bluest Eye* (1994). In the Southwest, Mexican American nannies took care of children of their white employers. In the American West, Asian American domestic workers have done the same. As mothering is passed down the race/class/nation hierarchy, each woman becomes a provider and hires a wife. But increasingly today, the pass-down of care crosses national borders. For example, Parrenas reported that Carmen Ronquillo had worked for $750 a month as project manager of food services at Clark Airforce base in the Philippines when the base closed. She could find no job that paid nearly as much. So, although she'd criticized her sister for leaving her family to migrate abroad, Carmen, too, left her husband and two teenagers to take a job as a maid for an architect and single mother of two in Rome. As she explained to Parrenas:

> When coming here, I mentally surrendered myself and forced my pride away from me to prepare myself. But I lost a lot of weight. I was not used to the work. You see, I had maids in the Philippines. I have a maid in the Philippines that has worked for me since my daughter was born twenty-four years ago. She is still with me. I paid her 300 pesos before and now I pay her 1,000 pesos.

[Speaking of her job in Rome] I am a little bit luckier than others because I run the entire household. My employer is a divorced woman who is an architect. She does not have time to run her household so I do all the shopping. I am the one budgeting, I am the one cooking [laughs] and I am the one cleaning too. She has a 24- and 26-year-old ... they still live with her. I stay with her because I feel at home with her. She never commands. She never orders me to do this and to do that.

Transfer of care takes its toll both on the Filipina child and on the mother. "When I saw my children, I thought, 'Oh children do grow up even without their mother.' I left my youngest when she was only five years old. She was already nine when I saw her again but she still wanted for me to carry her [weeps]. That hurt me because it showed me that my children missed out on a lot."

Sometimes the toll it takes on the domestic worker is overwhelming, and suggests that the nanny has not displaced her love onto an employer's child but simply continues to long intensely for her own child. As one woman told Parrenas:

The first two years I felt like I was going crazy. You have to believe me when I say that it was like I was having intense psychological problems. I would catch myself gazing at nothing, thinking about my child. Every moment, every second of the day, I felt like I was thinking about my baby. My youngest, you have to understand, I left when he was only two months old.... You know, whenever I receive a letter from my children, I cannot sleep. I cry. It's good that my job is more demanding at night.

Given the depth of this unhappiness, one might imagine that care chains are a minimal part of the whole global show. But it seems that this is not the case, at least in the Philippines. Since the early 1990s, 55 percent of migrants out of the Philippines have been women and, next to electronic manufacturing, their remittances make up the major source of foreign currency in the Philippines. Recent improvements in the economy have not reduced female emigration, which continues to increase. In addition, migrants are not drawn from the poorest class, but often include college-educated teachers, small businesswomen, secretaries: in Parrenas's study, over half of the nannies she interviewed had college degrees and most were married mothers in their thirties. In Parrenas's words, "it is a transnational division of labor that is shaped simultaneously by the system of global capitalism, the patriarchal system of the sending country and the patriarchal system of the receiving country."

Where are men in this picture? For the most part, men—and especially men at the top of the class ladder—leave child-rearing to women. Many of the husbands and fathers of Parrenas's domestic workers had migrated to the Arabian Peninsula and other places in search of better wages, relieving other men of "male work" while being replaced themselves at home. Others remained at home, responsible fathers caring or partly caring for their children. But other men were present in women's lives as the tyrannical or abandoning persons they needed to escape. Indeed, many of the women migrants Parrenas interviewed didn't just leave; they fled. As one migrant maid explained:

> You have to understand that my problems were very heavy before I left the Philippines. My husband was abusive. I couldn't even think about my children, the only thing I could think about was the opportunity to escape my situation. If my husband was not going to kill me, I was probably going to kill him.... He always beat me up and my parents wanted me to leave him for a long time. I left my children with my sister. I asked my husband for permission to leave the country and I told him that I was only going to be gone for two years. I was just telling him that so I could leave the country peacefully. In the plane ... I felt like a bird whose cage had been locked for many years ... I felt free.... Deep inside, I felt homesick for my children but I also felt free for being able to escape the most dire problem that was slowly killing me.

Or again, a former public school teacher back in the Philippines confided: "After three years of marriage, my husband left me for another woman. My husband supported us for just a little over a year. Then the support was stopped.... The letters stopped. I have not seen him since." In the absence of government aid, then, migration becomes a way of coping with abandonment.

Sometimes the husband of a female migrant worker is himself a migrant worker who takes turns with his wife migrating, but this isn't always enough to meet the needs of the children. One man worked in Saudi Arabia for ten years, coming home for a month each year. When he finally returned home for good, his wife set off to work as a maid in America while he took care of the children. As she explained to Parrenas:

> My children were very sad when I left them. My husband told me that when they came back home from the airport, my children could not touch their food and they wanted to cry. My son, whenever he writes me, always draws the head of Fido the dog with tears on the eyes. Whenever he goes to Mass on Sundays, he tells me that he misses me more because he sees his friends with their mothers. Then he comes home and cries. He says that he does not want his father to see him crying so he locks himself in his room.

OVER THE OCEAN

Just as global capitalism helps create a Third World supply of mothering, so it creates a First World demand for it. At the First World end, there has been a huge rise in the number of women in paid work—from 15 percent of mothers of children aged six and under in 1950, to 65 percent today. Indeed, American women now make up 45 percent of the American labor force, and three-quarters of mothers of children aged eighteen and under now work, as do 65 percent of mothers of children of six and under. In addition, according to a recent report by the international labor organization, the average number of hours of work have been rising in the United States.

Partly because a lot of American grandmothers and other female kin, who might otherwise have looked after a worker's children, now do paid work themselves, over the past thirty years a decreasing proportion of families have relied on relatives for their child-care, and more are looking for non-family care. Thus, at the First World end of care chains we find working parents who are grateful to find a good nanny or childcare provider and able to pay more than the nanny could earn in her native country.

In addition, many American families rely on out-of-home care for their elderly—a fact of which many nannies themselves paradoxically disapprove. As one of Parrenas's respondents, a Los Angeles elder-care worker, put it critically: "Domestics here are able to make a living from the elderly that families abandon. When they are older, the families do not want to take care of them. Some put them in convalescence homes, some put them in retirement homes and some hire private domestic workers." But at the same time, the elder-care chain, like the child-care chain, means that nannies cannot take care of their own ailing parents, and if their daughters also go abroad to work, they may do an "elder-care" version of a child-care chain—caring for First World elderly persons while a paid worker cares for their aged mother back in the Philippines.

First World women who hire nannies are themselves caught in a male-career pattern that has proved surprisingly resistant to change. While Parrenas did not interview the Los Angeles employers of Filipina maids and nannies, my own research for *The Second Shift* and *The Time Bind* sheds some light on the First World end of the chain. Women have joined the law, academia, medicine, business, but such professions are still organized for men with families who are free of family responsibilities. Most careers are based on a well-known pattern: doing professional work, competing with fellow professionals, getting credit for work, building a reputation, doing it while you are young, hoarding scarce time, and minimizing family life by finding someone else to do it. In the past, the professional was a man and the "someone else to do it" was a wife. The wife oversaw the family, which was itself a preindustrial, flexible institution absorbing the human vicissitudes of birth, sickness, death, that the workplace discarded. Today, men take on much more of the child-care and housework at home, but they still base their identity on demanding careers in the light of which children are a beloved impediment. Hence, the resistance to sharing care at home, and the search for care further "down" the global chain.

Among these First World mothers are those who give their emotional labor, in turn, to companies that hold themselves out to the worker as a "family." In my research on a multinational, Fortune 500 manufacturing company I call Amerco, I discovered a disproportionate number of women employed in the human side of the company: public relations, marketing, human resources. In all sectors of the company, women often helped others sort out problems—both personal and professional—at work. It was often the welcoming voice and "soft touch" of women workers that made Amerco seem like a family to other workers. Among the ultimate beneficiaries of various care chains we thus find large, multinational companies with strong work cultures. At the end of some care chains are company managers.

THREE PERSPECTIVES ON CARE CHAINS

Given Parrenas's portrait of this global care chain, and given the chain's grow-ing scope, it is worth asking how we are to respond to it. It would be good to know more than we currently do about such care chains. Some children back in the Philippines amid kin in their own community may be doing fine; we don't know. But once we know more, with what perspective are we to view it?

I can think of three ways to see care chains—through the eyes of the primordialist, the sunshine modernist, and (my own) the critical modernist. To the primordialist, the right thing would be for each of us to take care of only our own family, our own community in our own nation. If we all take care of our own primordial plots, a person with such a perspective would argue, everybody will be fine. The concept of displacement itself rests on the premise that some original first object of love gets first dibs and that second and third comers don't share that right. And for the primordialist, those first objects are members of one's most immediate family. In the end, the primordialist is an isolationist, a non-mixer, an anti-globalist. To such a person, the existence and the global nature of such care chains seem wrong. Because such care is usually done by women, primordialists often also believe that women should stay home to provide this primordial care.

For the sunshine modernist, on the other hand, care chains are an in-evitable part of globalization, which is itself uncritically accepted as good. Perhaps most sunshine modernists are uncritical of globalization because they don't know about the relation between the care provided in the First World and that provided in the Third World; a minority knows but is not concerned. The idea of displacement is hard for them to catch onto, for the primary focus of the nanny's love depends on what seems right in a context of laissez-faire marketization. If a supply of labor meets the demand for it, the sunshine modernist is satisfied. If the primordialist thinks such care chains are bad because they're global, the sunshine modernist thinks they're good because they're global. Either way, the issue of inequality of access to care disappears.

The critical modernist has a global sense of ethics. If she goes out to buy a pair of Nike shoes, she is concerned to learn how low the wage and how long the hours were for the Third World factory worker making them.

She applies the same moral concern to care. So she cares about the welfare of the Filipino child back home. Thus, for the critical modernist, globalization is a very mixed blessing. It brings with it new opportunities—and the nanny's access to good wages is an opportunity—but also new problems, including costs we have hardly begun to understand.

From the critical modernist perspective, globalization may be increasing inequities not simply in access to money, important as that is, but in access to care. Though it is by no means always the case, the poor maid's child may be getting less motherly care than the First World child. We needn't lapse into primordialism to sense that something may be amiss in the picture Parrenas offers us and to search for some solutions.

Although I don't have a solution, I suggest that one approach is to try to reduce incentives to migrate by addressing the causes of the migrant's economic desperation. Thus, the obvious goal is one of developing the Philippine economy. But even with such an obvious idea, we find the solution not so simple.

According to the migration specialist Douglas Massey, surprisingly underdevelopment isn't the cause of migration; development is. As Massey notes, "international migration ... does not stem from a lack of economic development, but from development itself." As Massey's research shows, American policy toward Mexico has been to encourage the flow of capital, goods, and information (through NAFTA) and to bar the flow of migrants (by reducing social services to illegal aliens and even legal resident aliens, and increasing border vigilance). But the more the economy of Mexico is stirred up, the more Mexicans want and need to migrate—not just to get higher wages, but to achieve greater security through alternative survival strategies. If members of a family are laid off at home, a migrant's monthly remittance can see them through, often by making a capital outlay in a small business, or paying for a child's education.

Also, the more development at home, the more opportunities to make a productive investment of capital back home, and the more need to diversify sources of income as a way of managing the greater risk associated with economic turmoil. Massey concludes, "International migration ... does not stem from a lack of economic development but from development itself ... the higher the waves (of migration) in a person's community and the higher the percentage of women employed in local manufacturing, the greater the probability of leaving on a first undocumented trip to the US." If development creates migration, and if, as critical modernists, we favor some form of development, we need to figure out more humane forms for the migration it is likely to cause.

Other solutions focus on other aspects of the care chain. Insofar as part of the motive for female migration is to flee abusive husbands, part of the solution would be to create local refuges. Another might be to alter migration policies so as to encourage migrating nannies to bring their children with them. Alternatively, employers, or even government subsidies, could help them make regular visits home.

Another more underlying part of the solution would be to raise the value of caring work, such that whoever did it got more credit as well as money for it and care wasn't such a "pass on" job. And now here's the rub. The value of the labor of raising a child—always low relative to the value of other kinds of labor—has, under the impact of globalization, sunk lower still. Children matter to their parents immeasurably, of course, but the labor of raising them does not earn much credit in the eyes of the world. When middle-class housewives raised children as an unpaid role, the work was dignified by the aura of middle-classness: that was the one up-side to the otherwise confining middle-class nineteenth- and early-twentieth-century American "cult of true womanhood." But when the unpaid work of raising a child became the paid work of child-care workers, the low market value of child-care work—less than that of dog-catchers or traffic meter collectors in the USA—not only reveals the abiding low value of caring work, but further lowers it.

The low value placed on caring work is not due to the absence of a need for it, or to the simplicity or ease of the work, but to the cultural politics underlying this global exchange. The declining value of childcare anywhere in the world can be compared with the declining value of basic food crops, relative to manufactured goods on the international market. Though clearly more necessary to life, crops such as wheat, rice, or cocoa fetch low and declining prices while the prices of manufactured goods (relative to primary goods) continue to soar on the world market. Just as the market price of primary produce keeps the Third World low in the community of nations, so the low market value of care keeps the status of the women who do it—and, by association, all women—low.

A final basic solution would be to involve fathers in caring for their children. If fathers shared the care of children, world-wide, care would spread laterally instead of being passed down a social class ladder. There is a cultural embrace of this idea in the USA but a lag in implementation.

In sum, according to the International Labour Organisation, half of the world's women between fifteen and sixty-four are in paid work. Between 1960 and 1980, sixty-nine out of eighty-eight countries for which data are available showed a growing proportion of women in paid work. Since 1950, the rate of increase has skyrocketed in the USA and has been high in Scandinavia and the UK, and moderate in France and Germany. If we want developed societies with women doctors, political leaders, teachers, bus drivers and computer programmers, we will need qualified people to help care for their children. And there is no reason why every society should not enjoy such loving paid child-care. It may even be true that Vicky Diaz is the person to provide it. At the same time, critical modernists would be wise to extend their concern to the possible hidden losers in the care chain. For these days, the personal is global.

15

Deportation and the Parent-Child Relationship

David B. Thronson

[....]

While citizenship and immigration laws certainly influence lives in a variety of profound ways, one core function they serve is to circumscribe the ability of persons to legally enter or remain in the United States. As such, laws that determine citizenship, the allocation of immigrant visas and relief from removal all have profound effects on the ability of individuals and families to decide where they will live. Family relationships, and in particular the parent-child relationship, play a prominent role in the structuring of immigration and nationality law.

As will be seen, immigration and citizenship provisions generally promote keeping children and parents together. Because the application of immigration and nationality laws mimics the results achieved by constitutional protections of the rights of children and parents in family integrity, it is easy to assume that these protections of family integrity are at work in shaping immigration and citizenship frameworks. Upon closer examination, however, it is apparent that other goals are predominantly served by immigration and citizenship provisions. Protecting children and their interests is not a priority of immigration law.

ALIGNING CHILDREN'S IMMIGRATION STATUS WITH THAT OF PARENTS

At the most general level, three major programs determine eligibility to immigrate to the United States: family-sponsored immigration, employment-based immigration, and diversity immigration. Outside these three major programs, other forms of immigration relief operate on much smaller scales and include provisions that prohibit the government from returning persons to particular countries where they would face persecution or torture.

Family-sponsored immigration provisions result, by far, in the largest number of determinations regarding eligibility to immigrate to the United States. Generally, family-sponsored immigration provisions permit citizens and legal permanent residents to petition for the immigration of certain family members who fall in particular categories. In particular, parents are able to petition for children who are under age twenty-one. Additionally, children may qualify as "derivative" to parents who are principal beneficiaries of the other two major programs, employment-based and diversity visas. As beneficiaries of parents' immigration petitions and as derivatives, children comprise approximately one-third of all legal immigration to the United States. Therefore, the parent-child relationship plays a significant role within the dominant framework of the immigration system.

The ability of parents to bring their children to the United States has led some to identify family unity as an important value underlying immigration law. But while family relationships do form the basis of much of legal immigration, narrow definitions of family and long wait times frustrate the actuality of preserving or restoring family integrity. Moreover, a claim that immigration and nationality law promote family integrity in general is too broad. To the extent that the statutory scheme of immigration law promotes the goal of family integrity, it does so only by providing parents with opportunities to align their children's status with their own. Children in this scheme are denied agency to extend immigration status to their parents. A closer examination of the statutory framework demonstrates this distinctive result.

First, for purposes of immigration law, a "child" only exists in relation to a parent. Meeting the definition of "child" requires satisfaction of qualifying conditions, all of which require demonstration of the dependency of the child on the parent. Further emphasizing notions of dependency, immigration law reserves the power to recognize and establish a parent-child relationship for immigration purposes to the parent, and makes it unavailable to a child. As a result, any immigration eligibility benefit that accrues to an individual based on being a "child" necessarily is filtered through a parent upon whom the child is dependent.

As noted above, within the family-related immigration framework, parents who qualify to immigrate often may petition for children or may include them as derivatives. Children, in contrast, can do neither for their parents. The qualifier "may" in describing the parents' options is worth noting, because the decision to include children in a petition is left to the discretion of the parent. Under immigration statutes, children cannot force parents to act on their behalf. While perhaps assuming that most parents will act in the best interests of their children, immigration statutes impose absolutely no obligation upon parents to do so.

To the extent that the framework for family-sponsored and derivative immigration tends to achieve family integrity, it does so by ceding control over a child's status to parents and by denying opportunities for children to achieve legal status as children without their parents. Parents who are successful in navigating the immigration system may include their children with them or may petition later for their children to join them. If the parents' attempts to immigrate fail, the attempts of their derivative children will fail as well. In other words, this framework is set up in a manner that seeks to ensure that children will not acquire any immigration rights denied to parents through family related immigration. The system is geared to assimilate children's status to that of their parents, not the other way around. In this way, children are passively advanced through the process by successful parents and are held back by unsuccessful parents. Either way, the family related immigration system anticipates children with their parents, not alone.

Importantly, although this version of family integrity does, in most instances, tend to keep children together with parents, it has no concern for where the family ends up or for children whose parents are unable to or choose not to assist them. [....]

WHEN CHILDREN DO NOT SHARE
STATUS WITH PARENTS

The overall tendency of immigration and naturalization law to assimilate children to their parents' status is not accomplished without exceptions. Despite the important role of family in establishing eligibility to immigrate to the United States, immigration rights, once achieved, are ultimately held by individuals and not by families. This means that it is entirely possible, and in certain circumstances likely, that parents and children will not share the same immigration or citizenship status. There are three primary ways in which this result occurs.

Unaccompanied Minors

For a wide array of reasons, thousands of children do arrive at the borders alone. In the absence of a parent, immigration law does not regard these "unaccompanied minors" as "children," and immigration law does not tailor substantive or procedural protections to their age or development. Unaccompanied minors, who are not "children" under immigration and nationality law definitions, sit uncomfortably outside the dominant framework in which family related immigration strips children of agency. Unaccompanied minors thus are situated at another extreme where they are forced to function as adults without accommodation based on their level of development.

Though excluded from any ability to claim an immigration benefit based on family, unaccompanied minors otherwise have the same rights as adults to file for immigration relief for which they might qualify, including such forms of relief as asylum or protection from removal pursuant to the Convention Against Torture. In addition, a form of immigration relief known as special immigrant juvenile status is available to some undocumented children who are dependent upon a juvenile court.

The narrowed range of immigration options available to unaccompanied minors are among the most complex, both procedurally and substantively. While the special difficulties faced by unaccompanied minors are outside the scope of this article, it is worth noting that these difficulties are compounded by the deeply ingrained notions of children only as dependents that consti- tute the dominant paradigm of immigration law. While many children benefit from the passive role of dependent through family related immigration, the dominance of this view makes the immigration system even more difficult for children who do not fit this pattern.

Children as unaccompanied minors and state dependents may acquire legal immigration status in the United States independently of their parents. When they do so, however, they are often unable to reunite with parents because the dominant paradigm still blocks them from petitioning for family members.

Deportation of Parents

Although the role of family is critical in shaping who qualifies to immigrate to the United States, when a person faces removal from the United States it is as an individual, not as a family unit. The deportation of parents, therefore, is a common avenue by which parents' immigration status loses alignment with that of their children. Removal proceedings may result in an order of deportation against a parent that does absolutely nothing to affect directly the immigration status of a child or other family members. As discussed below, if a child who is not deportable under immigration law leaves the country with the parent in this situation, it is on the basis of the parent-child relationship, not the mandate of immigration law.

Removals from the United States have increased since immigration law reforms in 1996 dramatically altered the number of criminal offenses that can lead to an individual's removal. Still, it is an inaccurate stereotype to conclude that most persons deported are criminals. Despite the increase in removals based on criminal grounds, "most removals take place because non-citizens do not have the requisite documents, such as visas or permanent residency papers, to stay and/or work in a foreign country."

As discussed below, situations in which parents are ordered removed while children remain settled in the United States with legal immigration status pose some of the most difficult questions.

Jus Soli and the Creation of Mixed Status Families

Finally, the citizenship concept of jus soli, the right of the land, extends US citizenship to children born in the United States. The Fourteenth Amendment provides that "all persons born or naturalized in the United States, and subject to the jurisdiction thereof, are citizens of the United States and of the State wherein they reside." With only a very few narrow exceptions, the Supreme Court has interpreted the Fourteenth Amendment to mean that all children born in the United States are US citizens at birth, regardless of the immigration status of their parents. In sharp contrast to the naturalization system, this constitutional rule often results in children attaining US citizenship even though their parents do not.

Through the three avenues just discussed, immigration of unaccompanied minors, removal of parents, and jus soil citizenship, children and parents often have disparate rights regarding the ability to reside legally in a particular country. It is in these situations, when the impulse of immigration and nationality law to assimilate children's status to that of parents is frustrated, that the intersection of immigration law and family law is most complex. In such situations, the parent-child relationship is perhaps most vulnerable.

WHEN IMMIGRATION LAW AND FAMILY INTEGRITY CLASH

The potential for tension between family integrity and the operation of immigration and nationality laws peaks when children hold claims to immigration and citizenship status in the United States that their parents do not share. In the reverse situation, immigration law is more likely to provide an avenue for parents to extend status to their children and thus preserve the option of living together in the United States. But the lack of agency for children in the statutory framework of immigration law denies children the ability to extend status to their parents. It is quite common that immigration law provides no legal means for children to live with the parents in the United States although there is no reason to question the parents' concern and competence regarding their children. On the other hand, because immigration and nationality law do not account for children's interests or parents' fitness, there is a grey area in which the application of immigration law may implicate child protection concerns.

When families settle in the United States and the intervention of immigration law results in a parent being ordered removed, the framework of immigration law burdens families with hard choices. Under the statutory framework, either children must stay in the United States and be separated from their removed parent or parents, or they must leave with their parents. The former option threatens family integrity and the latter diminishes children's right to stay in the United States. Unsurprisingly, families have challenged this framework, seeking a third option of keeping the family together in the United States. [....]

Keeping Parents in the United States

Parents' decisions to leave the United States are not always voluntary, and a number of constitutional theories have been articulated around the idea that the deportation of parents will result in the "de facto deportation" or "constructive deportation" of their US citizen children. In such instances where citizen children and non-citizen parents share a desire to remain together in the United States, the children's rights have been asserted as a means to overcome the removal of parents.

The Acosta Family

Lina Acosta's parents conceded their deportability under immigration laws shortly after Lina's birth in the United States, but they asserted that their deportation, "though admittedly valid as against them, will operate, if executed, to deny [Lina] the right which she has as an American citizen to continue to reside in the United States." In denying this claim, the court principally relied on three rationales.

First, the court's analysis adopted the critical assumption that parents can decide where the child will live even in the context of the parents' deportation and further presumed that parents generally will decide to keep their children with them. The child "must remain with her parents and go with them wherever they go." Alternatively, the parents could "decide that it would be best for her to remain with foster parents, if such arrangements could be made. But this would be their decision involving the custody and care of their child, taken in their capacity as her parents, not an election by [the child] herself to remain in the United States."

Second, the court acknowledged that children independently have rights, flowing from their citizenship status, to remain in the United States. Younger children, however, lack autonomy to exercise these rights and parents are presumed to be the guardians of their children's rights in such cases. Specifically, though a US citizen has a right to remain in the United States, "in the case of an infant below the age of discretion the right is purely theoretical ... since the infant is incapable of exercising it." When a "child cannot make a conscious choice of residence, whether in the United States or elsewhere, [she] merely desires, if she can be thought to have any choice, to be with her parents."

Third, the court emphasized the child's right of return. The child will, "as she grows older and reaches years of discretion be entitled to decide for herself where she wants to live and as an American citizen she may then, if she so chooses, return to the United States to live." The child's "return to Colombia with her parents, if they decide to take her with them as doubtless they will, will merely postpone, but not bar, her residence in the United States if she should ultimately choose to live here."

Under the court's approach, any decision about children staying or leaving is entrusted to parents, whether exercising their prerogative to decide where their children live or exercising the rights of the children because the children are not sufficiently mature to do so. The court views the children's possible removal from the United States not as a governmental decision but rather as a parental choice. Indeed, immigration laws do not empower the government to force a US citizen to leave the United States, and they do not block US citizen children's later decisions to return. The government cannot and does not order children to stay or leave, but the court finds no constitutional violation in imposing the choice upon parents.

Choiceless Choice

The court's reasoning in the case of Lina Acosta is highly representative of that employed in similar cases where children's immigration and citizenship rights are asserted to defeat parents' removal. This is true despite procedural variations, differences in ages and diverse articulations of the rights involved. Across these distinctions, these claims have been rejected uniformly by courts in virtually every circuit. Legal scholarship, even where in some cases advocating against the prevailing outcome, has similarly recognized the longstanding, consistent failure of these claims.

These cases thus solidly support the proposition that children's valid immigration or citizenship status alone is insufficient to overcome the removal of a parent from the United States. This is not to suggest that this conclusion is beyond challenge. It may be that the potential for serious harm to the child sufficiently affects the rationale to alter the result. Also, related arguments utilizing international human rights rationales have had better success in other countries and a broader human rights framework may provide a foundation for rethinking these cases, a task that is beyond the scope of this article. Nevertheless, the proposition that children's valid immigration or citizenship status alone is insufficient to overcome the removal of a parent from the United States is a firmly established starting point for courts considering the situation of citizen children whose parents face deportation.

This outcome should not be surprising. First, the rationale of the courts that parents in the first instance make decisions about where children live is consistent with decisions about family in the domestic context. Second, halting the deportation of parents on behalf of children would run counter to the dominant paradigm of immigration law in which it is children who assimilate to the status of the parent and not vice versa. As mentioned above, the concern of immigration law that children share their parents' immigration status is indifferent to place and is equally satisfied whether parents and children remain in the United States or leave.

A standard lament on these cases is that they fail to adequately value family integrity, but these decisions can be viewed from a more positive angle. While the families that file these cases certainly have not been successful in achieving their goal of remaining together in the United States, these cases all fundamentally reaffirm the strength of the parent-child relationship. This may be of little consolation for a family that faces excruciating choices of separating from children or taking them out of the country, but none of these cases begin to suggest that facing deportation makes parents unfit. These cases serve as a bulwark for families that face losing the ability to make the difficult choices themselves through state challenges to custody. In other words, decisions upholding de facto deportations validate the notion that fundamental rights in the parent-child relationship are not weakened by parents' lack of immigration status or even their imminent deportation. [....]

Suggested Further Readings for Part VI

Joanna Derby, *Divided by Borders: Mexican Migrants and Their Children* (Berkeley: University of California Press, 2010).

Barbara Ehrenreich and Arlie Russell Hochschild, *Global Woman: Nannies, Maids, and Sex Workers in the New Economy* (New York: Henry Holt and Company, 2004).

Cameron Lynn Macdonald, *Shadow Mothers: Nannies, Au Pairs, and the Micropolitics of Mothering* (Berkeley: University of California Press, 2011).

Martha Nussbaum, *Sex and Social Justice* (Oxford: Oxford University Press, 1999).

Rhacel Parrenas, *Servants of Globalization: Women, Migration, and Domestic Work* (Palo Alto, CA: Stanford University Press, 2001).

Bahira Trask, *Globalization and Families* (New York: Springer, 2010).

Joan Tronto, "A Feminist Democratic Ethics of Care and Global Care Workers: Citizenship and Responsibility," in *Feminist Ethics and Social Policy: Towards a New Global Political Economy of Care*, ed. Rianne Mahon and Fiona Robinson (Vancouver: University of British Columbia Press, 2012), 162–177.

Joan Tronto, "Privatizing Neo-Colonialism: Migrant Domestic Care Workers, Partial Citizenship, and Responsibility," in *Europeanization, Care and Gender: Global Complexities*, ed. H. M. Dahl, M. Keränen, and A. Kovalainen (Basingstoke: Palgrave, 2011), 165–181.

Allison Weir, "The Global Universal Caregiver: Imagining Women's Liberation in the New Millennium," *Constellations* 12, no. 3 (2005): 308–330.

About the
Contributors

Jean Bethke Elshtain is Laura Spelman Rockefeller professor of social and political ethics at the University of Chicago Divinity School.

Daniel Engster is professor of political science at the University of Texas–San Antonio.

Joel Feinberg (1926–2004) taught at Brown University, Princeton University, UCLA, Rockefeller University, and the University of Arizona, where he retired in 1994 as regents professor of philosophy and law.

Nancy Fraser is Henry A. and Louise Loeb professor of political and social science and a professor of philosophy at The New School in New York City.

Arlie Russell Hochschild is professor emerita of sociology at the University of California at Berkeley.

Traci M. Levy is professor of political science at Adelphi University.

Tamara Metz is professor of political science and humanities at Reed College.

Véronique Munoz-Dardé is professor of philosophy at the University of California–Berkeley and the University College–London.

Susan Moller Okin (1946–2004) was the Marta Sutton Weeks professor of ethics in society at Stanford University. She also taught at the Universities of Auckland, Vassar, Brandeis, and Harvard.

Frances E. Olsen is professor of law at UCLA.

Alison Dundes Renteln is professor of political science and anthropology and a member of the School of Policy, Planning, and Development at USC. She is also the vice chair and director of the Unruh Institute of Politics.

Mary Lyndon Shanley is professor of political science and the Margaret Stiles Halleck Chair at Vassar College.

Sarah Song is professor of political science at the University of California–Berkeley and a professor of law at the University of California–Berkeley Law School.

Judith Stacey is professor of social and cultural analysis and sociology at New York University.

David B. Thronson is professor of law at Michigan State University.

Credits

The readings included in this volume have been used with permission from the following sources. They appear in condensed form, and all footnotes, endnotes, and references have been omitted.

PART I

Judith Stacey. *Brave New Families*. Berkeley: University of California Press, 1998, 3–19, 268–271. Reprinted with permission of the publisher.

Jean Bethke Elshtain. "The Family and Civic Life." In *Rebuilding the Nest*, edited by David Blankenhorn, Steven Bayme, and Jean Bethke Elshtain. Milwaukee, WI: Family Service America, 1990. Reprinted with permission of the author.

Traci M. Levy. "Families as Relationships of Intimacy and Care." In *Justice, Politics, and the Family*, edited by Daniel Engster and Tamara Metz. Boulder: Paradigm Publishers, 2014. Published by permission of the author.

PART II

Susan Moller Okin. *Justice, Gender, and the Family*. New York: Basic Books, Inc. 1991, 134–186. Reprinted with permission of the publishers.

Nancy Fraser. "After the Family Wage." In *Political Theory* 22 (November 1994): 591–618. Taylor and Francis Group. Reprinted with permission of the publishers.

PART III

Véronique Munoz-Dardé. "Is the Family to Be Abolished Then?" In *Proceedings of the Aristotelian Society*, New Series 99 (1999): 37–56. Reprinted by courtesy of the Editor of the Aristotelian Society: © 1999.

Daniel Engster. "The Place of Parenting within a Liberal Theory of Justice: The Private Parenting Model, Parental Licenses, or Public Parenting Support?" In *Social*

Theory and Practice 36, no. 2 (April 2010): 233–262. Reprinted with permission of the publishers.

Joel Feinberg. "The Child's Right to an Open Future." In *Whose Child?: Children's Rights, Parental Authority and State Power,* edited by W. Aiken and H. La-Follette, 124–153. Totowa, NJ: Little Field Adams, 1980. Reprinted with permission of the publishers.

PART IV

Frances E. Olsen. "The Myth of State Intervention in the Family." In *University of Michigan Journal of Law Reform* 18, no. 4 (1985): 835–864. Reprinted with permission of the journal.

Mary Lyndon Shanley. "Just Marriage." In *The Boston Review* (2003) and *Just Marriage* by Mary Lyndon Shanley, Oxford, UK: Oxford University Press (2004). Copyright 2003 by Mary Lyndon Shanley. Reprinted with permission of the author.

Tamara Metz. "The Liberal Case for Disestablishing Marriage." In *Contemporary Political Theory* 6 (2007): 196–217. Palgrave Macmillan. Reprinted with permission of the author.

PART V

Alison Dundes Renteln. "The Cultural Defense: Children." In *The Moral and Political Status of Children,* edited by David Archard and Colin M. Macleod, 48–72. New York: Oxford University Press, 2002. Reprinted with permission of the publishers.

Sarah Song. *Justice, Gender, and the Politics of Multiculturalism.* Cambridge: Cambridge University Press, 2007, 142–168. Copyright 1957 Sarah Song. Reprinted with permission of the publishers.

PART VI

Arlie Russell Hochschild. "Global Care Chains and Emotional Surplus Value." In *Global Capitalism,* edited by Will Hutton and Anthony Giddens, 130–146. New York: Free Press, 2000. Copyright 1997 Arlie Russell Hochschild. Reprinted with permission of Georges Borchardt, Inc. on behalf of the author.

David B. Thronson. "Choiceless Choices: Deportation and the Parent-Child Relationship." In *Nevada Law Journal* 6 (Spring 2006): 1165–1214. Reprinted with permission of the author.